THE SERMON
AT THE TEMPLE
AND
THE SERMON
ON THE MOUNT

THE SERMON
AT THE TEMPLE
AND
THE SERMON
ON THE MOUNT
A LATTER-DAY SAINT APPROACH

John W. Welch

Deseret Book Company
Salt Lake City, Utah
and

Foundation for Ancient Research and Mormon Studies
Provo, Utah

Library of Congress Cataloging-in-Publication Data

Welch, John W. (John Woodland)
 The Sermon at the temple and the Sermon on the mount : a Latter-day Saint approach / by John W. Welch.
  p. cm.
 Includes bibliographical references.
 ISBN 0-87579-301-0
 1. Book of Mormon. Nephi, 3rd XII–XV – Criticism, interpretation, etc. 2. Bible. N.T. Matthew V–VII – Criticism, interpretation, etc. 3. Sermon on the mount – Criticism, interpretation, etc. I. Title.
BX8627.W37 1990
289.3'22 – dc20   90-34403
                                                            CIP

Printed in the United States of America
10   9   8   7   6   5   4   3   2   1

CONTENTS

CONTENTS

1

INTRODUCTION

No text in the Bible is more important or has had more influence on the history and character of Christianity than the Sermon on the Mount in Matthew 5-7. It would be hard to overstate the value of the Sermon on the Mount in shaping Christian ethics and in conveying to the world the teachings of Jesus and of early Christianity. It is known as the Great Sermon, *die Rede von Reden*, an "unparalleled address,"[1] and thousands of books and articles have analyzed it extensively and minutely.[2] It stands unsurpassed as the sermon of the Master *par excellence*.

Embedded in the Book of Mormon, in the account of

---

1. James E. Talmage, *Jesus the Christ* (Salt Lake City: Deseret Book, 1976), 727.

2. Among the general studies of the Sermon on the Mount are Georg Strecker, *The Sermon on the Mount: An Exegetical Commentary*, tr. O. C. Dean., Jr. (Nashville: Abingdon, 1988); Joachim Jeremias, *The Sermon on the Mount*, tr. N. Perrin (Philadelphia: Fortress, 1963); Harvey K. McArthur, *Understanding the Sermon on the Mount* (Westport, Connecticut: Greenwood, 1978). A valuable annotated listing of hundreds of works on the Sermon on the Mount is Warren S. Kissinger, *The Sermon on the Mount: A History of Interpretation and Bibliography*, American Theological Library Association Bibliography Series, No. 3 (Metuchen, New Jersey: Scarecrow Press, 1975).

the first day of Jesus' ministry among the Nephites at the temple in Bountiful (3 Nephi 11-18), are three chapters that are substantially the same as Matthew 5-7. The Book of Mormon account of what Jesus said that day I call the Sermon at the Temple. The materials in the two sermons are so profound that no single approach can capture their full meaning and significance. They can be studied profitably from several angles.

In this book I have gathered some thoughts together around one approach to the Sermon on the Mount that may be of special interest to Latter-day Saints. I explore the contours of the Sermon through its history, language, and temple context. While I draw upon many particular points from Christian scholars to enrich and corroborate my interpretations, I find that the unique insights afforded by 3 Nephi in the Book of Mormon bring the greatness of the Sermon on the Mount most dramatically into focus. The spires and peaks of that monumental sermon, towering from that everlasting hill, loom even larger as they are understood in the setting of Jesus' Sermon at the Temple.

Overview

The present study is divided into several phases. They are advanced as ideas to ponder and as theories to be considered. They are neither exhaustive nor definitive. In exploring a number of possibilities that will hopefully prove to be worth further reflection, they address a variety of issues and audiences.

In chapters 2, 3, and 4, I offer a Latter-day Saint interpretation of the Sermon that sees it in the context of a sacred temple experience, for that is the setting of Jesus' Sermon at the Temple. Seeing the teachings, instructions, doctrines, and commandments of the Sermon on the Mount in this way—in connection with the ceremonial stages and ordinances of covenant making—opens new insights into a unified meaning and comprehensive significance of the otherwise segmented Sermon on the Mount. I invite readers to ponder the prospects of the exceptional view of the Sermon that the Book of Mormon presents to us, for that view has far-reaching implications.

In chapter 5, I compare the words and phrases in the Sermon at the Temple with those of the Sermon on the Mount to show their points of uniqueness and independence. Subtle differences between these two texts give information about the very different settings for the sermons and the audiences that Jesus addressed each time he delivered it. My aim in this chapter is to enhance our understanding and appreciation of the Sermon at the Temple as a solid historical text and, at the same time, to offer further insights into the essential nature of the Sermon as a whole.

In chapter 6, I point out a number of elements in the Sermon that were derived from or were present in the common Israelite heritage generally shared by the Jews in Jerusalem and the Nephites in Bountiful. From the points developed in chapters 5 and 6, I strive to show that the Sermon on the Mount materials in 3 Nephi have not simply been spliced naively into the text of the Book of Mormon. The Sermon fits into the Book of Mormon context comfortably and appropriately.

In chapters 7, 8, and 9, I consider some implications raised by the presence of the text of the Sermon on the Mount in the Book of Mormon. The fact that King James language of the Matthean Sermon appears in 3 Nephi has spawned challenges from Book of Mormon critics, and it undoubtedly will continue to raise issues among lay and scholarly readers of the Book of Mormon. What does the text of the Sermon at the Temple tell us about the nature of the translation of the Book of Mormon? Can we account for the stylistic and linguistic similarities between the Sermon at the Temple and the King James translation of the

Sermon on the Mount? Does the Temple Sermon improve upon that English translation? Does the Sermon at the Temple erroneously follow a corrupted Greek text of the Bible? What of the synoptic question pursued so thoroughly by critical New Testament scholars? What can be learned by pursuing these avenues of inquiry?

The Need for a Unifying Interpretation

These, and many other questions, have always come with the territory of these texts, for despite the Sermon's acclaimed preeminence and apparent simplicity, it is also paradoxically inscrutable. What kind of a text is the Sermon on the Mount? What is its main theme or message? What should it mean to readers today? Is it a coherent speech, or a collection of unrelated sayings? Traditional approaches have failed to answer these questions satisfactorily.

The meaning of the Sermon on the Mount seems unfathomable and inexhaustible to most Bible scholars. Despite endless commentaries, the Sermon on the Mount has simply defied summarization. After centuries of New Testament scholarship, no adequate distillation or coherent logic of the Sermon on the Mount has been convincingly identified. As Hans Dieter Betz has recently summarized, "New Testament scholarship up to the present has offered no satisfactory explanation of this vitally important text."[1] "There is no section of the Bible which has been so quoted (by non-Christians as well as Christians), worked over, commented upon, argued about, taken apart and put together, preached and taught, praised and scorned, as has the Sermon on the Mount."[2]

---

1. Hans Dieter Betz, *Essays on the Sermon on the Mount* (Philadelphia: Fortress, 1985), ix.

2. John E. Burtness, "Life Style and Law: Some Reflections on Matthew 5:17," *Dialog* 14 (1975): 13.

The Sermon on the Mount has been variously interpreted since the earliest days of Christianity.[1] It has been viewed practically, ethically, spiritually, ecclesiastically, personally, and ascetically. In modern times, it still remains possible to "understand and interpret the Sermon on the Mount in a thousand different ways."[2]

Every possible tool of critical scholarship has been brought to bear on the Sermon on the Mount, and yet it still eludes and transcends explanation. It has been examined in great detail by textual critics who specialize in comparing the early New Testament manuscripts in their variant forms. For example, famous scholars such as Wellhausen, Bultmann, Klostermann, Dodd, and others have asserted that the third beatitude (Matthew 5:5) was not originally part of the text of the Sermon on the Mount since it switches places with the second beatitude in some early New Testament manuscripts, while others argue that such a conclusion is unwarranted.[3]

Analyses of the structural composition of the Sermon have also varied: "Concerning the overall structure of the first Gospel, nothing close to scholarly unanimity has yet been achieved."[4] Dale Allison focuses especially on triadic structures in the Sermon and finds similar three-part structures in the Mishnah.[5] Joachim Jeremias sees basically a

---

1. See Robert M. Grant, "The Sermon on the Mount in Early Christianity," *Semeia* 22 (1978): 215-31.

2. Dietrich Bonhoeffer, *The Cost of Discipleship*, tr. E. Mosbacher (New York: Harper and Row, 1970), 115.

3. See Robert A. Guelich, "The Matthean Beatitudes: 'Entrance Requirements' or Eschatological Blessings?" *Journal of Biblical Literature* 95 (1976): 423 n. 46. See, generally, McArthur, *Understanding the Sermon on the Mount*, 15.

4. Dale C. Allison, Jr., "The Structure of the Sermon on the Mount," *Journal of Biblical Literature* 106 (1987): 423, see 423-25.

5. Ibid.

three-part structure in the Sermon (covering controversy over interpreting scripture, controversy with the righteousness of the Pharisees, and the new righteousness of the disciples).[1]

Likewise, source criticism has yielded a kaleidoscope of possible designs[2] and authorship. For example, some have proposed that Matthew was personally responsible for writing the five beatitudes in Matthew 5:5, 7-10 that are absent in Luke 6:20-22.[3] The text has been combed for clues of Jewish or Hellenistic influences. David Flusser points out parallels between the *Thanksgiving Scroll* 18:14-15 from the Dead Sea community and Matthew 5:3-5, and Erik Sjöberg expounds at length upon the Judaic backgrounds of Matthew 6:22-23, while Betz finds in the same passage Hellenistic ideas and ancient Greek theories of vision.[4]

The theology, meaning, intended uses, and purposes of the Sermon in early Christian piety have been pondered. Betz and Jeremias both see the Sermon on the Mount as an early Christian *didache* that was taught to all new converts.

---

1. Jeremias, *Sermon on the Mount*, 23. See generally Alfred M. Perry, "The Framework of the Sermon on the Mount," *Journal of Biblical Literature* 54 (1935): 103-15.

2. Neil J. McEleney, "The Beatitudes of the Sermon on the Mount/ Plain," *Catholic Biblical Quarterly* 43 (1981): 1-3; C. M. Tuckett, "The Beatitudes: A Source-Critical Study, with a Reply by M. D. Goulder," *Novum Testamentum* 25 (1983): 193-216.

3. J. Dupont, *Les Béatitudes: Le problème littéraire — Les deux versions du Sermon sur la montagne et des Béatitudes*, 2nd ed. (Paris: Gabalda, 1969), 1:250-64; H. Frankmolle, "Die Makarismen (Matt 5:1-12; Luke 6:20-23) — Motive und Umfang der redaktionellen Komposition," *Biblische Zeitschrift* 15 (1971): 52-75; N. Walter, "Die Bearbeitung der Seligpreisungen durch Matthäus," *Texte und Untersuchungen* 102 (1968): 246-58.

4. See, for example, D. Flusser, "Blessed are the Poor in Spirit," *Israel Exploration Journal* 10 (1960): 1-13; Erik Sjöberg, "Das Licht in dir: Zur Deutung von Matth. 6,22f Par.," *Studia Theologica* (Lund: Gleerup, 1952), 5:89-105; Betz, *Essays on the Sermon on the Mount*, 71-88.

In their view (and I basically agree with them on this point), it was used to instruct "baptismal candidates or newly baptized Christians."[1] Krister Stendahl has somewhat similarly concluded that the Gospel of Matthew was produced for use in "a school for teachers and church leaders" and that for this reason the Sermon "assumes the form of a manual for teaching and administration within the church."[2]

Moreover, the Sermon on the Mount has been interpreted typologically. One view sees it as reflecting the five dimensions of the early Christian church and the main themes of its ecclesiastical history.[3] These five themes, formulated by Gerhard Ebeling and supposedly exhaustive of early Church history, are (1) the mystical ("seeing God," "seek and find"), (2) faith and theology, (3) orthodoxy versus heresy, (4) persecution and mission, and (5) Christian sin and ecclesiastical repentance. Going off in a much different but fascinating typological direction is W. D. Davies, who suggests that the Sermon on the Mount is none other than the new law of God given at a mountain, replicating the giving of the law to Moses on Mount Sinai, set in a five-part structure that mirrors the five books of the Pentateuch.[4]

Questions have been raised about the intended audience of the Sermon,[5] some suggesting that Jesus addressed himself only to the disciples, not to mankind in general.[6] Others

---

1. Betz, *Essays on the Sermon on the Mount*, 55–70; Jeremias, *Sermon on the Mount*, 22–35.

2. Krister Stendahl, *The School of Matthew* (Philadelphia: Fortress, 1968), 35.

3. Karlmann Beyschlag, "Zur Geschichte der Bergpredigt in der alten Kirche," *Zeitschrift für Theologie und Kirche* 74 (1977): 291–322.

4. W. D. Davies, *The Sermon on the Mount* (Cambridge: Cambridge University Press, 1966), 6–27.

5. Jack D. Kingsbury, "The Place, Structure, and Meaning of the Sermon on the Mount within Matthew," *Interpretation* 41 (1987): 131–43.

6. T. W. Manson, *Ethics and the Gospel* (New York: Scribner's, 1960), 51.

have puzzled over which early Christian communities might possibly have played a role in producing the Sermon on the Mount,[1] as well as the potential targets against whom its critical statements may have been aimed.[2]

Beside these various historical treatments, the Sermon on the Mount has been given an astonishingly wide variety of practical applications and interpretations in contemporary theology and religion: For some, the Sermon on the Mount makes nothing less than a demand for ethical perfection;[3] for some, it proclaims a set of ideals impossible to fulfill and is thus "a call to the Mercy Seat."[4] David Greenwood argues that the imperatives in the Sermon should not be thought of as law, for "a good law should be worded in such a way that at least the majority of those on whom it is imposed are capable of obeying it in all normal circumstances," and obviously the high demands of the Sermon on the Mount do not meet this criterion.[5] For others, it preaches an urgent and expedient interim ethic relevant only to the supreme apocalyptic crisis of the world at hand.[6] No wonder Joachim Jeremias has asked,

---

1. Betz, *Essays on the Sermon on the Mount*, 19–22, 65–69; Stendahl, *School of Matthew*, 13–35.

2. Betz, *Essays on the Sermon on the Mount*, 125–51; David Hill, "False Prophets and Charismatics: Structure and Interpretation in Matthew 7:15–23," *Biblica* 57 (1976): 327–48.

3. Hans Windisch, *Der Sinn der Bergpredigt* (Leipzig: Hinrich, 1929).

4. This is the view of Robert Frost, in McArthur, *Understanding the Sermon on the Mount*, 18.

5. David Greenwood, "Moral Obligation in the Sermon on the Mount," *Theological Studies* 31 (1970): 304, see 301–9.

6. See, for example, Albert Schweitzer, *The Mystery of the Kingdom of God*, tr. W. Lourie, (New York: Dodd and Mead, 1914), 97–99; see also the views summarized by Jeremias, *Sermon on the Mount*, 1–12. McArthur identifies twelve ethical approaches in *Understanding the Sermon on the Mount*, 105–48; Strecker discusses other types of exegesis in *Sermon on the Mount*, 15–23.

8

What is the meaning of the Sermon on the Mount? This is a profound question, and one which affects not only our preaching and teaching but also, when we really face up to it, the very roots of our existence. Since the very beginning of the church it has been a question with which all Christians have had to grapple, not only the theologians among them, and in the course of the centuries a whole range of answers has been given to it.[1]

This variety of approaches is pervasive. It is also prescriptive, for most of these interpretations reveal far more about the beliefs of the interpreters than about the meaning of the Sermon itself: "What each believes Jesus was, did, and said, determines the method by which each interpreter builds his bridge between Jesus and the twentieth century."[2]

Any study dealing with the Sermon on the Mount, therefore, enters into a soberingly vast field of exegesis and interpretation. Easy answers to any of the questions raised about the Sermon on the Mount are few in number and hard to come by. One way to view this array of opinions is to acknowledge that the living pliability of the Sermon on the Mount is both a great strength and a great weakness. Whoever a person is — from curious investigator, to recent initiate, or committed disciple — the Sermon on the Mount can communicate a wide range of ideas and feelings, from technical or practical concerns to pertinent eternal truths and moral imperatives.

Out of this diversity, little consensus has consequently emerged about the original purpose and organization of the Sermon on the Mount: "When one turns to questions about the Sermon's meaning and relevance, there is far from unanimity of opinion."[3] Some have concluded, for example,

---

1. Jeremias, *Sermon on the Mount,* 1.

2. Irvin W. Batdorf, "How Shall We Interpret the Sermon on the Mount?" *Journal of Bible and Religion* 27 (1959): 213, see 211-17.

3. Kissinger, *Sermon on the Mount,* xi.

that the Sermon on the Mount is an eclectic collection of isolated sayings of Jesus, which Matthew or early followers of Christ gathered together without a single theme or organized development. This argument receives some strength from the fact that certain verses in the Sermon on the Mount are also found in other Gospels but in different settings. Others, unsatisfied with that assessment, for it fails to explain the obvious strength of the Sermon as a whole, have attempted to bring all the disparate parts of the Sermon on the Mount under unifying main themes, such as Jesus' fulfillment of the law of Moses, or the golden rule, or freedom,[1] or the attainment of greater righteousness.[2] The main problem with the unifying approaches offered so far, however, is that no one of them can account completely for all of the text, for each of the suggested distillations selectively ignores many parts of the Sermon that do not happen to fit its particular theme, scheme, or constraints.

In the face of this uncertainty, it seems to me that the Sermon at the Temple, with its unifying and coherent understanding of the Sermon on the Mount, provides a welcome new perspective. It offers answers to questions about why the Sermon was given, what was being said, what kind of sermon it was, how all of its parts fit together, and what it all means. When Jesus first appeared to the Nephites at the temple in Bountiful, he instructed and blessed the Nephites for the entire day. His lengthy Sermon at the Temple enhances our understanding of the masterful Sermon on the Mount as much or more than any other source I know.

The Sermon at the Temple does this primarily by dis-

---

1. Peter Stuhlmacher, "Jesu vollkommenes Gesetz der Freiheit," *Zeitschrift für Theologie und Kirche* 79 (1982): 283–332.

2. Kingsbury, "The Place, Structure, and Meaning of the Sermon on the Mount," 136.

closing the *context* in which Jesus spoke these words on that occasion, a context in which this text can be completely comprehended, interpreted, and made relevant.

Knowing anything about the context of the Sermon on the Mount has long been a major element missing from our understanding of it. As Jeremias laments, "The instructions of the Sermon have been torn out of their original context,"[1] and thus he and others have sought to supply needed contexts by importing into the Sermon on the Mount the settings of parallel New Testament passages or by hypothesizing how the early Christians developed the Sermon on the Mount for use in their cultic teachings.

The Sermon at the Temple, however, presents an extensive report, offering a coherent view about the missing contextual setting, or, as Jeremias acutely senses, an understanding of what else preceded or accompanied the sayings in the Sermon on the Mount that is necessary to make them comprehensible.[2] Interestingly, Jeremias concludes that the heavy demands of the Sermon on the Mount make sense only if one assumes that the preaching of the gospel preceded and set the stage for those demands.

In Jeremias' view, five things are presupposed by the Sermon on the Mount: (1) a knowledge of the light of Christ, (2) the coming of the new age, (3) the expiration of the old law, (4) the unbounded goodness of God, and (5) the designation of the disciples as successors of the prophetic mission. These must be taken as givens in order for the Sermon on the Mount to make any sense.[3] Strikingly, these are among the main themes explicitly stated in 3 Nephi 9:19 and 11:3–12:2. These words form the prelude to and the first sections of the Sermon at the Temple, which report (1)

---

1. Jeremias, *Sermon on the Mount,* 30.

2. Ibid., 24–33.

3. Ibid., 26–29.

the brilliant appearance of the risen Christ, "the light and life of the world" (3 Nephi 11:11), (2) the commencement of a new era (see 3 Nephi 11:28–41), (3) the fulfillment of the law of blood sacrifice (see 3 Nephi 9:19), (4) evidence of Jesus' atoning suffering and goodness (see 3 Nephi 11:14–17), and (5) the ordination of disciples as servant-ministers (see 3 Nephi 11:18–22; 12:1). Thus, at the outset, the Sermon at the Temple states explicitly these background elements that only can be presumed to stand behind the Matthean text.

Knowing more about the immediate context of the Sermon at the Temple then adds many insights to our understanding of this text. Essentially, it serves in the establishment of a righteous people who enter into a covenant to become Christ's sons and daughters, to take upon them his name, and to keep his commandments. Further understanding emerges, in this light, by reading and examining the text closely. The result is an understanding of the Sermon as a whole. While it is, of course, true that we can take individual maxims in the Sermon out of context (such as "turn the other cheek" from Matthew 5:39, or "lay not up treasures on earth" from Matthew 6:19) and make good practical sense of them in many applications, doing this severs these sayings from their surroundings and roots. Cut off, they do not thrive. We can discern a greater range of religious significance, however, when we hear and understand them in the context in which Jesus set them. For those who have ears to hear and eyes to see, the Sermon at the Temple contains more of the fullness of the gospel than anyone has previously imagined, revealing and enriching the profound sacred truths of the Sermon on the Mount.

This contextual information, supplied solely by the Book of Mormon, offers some important keys to the Sermon on the Mount itself—to its internal coherence, purpose, and unity. These keys open new ideas about these words of Jesus, inviting study and reflection for years to come. Just as the Sermon on the Mount has provided fertile ground for spiritual and scholarly research for hundreds of years in Bible studies, the same will undoubtedly be the case with the Sermon at the Temple in Book of Mormon research. The following chapters strive to move in that direction.

2

THE TEMPLE CONTEXT
AND UNITY OF THE
SERMON AT THE TEMPLE

While the Sermon at the Temple contributes to our understanding of the Sermon on the Mount in several ways, the most important for me is how it unlocks the age-old mystery of the unity of the Sermon. The main reason that the Sermon on the Mount has remained a sealed text for most readers is the problem of discerning what holds it all together. Does the Sermon on the Mount have a single theme or logic, or is it a haphazard collection of disjointed sayings? To this question, the Sermon at the Temple offers clues to a most remarkable answer.

Simply stated, the Sermon at the Temple is a temple text. The temple context is what gives the Sermon its unity and, therefore, an exceptionally rich background against which it can be understood and appreciated. I therefore advance an interpretation of the Sermon that sees it not just as a moral or ethical discourse, but also as a sacred temple experience. This view, like any other interpretation, cannot be proved absolutely but can only be set forth for consideration, scrutiny, reflection, and for comparison with other possible analyses. And like any other interpretation, my theory undoubtedly has its weaknesses along with its strengths (although telling those two apart is not always

14

easy). Thus, if a reader knows of another interpretation that accounts better for every element in the text of the Sermon than does the approach I am suggesting, I would certainly encourage him or her to entertain that view. But of all the interpretations of the Sermon on the Mount that I have studied, I see the interpretation of it as a temple text as the most coherent and insightful. If my view on this is correct, it has far-reaching implications for how we should understand the Book of Mormon, the New Testament, and early Christianity, as well as the Latter-day Saint temple experience in general.

What follows therefore, especially in chapter 3, is an interpretive essay. Before getting to the individual details of that interpretation, I will first discuss the general elements of the temple setting, for they provide the basis for the ceremonial and covenantal interpretation that follows. This study is both exegetical, drawing meaning out of the text, and also interpretive, bringing meaning to the text. I recognize that I offer a new Latter-day Saint interpretation of the Sermon at the Temple and Sermon on the Mount. I have tried to write just the way I think and feel about this material. I would not expect people unfamiliar with the Latter-day Saint temple ceremony or doctrine to see spontaneously what I see. Still, I hope that any reader will be able to view and ponder the familiar landscape of the Sermon on the Mount from that fruitful vantage point, for the Sermon on the Mount can be understood by anyone as a text constituting and accompanying a covenant-making ritual.

Knowing something about the setting of a speech usually enhances our understanding of it. Where, when, and to whom a sermon is delivered often affects what its words intend, why the speaker selects certain phrases, and how its listeners and readers understand those words. Thus in search of greater understanding, biblical scholars have combed the scriptures for clues about the *Sitz im Leben* or

15

life setting of many prophetic discourses and cultic expressions. This has yielded valuable results in biblical studies. This is true also of research into the Book of Mormon.

In general, we know that we only see the tip of the iceberg in the scriptural record. When Jesus appeared to the Nephites in Bountiful in 3 Nephi, he said and did a great many more things than are recorded in 3 Nephi 11-28. Recall that not "even a hundredth part of the things which Jesus did truly teach unto the people" are reported (3 Nephi 26:6; cf. 17:16-17). Since the record is incomplete, readers must thoughtfully ponder the existing materials and carefully draw possible inferences from the background information that is given, trying to recreate a vivid picture of what transpired. The following background data can be gleaned from the text. It all points in the direction of a sacred covenant-making context.

As will be seen, the Sermon was definitely delivered at the temple, in connection with the issuing of commandments and the making of personal religious commitments, for the purpose of successfully withstanding the final day of judgment. It can probably also be associated with Jesus' other secret, sacred teachings, which, according to tradition, he delivered after his resurrection in Jerusalem. Moreover, all this may have transpired in Bountiful on a traditional holy day of convocation.

The Temple Location

First, the Sermon at the Temple was given in a temple setting—Jesus spoke at the temple in Bountiful (see 3 Nephi 11:1). Since he could have chosen to appear anywhere he wanted (at the marketplace, at the town gate, or any number of other places where people traditionally congregated), and since we may assume that he chose to appear where he did for some reason, his appearance at the temple presumably means that his words have something important to do with teachings and ordinances found within the temple.

It would not have surprised the Nephites that the Lord would choose to teach them at the temple. From what we know about their temples in the cities of Nephi and Zarahemla, these sacred places were obviously important religious and political centers for teaching (see Jacob 1:17; 2:2; people were routinely taught within its walls, see Mosiah 2:7); for preaching (see Alma 16:13); for imparting the mysteries (see Mosiah 2:9; Alma 12:9; 13:3, 16); for gathering for ceremonies, coronations, obligatory annual festivals, ordinances, and covenant renewals (see 2 Nephi 6–10; Jacob 2–3; Mosiah 1–6); for making royal proclamations (see Mosiah 2:30; 7:17); and for sacrificing "according to the law of Moses" (Mosiah 2:3). Nephite temples were patterned after the temple of Solomon (see 2 Nephi 5:16) and were built "after the manner of the Jews" (Alma 16:13) in layout and in many of their functions, but they were not its equal in size or splendor. What Jesus taught them in 3 Nephi 11–18 struck the Nephites as a marvelous transformation of their old order into a new one (see 3 Nephi 15:3).

Of course, some things taught in the temple may also be similar to things said outside the temple, and so it is not inconsistent with understanding the Sermon at the Temple as an esoteric or sacred text that Jesus should also have spoken parts of the Sermon on other occasions scattered throughout his public ministry in Palestine (for example, Luke 6 and 11). At the temple in particular, however, a single, systematic presentation of the essence of the gospel is to be expected and is found.

What is stated so explicitly in the Book of Mormon can only be symbolically inferred by New Testament scholars of the Sermon on the Mount. The "mount" may have been a quiet hillside in Galilee, but it also may well symbolize the "mountain of the Lord," a scriptural expression referring to the temple mount in Jerusalem itself. The possible connection between the sermon mount and the temple mount has not escaped the notice of biblical scholars. In Israel, the temple became synonymous with God's mountain (e.g., Isaiah 2:2 and Micah 4:1 call the temple in Jerusalem the "mountain of the Lord's house"). Just as God spoke to Moses from Mount Sinai, he continued to speak and act in Israel from his temple-palace on his chosen mount in Jerusalem, and the temple became "the architectural embodiment of the cosmic mountain."[1] Mount Zion in Jerusalem became the most important mountain in the world for the Jews, precisely because the temple was there. That low and undistinguished mound was nonetheless called, in the Bible, the world's tallest mountain, because God dwelt there.

That sacred place was thought to be protected from all evil enemies, who were powerless against that spiritual fortress, and life was said to flow forth from it in fertilizing streams. In this image of the temple, there came together for the ancient mind the linkage of things in heaven (where God sat upon his throne surrounded by his celestial council) and the earth, his footstool. It was a place set apart, and there the divine presence related to the world of man — ordering and stabilizing that world and acting upon it through natural and spiritual forces. At that point, the earth touched the divine sphere, just as mountain peaks reach the sky.[2] Thus, as W. D. Davies concludes, when Matthew

---

1. See John M. Lundquist, "What is a Temple? A Preliminary Typology," in H. Huffmon et al., eds., *The Quest for the Kingdom of God: Studies in Honor of George E. Mendenhall* (Winona Lake, Indiana: Eisenbrauns, 1983), 207; see also Donald W. Parry, "Sinai as Sanctuary and Mountain of God," in *By Study and Also by Faith: Essays in Honor of Hugh Nibley*, eds. J. Lundquist and S. Ricks, 2 vols. (Salt Lake City: Deseret Book and F.A.R.M.S., 1990), 1:482–500.

2. See, generally, Richard J. Clifford, *The Cosmic Mountain in Canaan and the Old Testament* (Cambridge: Harvard University Press, 1972), 7–8.

reports that Jesus spoke from a mount in Matthew 5-7, "probably no simple geographic mountain is intended. The mountain is the mountain of the New Moses, the New Sinai."[1] Understood this way, we can imagine no more appropriate place than the temple as the site of the Sermon at the Temple. In the Sermon at the Temple, the temple imagery is no longer veiled.

The Covenant-making Context

The temple in Israel has always been the shrine of the covenant, the home of the ark of the covenant, and the place where the covenant was renewed and perpetuated. Similarly, the Sermon at the Temple was delivered in a covenanting context. Its teachings were expressly designed to prepare people to enter into a covenant with Christ, for at the end of the Sermon the people sacramentally promised and witnessed that they were willing to do what Jesus had commanded them that day, to take upon them his name, and to partake of emblems to help them remember that he had shown his body to them and shed his blood for them (see 3 Nephi 18:1–11).

Moreover, many aspects of the Sermon at the Temple deal overtly with the gospel ordinances. For example, the Sermon on the Mount materials in the Sermon at the Temple appear immediately following Jesus' explanations of baptism, of the gift of the Holy Ghost, and of the rock upon which one should build, namely the covenantal relationship formed by repentance, baptism, and becoming as a little child (see 3 Nephi 11:38–39).

To a Nephite, the invitation of "becoming as a little child" would probably have reminded them of their own traditional covenant ritual, for at least since the days of King

---

1. Davies, *Sermon on the Mount*, 17, acknowledging that "not all scholars accept this view, but it is not to be dismissed cavalierly."

Benjamin they understood that "because of the covenant" they had made, they were "called the children of Christ, his sons, and his daughters" (Mosiah 5:7). Becoming a "child of God" may well also have reminded these people of the divine inheritance of the elect as the "sons and daughters" of God (see Mosiah 27:25-26)[1] who enter into God's presence, the theme on which the Sermon on the Mount also ends (see 3 Nephi 14:21). By both beginning (see 3 Nephi 11:39-40) and ending (see 3 Nephi 14:24-15:1) with this theme of entering into God's presence and withstanding the final judgment, the Sermon at the Temple gives added emphasis to the establishment of a covenantal relationship as a main purpose of the entire Sermon.

The metaphorical explanation of how a person must build upon this rock, instead of upon a sandy foundation (see 3 Nephi 11:39-40; 14:24-27), brackets the words of the Sermon on the Mount in 3 Nephi 12-14. The rock is the doctrine of repentance, baptism, and becoming God's child by spiritual rebirth. So we see that obedience to the commandments given in 3 Nephi 12-14 is not merely advisory or ethically desirable. Obedience to these stipulations is to be understood in connection with the making of a covenant through being baptized, receiving the gift of the Holy Ghost, and becoming a child of God fully blessed to inherit the Father's kingdom. These are among the requirements, the terms, of the covenant.

The Laws of the Covenant

Next, the teachings of the Sermon at the Temple were expressly given by way of commandment. Scholars have debated the basic character of the injunctions of the Sermon

---

1. See also H. Riesenfeld, "Guds söner och de heligas församling [Sons of God and the Congregation of the Holy Ones]," *Svensk Exegetisk Arsbok* 41-42 (1976-77): 179-88.

on the Mount: Do they form a new public order, a set of ideals, a set of commands, a law of the future kingdom but not of the present church, rules applicable only for a brief period before a shortly awaited coming of the kingdom, an existential claim of God on the individual, or general conditions of discipleship?[1] However, in one of the most significant sets of disclosures in the Sermon at the Temple, Jesus refers explicitly, emphatically, and consistently to his words as commandments (see 3 Nephi 12:19-20; 15:10; 18:10). They are necessary if the individual is to "come unto Jesus."

Just as the commands and laws promulgated in the making of the covenant at Sinai formed the basis of the Old Testament, the commandments of the Sermon at the Temple form the basis of this new covenant (or "testament") of Jesus Christ. For this reason, seeing the Book of Mormon as "Another Testament of Jesus Christ" is all the more meaningful, since the word *testament* in Greek literally means "covenant, . . . usually describing the entire relationship between God and the children of Israel."[2] As "Another Testament" or "Covenant," the Book of Mormon indeed reestablishes a modern-day understanding of God's commandments, which his people agree to obey by covenant, even the new and everlasting covenant (see D&C 21:1). Accordingly, the Doctrine and Covenants admonishes the Saints to "remember the new covenant, even the Book of Mormon" (D&C 84:57).

Seeing the Sermon on the Mount essentially as a set of commandments is not the normal approach of most inter-

---

1. See, for example, B. Friesen, "Approaches to the Interpretation and Application of the Sermon on the Mount," *Direction* 10 (1981): 19-25; Jeremias, *Sermon on the Mount*, 1-12.

2. See John W. Welch, "Word Studies — *Diatheke* — Testament," *Newsletter of the Religious Studies Center of Brigham Young University* (June 1987): 5.

preters, though this view has been proposed by some "ruthlessly honest" commentators.[1] Interestingly, this view has the support of the early Christian *Didache* 1:5, 4:13, and 13:7. For example, this so-called Teaching of the Twelve Apostles tells early members of the church to follow Jesus' instructions to give generously (quoting Matthew 5:41-42) and thereby not to "abandon the *commandments* of the Lord"; and it promises that "blessed is the man who gives according to the *commandment*, for he is without blame" (*Didache* 1:5; italics added). The Joseph Smith Translation of the Sermon (see JST, Matthew 5:21, 50; 6:30) reflects the same idea.

It remains unpopular, though, to see Jesus' words here as commandments figuring so prominently in his doctrine of salvation. This is especially the case among many Protestant scholars who see salvation by grace as primary, if not exclusive. Thus Martin Luther relegated the epistle of James (which declares that "faith without *works* is dead," James 2:26) to the straw pile[2] and called the Sermon on the Mount "the devil's masterpiece"[3] because in his opinion "the devil so masterfully distorts and perverts (*verdrehet und verkeret*) Christ's true meaning through his Apostle [Matthew] especially in the fifth chapter."[4] To this, Hans Windisch answers, "Let us be honest; let us free ourselves once and for all from that idealistic and Paulinizing exegesis! We must admit that the ethic of the Sermon on the Mount is every bit as much an obedience-ethic as is the ethic of the Old

---

1. See, for example, Windisch, *Der Sinn der Bergpredigt*, discussed by Jeremias, *Sermon on the Mount*, 2.

2. Martin Luther called the Epistle of James "*ein rechte stroern Epistel*" (a right strawy epistle) because it has "no Gospel quality to it," *D. Martin Luthers Werke* (Weimar: Böhlaus, 1906), 6:10.

3. "*Das heist ein meister stuck des Teuffels* [sic]." Ibid., 32:300.

4. Ibid.

Testament."[1] The Sermon at the Temple confirms this view, and more: Not only is the ethic of the Sermon on the Mount an obedience-ethic, the Sermon on the Mount also belongs every bit as much to the creation of a sacred covenant relationship between Jesus Christ and his people as did the Old Testament commandments, which belong unequivocally to the covenant made between Jehovah and the children of Israel (e.g., Exodus 19–24).

The Sacred Teachings of the Forty-day Literature

A further contextual clue is found in a disclosure by Jesus that may place the teachings of the Sermon in the same class as his post-resurrection teachings to his apostles in Palestine, namely that of the so-called forty-day literature. After basically rehearsing the Sermon on the Mount to the Nephites, Jesus told them that they had now "heard the things which I taught *before I ascended* to my Father" (3 Nephi 15:1; italics added). This may mean that Jesus reiterated the Sermon on the Mount to his apostles once again after his death and before his ascension. Otherwise, he could have said to the Nephites, "Behold, ye have heard the things which I taught *during my ministry* in Palestine." I suspect that Jesus taught his disciples the Sermon, or parts of it, many times during his ministry (e.g., when he began preaching in Galilee as reported in Matthew 5, when he sent out the apostles as missionaries as reported in JST, Matthew 5, and after his resurrection as reflected in 3 Nephi) and that his followers grew in understanding each time they heard it repeated.

Hugh Nibley, in several articles entitled "Christ among the Ruins," has demonstrated a number of connections between the Sermon at the Temple and the forty-day lit-

---

1. As paraphrased by Jeremias, *Sermon on the Mount*, 2.

erature.[1] Jesus addressed most of his teachings at that time to his apostles and instructed them in their priesthood duties, told them about their premortal existence, the creation of the world, and the purpose of this life, and explained how they could return to the glory of God through obedience to ordinances for the salvation of the living and the dead. He blessed them with an initiation or endowment, generally called the "mysteries," which emphasized garments, marriage, and prayer circles.[2]

Correspondences between this body of literature and the Sermon at the Temple enhance the possibility that the Sermon on the Mount played a role in the Palestinian post-resurrectional ministry as well. For example, I think it likely that the references in the Sermon to "raiment" and "clothe" (see Matthew 6:25 and 28-30) had something to do with what Jesus gave the apostles who were instructed to remain in Jerusalem after the resurrection "until ye be endued [i.e., endowed, or clothed] with power from on high" (Luke 24:49).[3] This view is corroborated by that fact that Joseph Smith taught that Peter and John received the "fulness of priesthood or the law of God" at the Mount of Transfiguration and that Peter "washed and anointed" all the apostles

---

1. "Christ among the Ruins," in N. Reynolds, ed., *Book of Mormon Authorship* (Provo: Religious Studies Center, 1982), 121–41; also *Ensign* 13 (1983): 14–19; reprinted in *The Prophetic Book of Mormon* (Salt Lake City: Deseret Book and F.A.R.M.S., 1989), in the *Collected Works of Hugh Nibley* (*CWHN*), 8:407–34.

2. Ibid; Hugh Nibley, "Evangelium Quadraginta Dierum: The Forty-day Mission of Christ—The Forgotten Heritage," in *Mormonism and Early Christianity* (Salt Lake City: Deseret Book and F.A.R.M.S., 1987), in *CWHN*, 4:10–44; see also John Gee, "Jesus Christ, Forty-Day Ministry," in *Encyclopedia of Mormonism* (New York: Macmillan, forthcoming).

3. The Greek word *enduo* means "to dress, to clothe someone," or to take on "characteristics, virtues, intentions." For further discussion, see John W. Welch, "*Enduo*," *Newsletter of the Religious Studies Center of Brigham Young University* (January 1990): 2.

and received "the endowment" on the day of Pentecost in Jerusalem.[1] President Heber C. Kimball similarly once remarked that Jesus had "inducted his Apostles into these ordinances [the holy endowments]."[2] Since the esoteric and post-resurrectional teachings of Jesus in the forty-day literature contain, above all, hints concerning the sacred mysteries Jesus taught to his apostles prior to his ascension,[3] the post-resurrectional context of the Sermon at the Temple invites the conclusion that the materials in the Sermon on the Mount are also at home as part of the sacred or secret teachings of Jesus.

Preparing to Pass the Final Judgment

Another thing the Sermon at the Temple accentuates is its orientation toward the day of judgment. Its concluding remarks expressly instruct the disciple how to pass through the final judgment, to enter into God's presence "in that day" (3 Nephi 14:21-23; Matthew 7:21-23). This purpose is stated more clearly in the Sermon at the Temple than in the Sermon on the Mount. In the Book of Mormon, Jesus expressly states that the purpose of the Sermon is to assist the disciple in surviving the eschatological day of judgment: "Whoso remembereth these sayings of mine and doeth them, him will I raise up at the last day" (3 Nephi 15:1). The purpose of this statement in the Sermon at the Temple is to encourage remembrance and to stimulate the people to keep the commandments that the Lord has given.

---

1. Joseph Fielding Smith, comp., *Teachings of the Prophet Joseph Smith* (Salt Lake City: Deseret Book, 1979), 158; Andrew F. Ehat and Lyndon W. Cook, *The Words of Joseph Smith* (Provo: Religious Studies Center, 1980), 211, 246, 285 n. 8, 331.

2. *Journal of Discourses*, 10:241. Robert J. Matthews concludes that this occurred "after the Savior's resurrection," in *A Sure Foundation: Answers to Difficult Gospel Questions* (Salt Lake City: Deseret Book, 1988), 112.

3. Nibley, "Evangelium Quadraginta Dierum," in *CWHN*, 4:10-44.

Elsewhere in the Book of Mormon, the first thing done after a covenant ceremony is, likewise, to appoint priests to exhort the people to remember their promises so they may withstand God's day of judgment (e.g., Mosiah 6:1-3; 2 Nephi 9:52). The disciple's salvation turns upon remembering and doing the things taught in the Sermon. Therefore, one should not think of the standards set forth in the Sermon as unreachable ideals. Observing this specific set of requirements is essential to eternal exaltation, for only thereby can the Lord raise us up at the last day. In this way, the speech embraces both this-worldly and other-worldly concerns. Its requirements impose standards of conduct upon ethical human behavior in this world, but at the same time it reveals the principles whereby the final judgment will proceed, which principles, if followed, will enable a person to survive the final judgment in the next world.

More Than Words Alone

Evidently the presentation of the Sermon at the Temple involved more than words alone. The Nephites heard many things, but they also saw things presented in an unusually powerful way (e.g., 3 Nephi 11:15). The amazed reaction of the righteous Nephites may indicate this. Even though they had long anticipated that the law of Moses would be superseded upon the coming of the Messiah, they were astonished at what Jesus taught on this occasion. They "marveled and wondered" (3 Nephi 15:2). The apostles in Galilee were likewise "astonished at his doctrine, for he taught them as one having authority" (Matthew 7:28-29). The authority Jesus made evident contributed significantly to their astonishment.

While the amazed reaction of the Nephites can be understood in several ways, it seems possible to me that it had something to do with the idea that what Jesus said and did somehow went beyond mere words or conventional dis-

26

course. Jesus presented things to these audiences in a very marvelous way. This was not an ordinary lecture or a simple, generic moral sermon. His presentation was far different from the logical thinking of the Scribes, which was well-known among the Jews; it also extended beyond the teaching of high moral standards, which had been common among the Nephites throughout their history. Included among the Nephite doctrines had always been powerful prohibitions against disputation, anger, strife, evil thoughts, greed, pride, and neglect of the poor. Why then should similar teachings of Jesus at the temple produce such an amazed reaction? It would seem that their amazement would have something to do with *how* the holy and glorified Jesus taught the principles, not just *what* he taught. The presentation must have been powerful, not just with dynamic intonation or forcefulness, but particularly with divine authority (*exousia*).

A Traditional Temple Occasion

Finally, one may wonder if Jesus did not appear to the Nephites at an auspicious time or on a ritually significant occasion. The record leaves it unclear exactly when Jesus appeared at the temple in Bountiful. Was it shortly after Jesus' death and resurrection at the beginning of the Nephite thirty-fourth year, or was it later in that year? Kent Brown and John Tvedtnes have both skillfully presented alternative arguments on this matter. The main question is how to understand the phrase "in the *ending* of the thirty and fourth year" in 3 Nephi 10:18, but neither is conclusive in interpreting its chronological significance.[1] There are good reasons to think that Christ's appearance did not occur immediately after his resurrection, yet there are equally ample

---

1. For a detailed discussion of the chronological issues, see S. Kent Brown and John A. Tvedtnes, with introduction by John W. Welch, "When Did Jesus Appear to the Nephites in Bountiful?" (Provo: F.A.R.M.S., 1989).

reasons for thinking that it was not at the very end of the thirty-fourth year either.

In light of the inconclusiveness and ambiguity here, it may be more fruitful to consider *what kind* of a gathering was likely involved instead of asking how long after the crucifixion Jesus' appearance in Bountiful was. Had the great multitude gathered together simply for an emergency civilian meeting, or had they assembled for another purpose? Since the Nephites had "gathered together . . . round about the temple" (3 Nephi 11:1) with "men, women, and children" (3 Nephi 17:25), one is reminded of King Benjamin's great covenant-renewal convocation assembly, when all his people gathered "round about" the temple, every man with his family in a traditional Feast of Tabernacles fashion (Mosiah 2:5; cf. Deuteronomy 31:9–13) and had "the mysteries of God . . . unfolded to [their] view" (Mosiah 2:9).

Also, since the size of the crowd in 3 Nephi did not increase as the day went on, apparently these Nephites had gathered for a specific purpose at the beginning of that day. Thus it seems likely that all the people in Bountiful had come to the temple on a scheduled religious festival or holy day. It is evident that these people would have been strict to observe their traditional religious laws, for they were among "the more righteous part of the people" (3 Nephi 10:12; cf. 9:13), the wicked having been destroyed. Moreover, the fact that women and children were present supports the idea that their meeting was not simply an emergency session of the city elders to consider the mundane needs for construction repairs and debris removal.[1] Although we

---

1. While Tvedtnes asserts that "the gathering of the people at the temple is not evidence that it was festival-time" (ibid., 11), his reasons for this are not persuasive to me. He claims that the multitude did not gather until the word had gone out that Jesus would appear again on the morrow (see 3 Nephi 19:1), but the crowd is called "a great multitude" even on the first day (3 Nephi 11:1). Those who came for the second

cannot be sure what festival it might have been, it seems likely to me that some festival was involved at the time the Nephites gathered in 3 Nephi.

Traditionally, all Israelites (and hence Nephites) were instructed to gather at the temple three appointed times each year, namely for the feasts of Passover, Pentecost, and Tabernacles: "Three times in the year all thy males shall appear before the Lord God" (Exodus 23:17). "At the end of every seven years . . . in the feast of tabernacles . . . all Israel [must come] to appear before the Lord thy God" at the temple, "men, and women, and children" (Deuteronomy 31:11-12).

Particularly important for the law of Moses and for the covenant of Israel with the Lord were two feasts, one called Shavuot in Hebrew (Pentecost in Greek), which came in June fifty days after Passover, and the other called Tabernacles, which followed closely after the Day of Atonement in the fall. These two festivals were each celebrated over a period of seven days, probably reminiscent of the seven days of the Exodus from Egypt and the seven periods of the creation.[1] There is considerable circumstantial evidence that the Nephites, who were strict in their observance of the law of Moses "in all things" (2 Nephi 5:10; see also Jarom 1:5; Alma 30:3; 3 Nephi 1:24), observed these essential Israelite festivals.[2] The purposes and themes of these ritual days

---

day apparently had to travel much of the night to be there (see 3 Nephi 19:3), so their absence on the first day should not preclude it from being considered a festival day observed by those living in the temple-city of Bountiful.

1. Abraham Bloch, *The Biblical and Historical Background of the Jewish Holy Days* (New York: KTAV, 1978), 182.

2. Regarding these holy convocations at the temple that the law of Moses required, see Exodus 23:14-19. Concerning the Book of Mormon, see the preliminary research reported in John W. Welch, comp., "King Benjamin's Speech in the Context of Ancient Israelite Festivals" (Provo: F.A.R.M.S., WEL-85c); F.A.R.M.S. Updates, "The Sons of the Passover" (August 1984) and "Abinadi and Pentecost" (September 1985).

related closely to covenant-making, law-giving, and prophetic instruction, which are also dominant themes in the Sermon at the Temple.

If the Nephites were assembled on one of these traditional holy days sometime after the signs of Jesus' death had been given, they probably would have wondered what they should do next. We know that they observed the law of Moses until Jesus proclaimed its fulfillment (see 3 Nephi 1:24–25; 15:2–8), but while Jesus' voice, which was heard out of the darkness, had announced the end of the Mosaic law at the time of his death (see 3 Nephi 9:17), no new instructions had yet been given to the Nephites about the new law that was to take its place. Indeed, when Jesus spoke to the Nephites in person at the temple of Bountiful, he reiterated the fact that the old law had been fulfilled (see 3 Nephi 12:18; 15:4), but they were still confused about what he meant by this (see 3 Nephi 15:2–3). Sooner or later, as they gathered at their temple, they must have wondered if it was still appropriate for them to continue using their old ritual order. Since it seems unlikely that they would have gone twelve months without addressing the implications of Christ's death for the continuation of their public rites and temple practices, this suggests that his appearance was probably not too long after his crucifixion and ascension.

We do not know how the Nephite ritual calendar in Bountiful related to the Israelite calendar in Jerusalem, for there had been no contact between the two for over six hundred years. It is impossible to determine which of the traditional festivals would have been observed in Zarahemla in the months following Jesus' crucifixion. Thus, it could have been around the Nephite time of Passover when Jesus appeared, as John Tvedtnes has suggested, or just before their New Year celebrations, as Kent Brown has proposed. Indeed, a year-rite gathering would make good sense of the occasion in 3 Nephi 11, for at such assemblages kings were typically crowned, laws promulgated, and covenants made or renewed.

If one can assume, however, that the two ritual calendars had not grown too far apart, the feast of Shavuot would have been celebrated in Bountiful a few months after the Passover crucifixion and shortly after the best known ascension of Jesus from Jerusalem, reported in Acts 1. Such a scenario would thus make good sense of the reference in 3 Nephi 10:18 to Christ's appearing in Bountiful "soon after" his ascension.[1]

Moreover, that date is close enough after the events of the destruction that the people could still "marvel" and "wonder" about the whole situation as they conversed about Christ and the signs of his death (see 3 Nephi 11:1–2). Such a date accommodates most of the information Brown has gathered about the settled condition of the people at the time of Jesus' appearance, and it also solves Tvedtnes's major problem by allowing time for records to have been kept between the time of the crucifixion and the appearance in Bountiful. The tension between the words "soon after the ascension" and the phrase "in the ending of the thirty and fourth year" (3 Nephi 10:18) remains unresolved, however, under any theory.

The hypothesis that Christ appeared at the feast of Shavuot in Bountiful also raises many interesting implications. No occasion more relevant than Shavuot can be imagined for the day on which to explain the fulfillment of the old law and the issuance of the new. According to recent scholarship, ancient Israelites may have celebrated, as part of Shavuot, the giving of the law to Moses and the revelation

---

1. John Sorenson notes in a recent study of seasonality in Book of Mormon warfare, however, that if the Nephites celebrated the grain harvest aspect of Shavuot and held this festival fifty days after the grain harvest in Mesoamerica, its date in the New World would have been sometime in December.

of the Ten Commandments on Mount Sinai.[1] That revelation was received about fifty days after the Exodus from
Egypt ("in the third month," Exodus 19:1), although it is
uncertain when the similar dates of this theophany and of
the early summer festival of Shavuot became associated.
The obvious connections between three of the Ten Commandments in Exodus 20 and Jesus' teachings about murder, adultery, and oaths in Matthew 5 and 3 Nephi 12 afford
another possible link between the day on which the Nephites
would have traditionally celebrated the giving of the Ten
Commandments and the time when Jesus taught the new
understanding of those very commandments.

In addition, Shavuot was a day for remembering great
spiritual manifestations. Thus, the Holy Ghost was man-
ifest as tongues of fire to the saints gathered for Pentecost
(the Greek name for Shavuot) that same year in Jerusalem
(see Acts 2:1-4). Shavuot came to be associated with the
day on which the Lord came down in smoke and flame on
Mount Sinai and appeared to Moses on behalf of the host
of Israel. Now Jesus had come down and appeared to all
gathered in Bountiful. Indeed, the ancient model for Shavuot
was the three-day ritual the Israelites observed before the
law was given at Sinai (see Exodus 19:15), and Jesus similarly "did teach the [Nephites] for the space of three days"
(3 Nephi 26:13; see also 11:1-8; 19:4-15; after which sub-
sequent appearances followed, see 26:13; 27:2). Thus, while
the suggestion that Jesus appeared at Bountiful on Shavuot
or any other particular holy day remains tentative, the choice
of Shavuot is attractive and symbolically meaningful.

In any event, as the Nephites had washed and presented
themselves ritually clean before the Lord at the temple, the

---

1. Moshe Weinfeld, "The Decalogue: Its Significance, Uniqueness,
and Place in Israel's Tradition," in E. Firmage, B. Weiss, and J. Welch,
eds., *Religion and Law: Biblical-Judaic and Islamic Perspectives* (Winona
Lake, Indiana: Eisenbrauns, 1989), 38-47.

question must have forcefully arisen again, as it had a generation earlier when the sign of Jesus' birth was seen (see 3 Nephi 1:24), asking what priestly functions this branch of Israel should continue to perform at its temple now that Jesus had lived and died. Indeed, their conversation "about this Jesus Christ, of whom the sign had been given concerning his death" (3 Nephi 11:2) immediately preceded, if not precipitated, the marvelous manifestation which they experienced.

What Jesus then taught them would have been understood, implicitly if not explicitly, as the new doctrines and ordinances the Nephites were to observe in their temples from that point forward in place of their old temple rituals and performances. Those earlier Nephite ordinances, as I have discussed elsewhere,[1] were after the order of Melchizedek and were given symbolically, "in a manner that thereby the people might know in what manner to look forward to [Christ] for redemption" (Alma 13:2, 16). The new order no longer looked forward to Christ, but rather celebrated and looked back on the fulfillment of his atoning sacrifice (see 3 Nephi 11:11).

All this combines to indicate that the Sermon at the Temple is no simple ethical or abstract doctrinal discourse. It is rooted in and around the temple and its covenants and commandments. It prepared those righteous participants to pass successfully by the judgments of God. It instructed them in the new ordinances of the priesthood in a wondrous and marvelous way. Accordingly, we turn our attention next toward an understanding of the possible ritual elements in the Sermon at the Temple.

---

1. John W. Welch, "The Melchizedek Materials in Alma 13," in *By Study and Also by Faith: Essays in Honor of Hugh Nibley*, eds. J. Lundquist and S. Ricks, 2 vols. (Salt Lake City: Deseret Book and F.A.R.M.S., 1990), 2:238–72.

3

TOWARD AN UNDERSTANDING
OF THE SERMON
AS A TEMPLE TEXT

In the limited time Jesus spent with the Nephites, he taught them things of ultimate importance. He gave them a series of commandments, which they then agreed to obey. They were solemnly admonished to "keep these sayings" so that they would "come not under condemnation; for wo unto him whom the Father condemneth" (3 Nephi 18:33). This was serious, sacred business. Although the Savior forbade the disciples to write or speak some of the things they saw and heard (see 3 Nephi 26:18), and while a person can interpret this Christophany in many ways, the recorded material lends itself readily to a ritual understanding. The types of actions, pronouncements, instructions, roles, symbols, images, and injunctions found in the Sermon at the Temple are ritually repeatable. By considering the sequence and substance of these materials, we can visualize the outlines—sometimes faintly, other times quite distinctly—of the solemn, ceremony-like experience Jesus presented to those he met at the temple.

The temple setting of the Sermon, accordingly, invites us to examine each of its momentous elements with a temple context in mind. In the following pages, I shall explore the forty-eight elements of the Sermon that I have

34

identified, examining in particular their possible roles in establishing a covenant relationship between God and his people and the capacity of those elements to be ritualized. For corroboration and elaboration, I draw upon various ritual aspects of early Christianity, Near Eastern temple typology, continuities between Jesus' Sermon and Israelite temple practices or cultic texts, and modern Latter-day scriptures and teachings. These supplemental points, however, are secondary. The primary objective is to move toward an understanding of the Sermon at the Temple itself.

1. A thrice-repeated announcement from above. The Sermon at the Temple begins with a soft, small, piercing voice speaking out of heaven (see 3 Nephi 11:3–5). At first the people could not understand it, but the voice repeated exactly the same announcement three times,[1] and the words were better comprehended each time they were repeated. At first, this small piercing voice may have sounded faint and broken; something like this perhaps: "Behold . . . Son, . . . well pleased, in whom I have glorified . . . hear . . . " (3 Nephi 11:7), but the words increased in clarity each time they were repeated.

2. Opening the ears and eyes. Total silence fell upon the people as they riveted their attention toward the sound. Upon the third hearing of the voice, the people are said to have opened "their ears to hear it; and their eyes were towards the sound thereof; and they did look steadfastly towards heaven, from whence the sound came" (3 Nephi 11:5). The opening of the ears and eyes can mark the beginning of a ritual ceremony (as it expressly does in Mosiah 2:9) and can symbolize the commencement of an opening

---

1. By way of interest, one may compare the research of Dale C. Allison, displaying the triadic nature of much of the Sermon on the Mount, a feature present also in the Mishnah ("The Structure of the Sermon on the Mount," 429–43).

35

of the mysteries and a deeper understanding of what is truly being said and done.

When the voice came the third time, "they did understand the voice" (3 Nephi 11:6). Such a call to attention, the *silentium*, typically opened many solemn Old World religious assemblies.[1] In opening the eyes and ears of the people, it may be compared functionally to an early Christian purificatory anointing of the eyes and ears "that you might receive hearing ears of the mysteries of God."[2] Not all people are intended to hear and know the mysteries of God; only those who have ears to hear and eyes to see. For this reason, Jesus spoke parables to the masses in Palestine; yet to his disciples, it was given "to know the mysteries of the kingdom of heaven; . . . blessed are your eyes, for they see: and your ears, for they hear" (Matthew 13:11, 16). Their eyes and ears were opened.

3. Delegation of duty by the Father to the Son. The people then understood the words of the Father as he introduced the Son: "Behold my Beloved Son, in whom I am well pleased, in whom I have glorified my name—hear ye him" (3 Nephi 11:7). The general pattern this reveals is how the Father himself does not personally minister to beings on earth, but does all things by sending the Son as his representative. The Son has the obligation to carry out his stewardship, and upon the completion of his assignment, he returns and apparently reports to the Father. Thus, at the conclusion of the Sermon at the Temple, Jesus says, "Now I go unto the Father, because it is expedient that I should go unto the Father for your sakes" (3 Nephi 18:35), whereupon Jesus "ascended into heaven," as the disciples bore record (3 Nephi 18:39).

---

1. Hugh Nibley, *Approach to the Book of Mormon* (Salt Lake City: Deseret Book, 1957), in *CWHN* 6:300 n. 10.

2. Hugh Nibley, *The Message of the Joseph Smith Papyri: An Egyptian Endowment* (Salt Lake City: Deseret Book, 1975), 280.

4. *Coming down.* After the Father's words, Jesus then appeared, "descending out of heaven . . . clothed in a white robe" (3 Nephi 11:8). Graphically, he came down with teachings and instructions from above. He came robed in garments worthy of mention, but not receiving further description—elements rich with possible ritual implementation and significance.[1]

5. *Silence.* While Jesus came down, the mouths of the people remained shut. "They durst not open their mouths, even one to another, and wist not what it meant" (3 Nephi 11:8). I assume that they remained in this state of profound silence, deep respect, reverence, and awe for several hours, as the two thousand five hundred people (see 3 Nephi 17:25) present stepped forward, one at a time, to touch their Lord.

6. *Identification by marks on the hand.* At first the people were confused and cautious, not knowing who had appeared to them. Even though the words of the Father had proclaimed the Son, the people still "thought it was an angel that had appeared unto them" (3 Nephi 11:8). In Hebrew (*mal'ak*) and Greek (*aggelos*), the words for "angel" and "messenger" are one and the same. Apparently the people were not sure whether they had been greeted by a messenger of light, or perhaps even of darkness, or by the Lord himself.

That confusion was removed only as Jesus "stretched forth his hand" and identified himself, saying, "I am Jesus Christ, whom the prophets testified shall come into the world" (3 Nephi 11:9–10). By these words and the extension of his hands, the people recognized him as the truest messenger, the Lord and Savior Jesus Christ, as had been prophesied. Old Testament prophets had said that the Lord would be known by the marks in his hands: "They shall look upon me whom they have pierced, . . . and one shall say unto him,

---

1. See Hugh Nibley, "Sacred Vestments," F.A.R.M.S. Preliminary Report, 1987.

What are these wounds in thine hands? Then he shall answer, Those with which I was wounded in the house of my friends" (Zechariah 12:10; 13:6). Early Christians also said, "I extended my hands and approached my Lord, for the expansion of my hands is His sign" (*Odes of Solomon* 42:1).

7. *Falling down.* Upon recognizing the divine visitor as the Lord who had taken upon himself the sins of the world, the multitude "fell to the earth" (3 Nephi 11:12). Bowing down—or more dramatically, full prostration—is not only an instinctive response when coming into the presence of a superior being, but it is also a common element of ritual. Prostration, particularly in a temple context, had long been a customary part of the Nephite covenant-making ceremony (see Mosiah 4:1).

8. *Personally touching the wounds.* The Lord then asked all the people to "arise and come forth . . . that ye may thrust your hands into my side, and also that ye may feel the prints of the nails in my hands and in my feet" (3 Nephi 11:14). All the people then went forth and placed their hands into his side and felt the nail prints in his hands and in his feet, "and did see with their eyes and did feel with their hands, and did know of a surety and did bear record" (3 Nephi 11:15). Thus their knowledge was made sure that he was "the God of Israel and the God of the whole earth, . . . slain for the sins of the world" (3 Nephi 11:14). They personally felt the signs of his suffering and death. Since there were two thousand five hundred souls present at this assembly, no more than a brief contact would have been possible under normal circumstances.

9. *Hosanna Shout and falling down a second time.* The experience continued when, in unison, the company sang out with one accord, "Hosanna! Blessed be the name of the Most High God!" (3 Nephi 11:17), reminiscent of Melchizedek's blessing of Abraham, "Blessed be the most high

God!" (Genesis 14:20). At this point their mouths were truly opened.[1]

The Hosanna Shout, meaning "Save Now," is puzzling to scholars. It has been alternatively interpreted as an intercessory prayer addressed to God, asking that assistance be given "to his Messiah," or as a "royal supplication addressed to the Messiah," or as "a call of triumphant joy," sometimes chanted as *lulav* branches were waved in the air.[2] "Whatever was the original Hebrew or Aramaic word for Hosanna, it must have conveyed a particular Messianic significance,"[3] associated by some with the anticipated Messianic cleansing of the temple.[4]

The origins of the Hosanna Shout are traceable at least as far back as the familiar *Hallel*, an ancient festival hymn that was especially at home in the temple of Jerusalem: "Save now [Hosanna], I beseech thee, O Lord: O Lord, I beseech thee, send now prosperity. Blessed be he that cometh in the name of the Lord; we have blessed you out of the house of the Lord" (Psalm 118:25–26). This hymn was well-known in Israel, being sung in postbiblical Judaism on the high holy days; it was also used as a liturgical cry in the worship of the early Christian community, particularly at the sacrament of the Lord's Supper.[5] Its aptness to the occasion at the temple in Bountiful is evident. The fact that the people all cried out in unison indicates that they spon-

---

1. For shades of the Egyptian initiatory "Opening of the Mouth" ceremony, see Nibley, *Message of the Joseph Smith Papyri*, 106–13.

2. Various views are summarized in Eric Werner, " 'Hosanna' in the Gospels," *Journal of Biblical Literature* 65 (1946): 97–122, esp. 106–11.

3. Ibid., 106.

4. J. Spencer Kennard, Jr., " 'Hosanna' and the Purpose of Jesus," *Journal of Biblical Literature* 67 (1948): 171–76.

5. G. Kittel, ed., *Theological Dictionary of the New Testament* (Grand Rapids, Michigan: Eerdmans, 1964), 9:683–84; hereafter cited as *TDNT*; Eric Werner, *The Sacred Bridge* (New York: Schocken, 1970), 267.

taneously broke forth with a familiar liturgical expression. They then fell down again at Jesus' feet and worshipped him (see 3 Nephi 11:17).

10. *Ordination to the priesthood.* Next, ordaining men to the priesthood was necessary. Jesus first ordained Nephi, giving him the authority normally associated by Latter-day Saints with the Aaronic Priesthood, namely the power to baptize the people. The Lord asked him to arise and come forth; he went forth and bowed himself before the Lord and kissed Jesus' feet, whereupon the Lord commanded him to arise. Nephi then arose and stood before Jesus, who ordained him and gave him "power that [he] shall baptize this people when [the Lord] again ascended into heaven" (3 Nephi 11:21). In addition, the Lord called eleven others and similarly ordained them (see 3 Nephi 11:22; 19:4). At the end of the day Jesus would give these twelve the "power to give the Holy Ghost" (3 Nephi 18:37), an authority allowing them to officiate in the Melchizedek Priesthood.

11. *Baptism explained.* Jesus then explained the manner of baptism, complete with the specific words of the baptismal prayer, calling the candidate by his own given name (see 3 Nephi 11:23–28). This washing and purifying ordinance stands in this sequence as a necessary first step toward the kingdom of God. These baptisms were not carried out immediately, but they were performed pursuant to these instructions at the beginning of the next day (see 3 Nephi 19:10–13). Perhaps those baptisms were viewed, among other things, as taking the place of the washings that Israelites practiced before coming up to the temple traditionally and that are precedented as early as Exodus 19:10.

12. *Assuring the absence of evil.* Jesus next took steps to assure that there were no disputations, contentions, or any influences of the devil among this people (see 3 Nephi 11:28–30). The Sermon at the Temple calls these the influences "of the devil, who is the father of contention" (3 Nephi

11:29). With a simple authoritative statement, Jesus asserted that "such things should be done away" (3 Nephi 11:30). This declaration fills the role of warding off the presence or influence of Satan—a standard element in ritual drama—and I assume that for this reason Satan's personal presence is not indicated anywhere again in the Sermon. One of the purposes of Jesus' teaching is to give the righteous the ability to be delivered "from evil," as the Lord's Prayer requests later in the Sermon (see 3 Nephi 13:12). The Greek for this can be read, "deliver us from the Evil One" (Matthew 6:13). Another power apparently given to the righteous is the ability to "cast out devils" (3 Nephi 14:22), although the Sermon warns that some will exercise this power unrighteously.

13. Witnesses. Jesus then identified three witnesses who would bear record of his doctrine. On this unique occasion, Jesus, God the Father, and the Holy Ghost bore record of the doctrine and of one another (see 3 Nephi 11:35–36). Filling a covenantal role that is familiar from several other occurrences in scripture (e.g., Genesis 18:2; Deuteronomy 4:26; 19:15; 2 Nephi 11:3), these three stand together at the commencement of this dispensation of the new law to the Nephites to witness of the gospel.

14. Teaching the Gospel. Having dispelled evil, Jesus' next concern was that all be taught his true gospel. Twice he defined his doctrine in exactly the same terms. It is the gospel of repentance, baptism, and becoming as a little child, to whom Jesus promises the gift of the Holy Ghost: "Again I say unto you, ye must repent, and become as a little child, and be baptized in my name, or ye can in nowise receive these things. And again I say unto you, ye must repent, and be baptized in my name, and become as a little child, or ye can in nowise inherit the kingdom of God" (3 Nephi 11:37–38). Whoever believes these things and does them, "unto him will the Father bear record of me, for he will visit him

41

with fire and with the Holy Ghost" (3 Nephi 11:35). This doctrine is essential (see 3 Nephi 11:34, 40). Jesus then commanded his ordained disciples to "go forth unto this people, and declare the words which I have spoken, unto the ends of the earth" (3 Nephi 11:41). The clear intention is that all people should have an opportunity to receive these things, or, in other words, that the gospel be received by all of Adam's posterity.

15. *Commending his disciples unto the people.* Jesus then turned to the multitude and blessed them, admonishing them to give strict heed to the words of the twelve: "He stretched forth his hand unto the multitude, and cried unto them, saying: Blessed are ye if ye shall give heed unto the words of these twelve whom I have chosen from among you to minister unto you, and to be your servants," and Jesus certified that he had "given [them] power" (3 Nephi 12:1). He blessed all who would believe their instruction and accept the people's words (cf. John 17), provided they entered into the covenant of baptism, received the Holy Ghost, and obtained remission of their sins (see 3 Nephi 12:2).

16. *Blessings promised.* Several blessings, well known as the Beatitudes, were then bestowed upon all the people (see 3 Nephi 12:3-12). The repetition of the word "all" in these Beatitudes emphasizes the fact that the blessings and promises therein were bestowed upon each individual present there. As candidates for Zion, they are typified as humble, compassionate, long-suffering peacemakers, who love righteousness, who will see God's face, and who will be his eternal children:

> Yea, blessed are the poor in spirit who come unto me, for theirs is the kingdom of heaven.
> And again, blessed are all they that mourn, for they shall be comforted.
> And blessed are the meek, for they shall inherit the earth.

And blessed are all they who do hunger and thirst after righteousness, for they shall be filled with the Holy Ghost.

And blessed are the merciful, for they shall obtain mercy.

And blessed are all the pure in heart, for they shall see God.

And blessed are all the peacemakers, for they shall be called the children of God.

And blessed are all they who are persecuted for my name's sake, for theirs is the kingdom of heaven.

And blessed are ye when men shall revile you and persecute, and shall say all manner of evil against you falsely, for my sake; for ye shall have great joy and be exceedingly glad, for great shall be your reward in heaven; for so persecuted they the prophets who were before you. (3 Nephi 12:3–12).

These blessings describe and promise the ultimate benefits that the faithful will receive if they obey in righteousness the principles that Jesus is about to deliver to them. He promises them blessings in nine different respects. Theirs is the kingdom of heaven, the earth, peace, comfort, mercy; they will see God, be filled with the Holy Ghost, and be called the children of God. Jesus blesses them further so they may be able to bear up under the persecutions and revilings that will be heaped upon them.

Seeing such blessings in a ritual or temple context is natural. Other texts similar in form to the Beatitudes can be found in several apocryphal, pseudepigraphic, and Greek religious texts that had cultic usages and apocalyptic significance (e.g., the *Homeric Hymn to Demeter* and *4 Ezra* 8:46–54). In *2 Enoch* 42, for example, one reads of an ascent into "the paradise of Edem [sic]," where a divine figure appears before Adam and his righteous posterity and rewards them with eternal light and life. Among the nine beatitudes he speaks to them are these: "Happy is the person who reverences the name of the Lord; . . . happy is he who

43

carries out righteous judgment; . . . happy is he who clothes the naked with his garment, and to the hungry gives his bread; . . . happy is he in whom is the truth, so that he may speak the truth to his neighbor; . . . happy is he who has compassion on his lips and gentleness in his heart; happy is he who understands all the works of the Lord, performed by the Lord."[1]

In *2 Enoch* 51–53, one is further taught that "it is good to go to the Lord's temple" three times a day to praise God by speaking a matched list of seven blessings and curses, including: "Happy is the person who opens his lips for praise of the God of Sabaoth, . . . cursed is every person who opens his heart for insulting, and insults the poor and slanders his neighbor, because that person slanders God; . . . happy—who cultivates the love of peace; cursed—who disturbs those who are peaceful. . . . All these things (will be weighed) in the balances and exposed in the books on the great judgment day."[2] It appears that these and other similar texts were regularly used in ancient cultic ceremonies, and thus Hans Dieter Betz sees a close parallel between the Beatitudes in the Sermon on the Mount and the initiation rituals of ancient mystery religions, for both "impart to their adherents, in initiations of the most various kinds, the secrets of the world beyond and their own lot at present."[3] In other words, toward the beginning of the ceremony, the

---

1. Charlesworth, *Old Testament Pseudepigrapha*, 1:168.

2. Ibid., 1:178–81.

3. Betz, *Essays on the Sermon on the Mount*, 30; see, generally, 26–33. "The second line of the macarism in Matt. 5:3 is, therefore, to be regarded as an eschatological verdict reached on the basis of knowledge about the fate of humankind in the afterlife. There is thus a remarkable parallel within the phenomenology of religion between the ancient Greek mysteries of Demeter and other mysteries, and Jewish apocalyptic. . . . It is for this reason that the verdict awaited at the last judgment, both in the mysteries and in Jewish apocalyptic, can already be rendered in the earthly present." Ibid., 30.

people are given a glimpse of the heights to which they may rise—the kingdoms and qualities—if they are true and faithful and become the people of Zion, the pure in heart (see Matthew 5:8; D&C 97:21).

Others have seen in the Beatitudes "entrance-requirements" for the Kingdom[1] and what Georg Strecker calls "the conditions that must be fulfilled in order to gain entrance to the holy of holies."[2] This view is supported by the fact that several of the requirements for entrance into the temple in Jerusalem are strikingly comparable to certain phrases in the Beatitudes. For example, to enter that temple one must be "pure in heart" and "seek [the Lord's] face" in order to stand in his holy place (Psalms 24:3-6). When Jesus accordingly blesses "the pure in heart" who shall "see God," he is alluding to those who are worthy to enter the temple. The "overriding meaning of seeing God and standing before him, as far as the Old Testament is concerned . . . has to do with his mercy-presence in the temple."[3] Strecker hastens to qualify this with the assertion that Jesus "teaches not cultic but eschatological virtues. They refer to entrance not into the earthly temple but into the kingdom of God,"[4] but it seems to me that this assessment is too narrow. To discard the efficacy and the present significance of the temple in earliest Christianity ignores the fact that

---

1. H. Windisch, *The Meaning of the Sermon on the Mount* (Philadelphia: Westminster, 1951), 26-27, 87-88. Robert A. Guelich, "The Matthean Beatitudes: 'Entrance Requirements' or Eschatological Blessings?" *Journal of Biblical Literature* 95 (1976): 415-34, argues that both factors are present in the Beatitudes, which presuppose the creation of a new relationship between man and God, implicit to which is an eschatological dimension, especially in connection with Isaiah 61.

2. Strecker, *Sermon on the Mount*, 33 n. 28.

3. Hermann Strack and Paul Billerbeck, *Kommentar zum neuen Testament aus Talmud und Midrasch* (Munich: Beck, 1922), 1:206.

4. Strecker, *Sermon on the Mount*, 33 n. 28.

all aspects of the old were not destroyed, but they simply were fulfilled and became new in Christ.

Likewise, the thrust of the first few beatitudes is to be similarly understood: The meek and the poor and the hungry are the ones who will be "endowed with the supreme gift of divine bliss, with the Holy Spirit."[1] Such a view is also consonant with a powerful passage in the Doctrine and Covenants regarding the Kirtland Temple, which likewise employs the terminology of the sixth beatitude to promise the righteous the blessings of the temple: "Yea, and my presence shall be there, for I will come into it, and *all the pure in heart* that shall come into it *shall see God*" (D&C 97:16; italics added).

17. The people invited to become the salt of the earth. The Lord next offers the people a special status, with a caution. He says, "I give unto you to be the salt of the earth; but if the salt shall lose its savor, . . . the salt shall be thenceforth good for nothing, but to be cast out and to be trodden under foot of men" (3 Nephi 12:13). This is an invitation to enter into a covenant with the Lord, carrying with it a solemn warning that those who violate the covenant will be cast out and trampled under foot (although one continues to invite them back; 3 Nephi 18:32–33). The covenant connection here, for Latter-day Saints, is found most clearly in the Doctrine and Covenants, which explains that those who enter into the everlasting covenant "are accounted as the salt of the earth" (D&C 101:39; cf. Numbers 18:19), a theme Elder Delbert L. Stapley developed in his General Conference talk entitled "Salt of the Earth."[2]

Among biblical commentaries, of course, a wide variety of meanings have been attributed to this particular meta-

---

1. D. Flusser, "Blessed are the Poor in Spirit," *Israel Exploration Journal* 10 (1960): 6.

2. *Improvement Era* 67 (December 1964): 1069–71.

phor. Wolfgang Nauch presents evidence, largely from rabbinic sources, that the reference to "salt" in Matthew 5 was "taken from a certain code of instruction for the disciples of Scribes," requiring them to be "modest and (of) humble spirit, industrious and salted, suffering insult and (they should be) liked by all men."[1] The concept of salt, according to his view, demands suffering, purification, and wisdom of the true disciple.

Implicit in Jesus' words here about salt, earth, and light may also be hints of certain creation themes: the doctrine of the Two Ways, the separation of opposites, light and dark, and heaven and earth. This principle of opposition is fundamental to the Sermon on the Mount. It surfaces again, for example, in the doctrine of the Two Ways in Matthew 7:13. Such creation themes were not confined to wisdom literature in the Bible, but were equally found in ritual. Indeed, some scholars have identified the creation account of Genesis as playing a key role in ancient Israelite temple ritual, although the details remain obscure. In Jesus' words, however, the old symbolism has been imbued with new, additional meaning:[2] Instead of the old imperative, "*Let* there be *light*" (Genesis 1:3), Jesus now issues the new injunction, "*Let* your *light* so shine before this people, that they may see your good works" (3 Nephi 12:16). Just as

---

1. "Salt as a Metaphor in Instructions for Discipleship," *Studia Theologica* 6 (1953): 165–66, see 165–78.

2. Discussed in Stephen D. Ricks, "Liturgy and Cosmogony: The Ritual Use of Creation Accounts in the Ancient Near East," F.A.R.M.S. Preliminary Report, 1981. Ricks cites Arieh Toeg, "Genesis 1 and the Sabbath [Hebrew]," *Beth Miqra* 50 (1972): 290; Moshe Weinfeld, "Sabbath, Temple Building, and the Enthronement of the Lord [Hebrew]," *Beth Miqra* 69 (1977): 188–89; and Peter J. Kearney, "Creation and Liturgy: The P Redaction of Ex 25–40," *Zeitschrift für die alttestamentliche Wissenschaft* 89 (1977): 375–78. These articles explore the relationships between the creation account and the temple, particularly the instructions for the construction of the tabernacle in Exodus 25–31.

the Creator looked at the creation and pronounced his works to be good, Jesus now invites each disciple to become a creator of "good works," that when they are seen, men may glorify God. With this, Jesus is forming a new heaven and new earth, a new creative act and new creation.

18. *A first set of laws explained.* Formal instruction to the people begins in earnest as Jesus next turns to teach and explain the essence of three of the Ten Commandments and of the law of Moses, the law administered anciently by the Aaronic Priesthood. He explains that this law has not been destroyed. In its fulfilled form, it still has an essential place in the righteous life: "Think not that I am come to destroy the law or the prophets. I am not come to destroy but to fulfil; for verily I say unto you, one jot nor one tittle hath not passed away from the law, but in me it hath all been fulfilled" (3 Nephi 12:17-18).

19. *Obedience and sacrifice.* First, Jesus teaches the companion principles of obedience to the Lord and of sacrifice. He exhorts the people to obey the commandments that he issues at this time: "I have given you the law and the commandments of my Father, that ye shall believe in me, and that ye shall repent of your sins, and come unto me with a broken heart and a contrite spirit. Behold, ye have the commandments before you, and the law is fulfilled. Therefore come unto me and be ye saved; for verily I say unto you, that except ye shall keep my commandments, which I have commanded you at this time, ye shall in no case enter into the kingdom of heaven" (3 Nephi 12:19-20). He requires the people to exercise faith, repentance, and obedience, which constitutes coming unto him "with a broken heart and a contrite spirit" (3 Nephi 12:19). The offering of a broken heart and a contrite spirit is none other than the new law of sacrifice, as the voice of the Lord had explained earlier from heaven (see 3 Nephi 9:19-20). This new law of obedience and sacrifice superseded the practices

of sacrifice under the law of Moses and put an end to "the shedding of blood" (3 Nephi 9:19).

20. Prohibition against anger, ill-speaking, and ridicule of brethren. Second, Jesus upgraded the old law against murder into a higher prohibition against becoming angry or speaking derisively or critically about one's brother: "Ye have heard that it hath been said by them of old time, and it is also written before you, that thou shalt not kill, and whosoever shall kill shall be in danger of the judgment of God; but I say unto you, that whosoever is angry with his brother shall be in danger of his judgment. And whosoever shall say to his brother, Raca, shall be in danger of the council; and whosoever shall say, Thou fool, shall be in danger of hell fire" (3 Nephi 12:21–22).

In the brotherhood of a priesthood setting, I interpret this as amounting especially to a prohibition against speaking evil against any other priesthood brother, let alone against God. In effect, it prohibits all manner of evil or unholy speaking against any brother, and thus all the more so against the Lord's anointed leaders. According to the Sermon at the Temple, anyone who is angry with a brother is said to be in danger of *his* judgment (the implication is that the offended person is a "brother" who has power to render judgment). Anyone who calls his brother "Raca" is in danger of being brought before "the council," that is, the elders in charge of administering the kingdom. Those who persist in such misconduct are in danger of hellfire. Since the word "Raca" means "empty-head," the thrust of this injunction is that laughing at a brother's foolishness (that is, what to a lay member may seem to be foolishness) is prohibited.

Such provisions and disciplinary procedures are especially pertinent to a community of covenanters, as the evidence that Manfred Weise and others have marshalled regarding rules of discipline at Qumran and in the earliest

Christian community tends to show.[1] According to one of
the rules of the Dead Sea community found in the *Manual
of Discipline* 7:8, "anger against a fellow-member of the
society could not be tolerated under any circumstances,"
and they applied a punishment "in any case of a member
harbouring angry feelings."[2] Indeed, the *Manual of Discipline* 1:16–2:18 concludes its covenant-making ceremony
by subjecting those who enter into the covenant unworthily
to judgments of the community council and to punishments
similar to those mentioned in Matthew 5:21–22. Weise argues that comparable councils were also convened in the
early Church, as evidenced in 1 Corinthians 5:4–5, 1 Timothy 1:20, and the writings of Ignatius,[3] specifically for the
purpose of disciplining those who affronted Christ by insulting those people in whom Christ's spirit dwelt. Such
deprecations are "not merely chidings in a banal sense,
rather they insult to the core the community of God, viz.,
the covenant-community (*Verbundenheit*) of God. Therein
lies their seriousness."[4]

21. *Reconciliation necessary before proceeding further.*
In 3 Nephi 12:23–24, Jesus interrupts the instruction to
explain that, if anyone desires to come unto him, he or she
should have no hard feelings against any brother or sister:
"Therefore, if ye shall come unto me, or shall desire to come
unto me, and rememberest that thy brother hath aught
against thee—go thy way unto thy brother, and first be

---

1. Manfred Weise, "Mt 5:21f—ein Zeugnis sakraler Rechtsprechung
in der Urgemeinde," *Zeitschrift der neutestamentliche Wissenschaft* 49
(1958): 116–23.

2. P. Wernberg-Moeller, "A Semitic Idiom in Matt. V. 22," *New
Testament Studies* 3 (1956): 72.

3. Ignatius uses the word "council" (*synhedrion*) in reference to a
"council of the apostles." See *TDNT* 7:871.

4. Weise, "Mt 5:21f—ein Zeugnis sakraler Rechtsprechung in der
Urgemeinde," 123.

reconciled to thy brother, and then come unto me with full purpose of heart, and I will receive you" (3 Nephi 12:23–24). No disciple can come unto Christ until first being reconciled with his brothers and sisters. Then one can come with "full purpose of heart" to be received by Christ.

Some scholars have seen this passage as an intrusive interruption in the flow of thought in the Sermon on the Mount because it breaks up the rhythm of the antitheses between the old and the new in Matthew 5. It makes good sense, however, in the context of insuring that the listeners are in the proper state of mind to go forward ritually toward the holy altar. Indeed, the Sermon on the Mount tells the disciple to leave his sacrifice on the altar and first go and reconcile himself with his brother before proceeding (see Matthew 5:24). In order to facilitate this reconciliation, Jesus admonishes the people to settle all their controversies quickly and to avoid going to court, looking forward instead to the fact that another day of judgment will be far more important than any earthly day in court.

22. Chastity. The next subject addressed is the law of chastity: "Behold, it is written by them of old time, that thou shalt not commit adultery; but I say unto you, that whosoever looketh on a woman, to lust after her, hath committed adultery already in his heart. Behold, I give unto you a commandment, that ye suffer none of these things to enter into your heart; for it is better that ye should deny yourselves of these things, wherein ye will take up your cross, than that ye should be cast into hell" (3 Nephi 12:27–30). The new law imposes a strict prohibition against sexual intercourse outside of marriage and, intensifying the rules that prevailed under the old law, requires purity of heart and denial of these things. In committing to live by this law, the righteous bear a heavy responsibility and are symbolically crucified themselves—"wherein ye will take up your cross" (3 Nephi 12:30).

Unlike the Sermon on the Mount, the Sermon at the Temple mentions no penalty concerning the unchaste eye that should be cast out if it offends (see Matthew 5:29). This has been a troublesome point for many biblical commentators, for Jewish attitudes around the time of Jesus were strongly set against any punishment that took the form of bodily mutilation.[1] It is unlikely, of course, that Jesus demanded actual self-mutilation of his disciples, and the Sermon at the Temple contains no such implication, for it does not speak in any way here of actual bodily mutilation; the mode appears to be figurative (see also JST, Matthew 5:34, "Now this I speak, a parable concerning your sins"). All references to plucking out the eye or to cutting off the hand that offends are absent in the Book of Mormon text, suggesting that this problematic verse in the Sermon on the Mount, on its face, does not fully reflect Jesus' original intent. Instead, the Sermon at the Temple speaks at this point of a total commitment—of the disciple taking up a symbolic cross, a symbol of capital punishment.

This demands that the righteous strictly exercise the virtue of self-control, and it also reflects a warning that, if a person violates the law of chastity, the penalty will involve serious consequences. In particular, the disciple must be willing to deny himself these things and, in so doing, "cross" himself (Alma 39:9) or, in Jesus' words, "take up your cross" (3 Nephi 12:30). The image this may bring to mind is that of a covenanter taking this obligation very seriously, for hanging or exposing a body on a tree or on a cross was part of the standard punishment under the law of Moses for any person who committed a sin worthy of death. This form of punishment was apparently known to the Nephites through the Brass Plates and the writings of the prophet

---

1. J. Schattenmann, "Jesus and Pythagoras," *Kairos* 21 (1979): 215–20.

Zenos (see 1 Nephi 19:13). Deuteronomy 21:22 speaks of exposing the body of the culprit "on a tree," a practice observed by the Nephites (see 3 Nephi 4:28), which Peter connected with the death of Jesus on the cross (see Acts 10:39). Thus, with this teaching in the Sermon at the Temple, one possibly confronts the idea that the disciple must be willing to take upon himself the very form of mortal punishment that Jesus himself suffered. As a practical matter in early Christianity, the punishment of those violating this covenant of chastity probably took the form of excommunication, understanding being "cut off" in Matthew 5:30 as "a communal parable."[1]

23. *Marriages of covenanters are not to be dissolved except for fornication.* In connection with the law of chastity, Jesus teaches the importance of marriage by superseding the old law of divorcement with the new law of marriage: "It hath been written, that whosoever shall put away his wife, let him give her a writing of divorcement. Verily, verily, I say unto you, that whosoever shall put away his wife, saving for the cause of fornication, causeth her to commit adultery; and whoso shall marry her who is divorced committeth adultery" (3 Nephi 12:31–32). Husbands are not to put their wives away, and wives are not to remarry. For centuries, commentators have struggled to understand the intended application of this radical prohibition against divorce. The context of the Sermon at the Temple suggests that this very demanding restriction applies only to husbands and wives who are bound by the eternal covenant relationship involved here. This explains the strictness of the rule completely, for eternal marriages can be dissolved only by proper authority and on justifiable grounds. Until they are so divorced, a couple remains covenantally married.

---

1. Helmut Koester, "Using Quintilian to Interpret Mark," *Biblical Archaeology Review* 6 (May/June 1980): 44–45; cf. 2 Nephi 1:17; 5:20; Mosiah 5:11–12.

24. Oaths sworn by saying Yes or No. Instructions are then given regarding the swearing of oaths (see 3 Nephi 12:33–37), in particular that Jesus' followers should "Let [their] communication be Yea, yea; Nay, nay; for whatsoever cometh of more than these is evil." Some biblical commentators have found this section in the Sermon on the Mount odd because it does not continue logically with the sequence of commandments in the Decalogue, as one might expect Jesus to follow if he were simply giving a commentary on the Ten Commandments. Instead, instructions are given on how religious commitments are to be made: The swearing of oaths (which often accompanied the making of covenants[1]) should not be by the heavens or by the earth or by one's head, but simply by saying "yes" or "no." That is sufficient. A rabbinic aphorism suggests a similar sentiment: "Let your Yes and No both be righteous. Do not speak with your mouth what you do not mean in your heart."[2] In a ritual context, any more than this is superfluous or perhaps devious; more is not required and is to be avoided. While these words about oaths apply in numerous life settings, they are most pertinent when people are making, or are about to make, solemn oaths to the Lord.

This interpretation holds that Jesus was not opposed to covenantal promises per se, only to oaths sworn in the wrong way. What he objects to is such casuistry that asks whether one is bound if one swears by temple gold but not if one swears by the temple, or whether one is bound on an oath by the offering but not on an oath by the altar (see Matthew 23:16–19). In Matthew 23, which seems to reflect most clearly the historical teaching of Jesus on oaths, "there is no total ban on oaths."[3] Indeed, Jesus' point is that one should look

---

1. *TDNT* 5:460.

2. Paul S. Minear, "Yes or No: The Demand for Honesty in the Early Church," *Novum Testamentum* 13 (1971): 1–13.

3. Ibid., 4.

in one's oaths to the deity behind the temple, behind the altar, and in the heavens, who sanctifies them all: "Whoso shall swear by the temple, sweareth by it, *and by him that dwelleth therein*; and he that shall swear by heaven, sweareth by the throne of God, *and by him that sitteth thereon*" (Matthew 23:21–22; italics added). The point is that all oaths are ultimately oaths by and before God. "All oaths directly or indirectly appeal to God; all are therefore binding since they call on him to guarantee their fulfillment."[1] Thus early Christians were told that they should be different from those at Qumran who swore horrific oaths or from others who regularly swore commercial or legal oaths in the temple of Herod. They were told to avoid the forms of all such oaths—neither *by* the heaven, nor *by* the earth.

To be sure, some have read Matthew 5:33 and James 5:12 as forbidding all oaths or promises ("swear not *at all*," "swear *no* other oath"), but this does not capture what appears to be the historical intent of Jesus (as reflected explicitly in Matthew 23),[2] and these two texts can be interpreted otherwise: I read the Greek in James 5:12 as telling Christians not to swear an oath by heaven, or by earth, or by any *other such thing* (*allon tina*).[3] James admonishes his followers to let their "yes" really be a "yes" and their "no" really be a "no" and to keep their solemn promises "so that they not fall under the judgment [of the Lord]." Disciples of Jesus are not to be uncommitted, but should let their

---

1. Ibid., 5.

2. Minear finds that the accent originally fell, not on the ban against oaths, but on the demand for radical honesty. Ibid., 3.

3. The Greek grammar in this verse is odd. "By heaven" and "by earth" are in the accusative case, leaving it unclear how to read *allon tina orkon*, which is equally in the accusative: that is, does it mean "an oath *by* any other thing" or "any kind of oath"? If the sense is "neither by heaven, nor by earth, nor by anything in between," the meaning of James 5:12 is essentially the same as Matthew 23.

sacred "word (*logos*) be yes, yes, no, no" (Matthew 5:37). From a Latter-day Saint point of view, the most important commitments a person can ever say "yes" or "no" to are those made in covenants with God.[1]

25. *Love of enemies.* The rules of loving one's neighbor, turning the other cheek, going the extra mile, giving the poor more than is asked, loving enemies, and doing good to all people are given next: "And behold, it is written, an eye for an eye, and a tooth for a tooth; but I say unto you, that ye shall not resist evil, but whosoever shall smite thee on thy right cheek, turn to him the other also; and if any man will sue thee at the law and take away thy coat, let him have thy cloak also; and whosoever shall compel thee to go a mile, go with him twain. Give to him that asketh thee, and from him that would borrow of thee turn thou not away. And behold it is written also, that thou shalt love thy neighbor and hate thine enemy; but behold I say unto you, love your enemies, bless them that curse you, do good to them that hate you, and pray for them who despitefully use you and persecute you; that ye may be the children of your Father who is in heaven; for he maketh his sun to rise on the evil and on the good" (3 Nephi 12:38–45).

Although the law of the Gospel is never expressly defined in scripture, I understand this law to be the law of love and generosity: "Thou shalt love the Lord thy God with all thy heart, and with all thy soul, and with all thy mind. This is the first and great commandment, and the second is like unto it, Thou shalt love thy neighbor as thyself" (Matthew

---

1. The bilateral covenantal nature of early Christian ordinances such as baptism and the sacrament is not well documented in the Bible, but it is in the Book of Mormon; see Richard L. Anderson, "Religious Validity: The Sacramental Covenant in 3 Nephi," F.A.R.M.S. 1988 Book of Mormon Lecture (Provo: F.A.R.M.S., 1989), reprinted in *By Study and Also by Faith: Essays in Honor of Hugh Nibley*, eds. J. Lundquist and S. Ricks (Salt Lake City: Deseret Book and F.A.R.M.S., 1990), 2:1–51.

22:37-39; quoting Deuteronomy 6:5; see also D&C 59:5-6). "If any man shall take of the abundance which I have made, and impart not his portion, according to *the law of my gospel,* unto the poor and the needy, he shall, with the wicked, lift up his eyes in hell, being in torment" (D&C 104:18; italics added).

In all dispensations, covenant people have been required to give to the poor and to lend to those who ask. This was required of the children of Israel (see Deuteronomy 15:7-11) and of the people of King Benjamin (see Mosiah 4:16-26) as a condition of their covenant. Thus Jesus' commandment that one must "give to him that asketh . . . and from him that would borrow of thee turn not thou away" (Matthew 5:42) not only captures the essence of the law of the gospel regarding love and generosity, but also incorporates a traditional Israelite and Nephite covenantal condition. Indeed, Jesus emphasizes that this law is old as well as new—"those things which were of old time . . . in me are all fulfilled" (3 Nephi 12:46-47)—and it can be seen that this law of the gospel is truly taught in the scriptures of all dispensations.

26. Transition into a higher order. At this point in the Sermon, the disciples have reached a plateau: "Therefore I would that ye should be perfect" (3 Nephi 12:48). The word "therefore" marks a transition in the design of the Sermon: On the one hand, it looks back over the instruction given thus far about the law of Moses, while on the other hand, it looks forward to yet a greater order to be required if the people are to become "perfect."

Although it is possible that the word "perfect" has only a straightforward ethical or religious meaning here,[1] reflect-

---

1. On perfection as our eternal goal, having the flaws and errors removed, see Gerald N. Lund, "I Have a Question," *Ensign* (August 1986): 39-41. Talmage, *Jesus the Christ,* 248 n. 5, minimalizes the concept to

ing perfect or "undivided obedience to God" and "unlimited love,"[1] there is a stronger possibility that the word carries a ceremonial connotation in this particular text. It seems to me that, in this verse, Jesus is expressing his desire that the disciples now advance from one level to a next level, to go on to become "perfect," "finished," or "completed" in their instruction and endowment. In addition to the ritual context of the Sermon — the context usually determining the sense in which the intended "completeness" consists[2] — several reasons support this understanding.

First, the Greek word translated into English as "perfect" in Matthew 5:48 is *teleios*. This important word is used in Greek religious literature to describe the person who has become fully initiated in the rituals of the religion. *Teleios* is "a technical term of the mystery religions, which refers to one initiated into the mystic rites, the initiate."[3] The word is used in Hebrews 5:14–6:1 to distinguish between the initial teachings and the full instruction; and in Hebrews 9:11 it refers to the heavenly temple. Generally in

---

"Be ye relatively perfect." See also W. Bauer, W. F. Arndt, and F. W. Gingrich, *A Greek-English Lexicon of the New Testament* (Chicago: University of Chicago Press, 1957), 816–17, hereafter *GELNT*, giving the meanings of *teleios* as "having attained the end or purpose, complete, perfect," "full-grown, mature, adult," "complete," "fully developed in a moral sense"; E. Kenneth Lee, "Hard Sayings — I," *Theology* 66 (1963): 318–20; E. Yarnold, "Teleios in St. Matthew's Gospel," *Studia Evangelica* 4, in *Texte und Untersuchungen* 102 (1968): 269–73, identifying three meanings of *teleios* in Matthew: Pharisaically perfect in keeping the laws, lacking in nothing, and fully grown.

1. This is the preferred meaning suggested in the Protestant view; see *TDNT* 8:73, 75.

2. Yarnold, "Teleios in St. Matthew's Gospel," 271.

3. *GELNT*, 817, citing sources; referring also to Philippians 3:15; Colossians 1:28; see also Demosthenes, *De Corona* 259, in C. A. Vince, tr., *Demosthenes* (Cambridge: Harvard University Press, 1971), 190–91, where *telousei* is translated as "initiations" into the mystery religions; *TDNT* 8:69.

the Epistle to the Hebrews, its usage follows a "special use" from Hellenistic Judaism, where the word *teleioō* means "to put someone in the position in which he can come, or stand, before God."[1] Thus, in its ritual connotations, this word refers to preparing a person to be presented to come before God "in priestly action"[2] or "to qualify for the cultus."[3] Early Christians continued to use this word in this way in connection with their sacraments and ordinances.[4]

Most intriguing in this regard is the letter of Clement of Alexandria describing the existence (c. 200 A.D.) of a *second* Gospel of Mark, reporting the Lord's doings as recounted by Peter and going beyond the public Gospel of Mark now found in the New Testament.[5] This so-called Secret Gospel of Mark according to Clement, contained things "for the use of those who were being perfected (*teleioumenon*). Nevertheless, he [Mark] did not divulge the things not to be uttered, nor did he write down the hierophantic [priesthood] teaching (*hierophantiken didaskalian*) of the Lord, but . . . brought in certain sayings of which he knew the interpretation would, as a mystagogue, lead the hearers into the innermost sanctuary of that truth hidden by seven veils."[6] The copy was read "only to those who are being initiated (*tous muoumenous*) into the great mysteries (*ta megala mysteria*)."[7] Thus, although almost nothing is known about these sacred and secret teachings of Jesus

---

1. *TDNT* 8:82; citing Hebrews 7:19; 10:1.

2. *TDNT* 8:83.

3. Ibid., 8:85.

4. H. Stephanus, *Thesaurus Graecae Linguae* (Graz: Akademische Druck- und Verlaganstalt, 1954), 8:1961, "gradibus ad sacramentorum participationem, *ton hagiasmaton metochen, admittebantur.*"

5. Morton Smith, *Clement of Alexandria and a Secret Gospel of Mark* (Cambridge: Harvard University Press, 1973).

6. Ibid., 446 (Morton Smith's translation).

7. Ibid.

mentioned by Clement (who died 215 A.D.), there can be little doubt that such esoteric, orthodox teachings existed in Alexandria and that some early Christians had been "perfected" by learning those priesthood teachings. The suggestion that the words of the Sermon, explicitly inviting its followers to become "perfected," may have stood in a similar tradition is, therefore, not without precedent in early Christianity.

Moreover, the cultic use of the Hebrew term *shalom* may provide a concrete link between the Nephites and this Greek and Christian use of *teleios*. John Durham has explored in detail the fundamental meanings of *shalom*, especially in Numbers 6:26 and in certain of the Psalms, and concludes that it was used as a cultic term referring to a gift or endowment to or of God that "can be received only in his Presence,"[1] "a blessing specially connected to theophany or the immanent Presence of God,"[2] specifically as appearing in the Temple of Solomon and represented "within the Israelite cult" and liturgy.[3] Buruch LeVine similarly analyzes the function of the *shelamim* sacrifices as producing "complete," or perfect, "harmony with the deity, . . . characteristic of the covenant relationship as well as of the ritual experience of communion."[4]

Durham, along with several others, sees this Israelite concept in the word *teleios* in Matthew 5:48.[5] "Matthew does not use *teleios* in the Greek sense of the perfect ethical personality, but in the Old Testament sense of the whole-

---

1. John I. Durham, "Shalom and the Presence of God," in *Proclamation and Presence* (Richmond, Virginia: John Knox, 1970), 292.

2. Ibid., 281.

3. Ibid., 286–92.

4. Baruch A. Levine, *In the Presence of the Lord* (Leiden: Brill, 1974), 35–36.

5. Durham, "Shalom and the Presence of God," 293 n. 135.

ness of consecration to God."[1] It tends toward the meaning of "living up to an agreement or covenant without fault: as the Father keeps the covenants he makes with us. . . . *Teleioi* is a locus technicus from the Mysteries: the completely initiated who has both qualified for initiation and completed it is *teleios*, lit. 'gone all the way,' fulfilling all requirements, every last provision of God's command. The hardest rules are what will decide the *teletios*, the final test—the Law of Consecration."[2] Thus, although we do not know what word Jesus used when he spoke to the Nephites that has been translated "perfect" in 3 Nephi 12:48, there is reason to believe that they would have known from their Israelite heritage a word like *shalom* similar in cultic content to the Greek word *teleios*.

Accordingly, in commanding the people to "be perfect even as I, or your Father who is in heaven is perfect" (3 Nephi 12:48), it seems that Jesus had several things in mind besides "perfection" as we usually think of it. Whatever he meant, it involved the idea of becoming like God ("even as I or your Father who is in heaven"), which occurs by seeing God (see 1 John 3:2) and knowing God (see John 17:3). These ultimate realities can be represented ceremoniously in this world, for as Joseph Smith taught, it is through his ordinances that we are "instructed more perfectly."[3]

Finally, the style of the Sermon shifts into a different mode after this invitation to become perfect. The next sec-

---

1. G. Bornkamm, G. Barth, and H. Held, *Tradition and Interpretation in Matthew* (London: SCM, 1963), 101; see also Strack and Billerbeck, *Kommentar zum neuen Testament*, 1:386.

2. Hugh Nibley, unpublished notes from his Sunday School class on the New Testament, on Matthew 5:48, in the F.A.R.M.S. Hugh Nibley Archive.

3. *History of the Church*, 2:312; discussed in Truman G. Madsen, "Mormonism and the New-Making Morality," James E. Talmage Lecture Series, February 24, 1971.

tion of the Sermon, contains no reference to the old law of Moses. If Matthew 5 (or 3 Nephi 12) is about *the law* (Moses), then Matthew 6 (or 3 Nephi 13) distills *the prophets* (represented by the spirit of Elijah; see Matthew 17:3), for the Sermon as a whole embraces both the law and the prophets (see 3 Nephi 12:17; 14:12). Stylistically there is also a sharp contrast between Matthew 5 (or 3 Nephi 12) and Matthew 6 (or 3 Nephi 13), so much so that many biblical commentators have suspected Matthew 6:1-18 of being a later intrusion into the text. That suspicion dissolves, however, if one sees that the text has simply moved on to a new stage of the experience, thus accounting for the different world to which it seems to belong. In this higher level there will be greater emphasis on secret and inward righteousness, as well as controlling the needs of the flesh and of this world. Thus the text next presents a second set of requirements by discussing almsgiving, prayer, forgiveness, fasting, and total dedication of all that one has to God.

27. *Giving to the poor.* Almsgiving is the first requirement of the higher order (see 3 Nephi 13:1-4). If done in secret, it will reap open rewards. This rule is a natural conjunction of the law of the gospel (see D&C 104:18) and the law of consecration. Vermes believes that Jesus' requirement that alms must be given in secret alludes to the "Chamber of Secrets" in the Temple of Herod mentioned in the Mishnah,[1] into which "the devout used to put their gifts in secret and the poor of good family received support therefrom in secret."[2] But giving to the poor has long been a requirement placed upon the Lord's covenant people.[3]

---

1. Mishnah, *Shekalim* 5:6.

2. G. Vermes, *Jesus the Jew* (London: Collins, 1973), 78.

3. For a broad and sensitive treatment of this subject in the biblical period, see Leon Epsztein, *Social Justice in the Ancient Near East and the People of the Bible* (London: SCM, 1986).

King Benjamin emphasized it as one of the main spiritual attributes of a righteous, covenant person: "Ye yourselves will succor those that stand in need of your succor" (Mosiah 4:16). Giving to the poor, he stipulated, is necessary in "retaining a remission of your sins from day to day" and is an essential prerequisite for entering into a covenant with God, having "no more disposition to do evil, but to do good continually" (Mosiah 4:26; 5:2, 5).

28. *The order of prayer.* After the instructions about praying in public and alone in private (see 3 Nephi 13:5-6), the English pronouns shift from a singular "thou" to a plural "ye." This may indicate that the Lord first taught the people how to pray individually in private ("when thou [singular] prayest, enter into thy closet"), then offered instruction in group prayer ("after this manner pray ye [plural]").[1] He then offered the Lord's Prayer: "After this manner therefore pray ye: Our Father who art in heaven, hallowed be thy name. Thy will be done on earth as it is in heaven. And forgive us our debts, as we forgive our debtors. And lead us not into temptation, but deliver us from evil. For thine is the kingdom, and the power, and the glory, forever. Amen" (3 Nephi 13:9-13).

From the earliest Christian times, the Lord's Prayer was "basically a prayer used by a group,"[2] and several early Christian texts document the use of sacred group prayers, with the participants standing in a circle around Jesus at the center.[3] The Lord's Prayer was undoubtedly intended as a pattern or model for group prayers. Jesus probably taught something like it on several occasions and fluidly modified

---

1. In Matthew 6:6 the Greek is also singular while in 6:7-9 it is plural, although in 6:5 the Greek is plural.

2. Gordon J. Bahr, "The Use of the Lord's Prayer in the Primitive Church," *Journal of Biblical Literature* 84 (1965): 155-56.

3. See Hugh W. Nibley, "The Early Christian Prayer Circle," *BYU Studies* 19 (1978): 41-78; in *CWHN* 4:45-99.

it somewhat each time, as reflected in the fact that no two texts of the prayer are quite the same (see Matthew 6:9–13; Luke 11:2–4; and 3 Nephi 13:9–13; *Didache* 8 offers yet a fourth, apparently independent, version). The early church father Origen understood the Lord's Prayer to be only a model or outline,[1] and the rabbis similarly expressed "strong prohibitions against reciting a fixed prayer," recommending that in saying a set personal prayer one should vary it a little each time.[2]

Hugh Nibley has seen in the structure of the Lord's Prayer more than a polite request or legal petition.[3] He maintains that it is rather an archetype of the "mysteries or ceremonies" that bring down to earth the pattern of heaven ("on earth exactly as it is in heaven"), "to which our present tie and password is the name" ("hallowed be thy name").[4] Like the typical elements of the mysteries, the prayer synoptically covers an *archē* (beginning in heaven, father of spirits), an *omphalus* (history, this world, bread, debts, temptation, and cry for deliverance), and *sphragis* (end of the world, seal, kingdom, and glory).[5]

A further connection between the Lord's Prayer and sacred ritual is evident in the description of the doxology that

---

1. Bahr, "The Use of the Lord's Prayer in the Primitive Church," 153.

2. Ibid., 157; see also Hans Dieter Betz, "The Lord's Prayer," presented at the Annual Meeting of the Society of Biblical Literature, Chicago, 1988.

3. See Joseph Heinemann, *Prayer in the Talmud* (Berlin: de Gruyter, 1977), 193–217, discussing the "law court patterns" in similar prayers, where one presents a plea to the divine judge, gives the facts, defends himself, and asks for judgment in his favor.

4. Hugh Nibley, unpublished notes from his Sunday School class on the New Testament, at Matthew 6:9–13, in the F.A.R.M.S. Hugh Nibley Archive.

5. Ibid; see also Raymond E. Brown, "The Pater Noster as an Eschatalogical Prayer," in *New Testament Essays* (London: 1965).

the children of Israel exclaimed in the temple of Jerusalem on the Day of Atonement. As Strack and Billerbeck explain, after the High Priest had transferred the sins of the people to the scapegoat, driven it out into the wilderness, and said the words, "that ye may be clean from all your sins before the Lord" (Leviticus 16:30), then

> the priests and the people, who were standing in the Forecourt of the Temple, when they heard the name of the Lord clearly uttered, as soon as it came out of the mouth of the High Priest, bowed their knees and threw themselves down and fell on their faces and said, "Praised be the name of his glorious kingdom forever and eternally!" In the Temple [*im Heiligtum*] one did not simply answer "Amen!" How did one answer? "Praised be the name of his glorious kingdom forever and eternally!" . . . How do we know that people answered this way upon each benediction [in the Temple]? The scripture teaches, saying, "He is to be exalted with every praise and adulation."[1]

Thus, in the temple, the faithful answered the High Priest not only with a simple "amen," but also with praises of God, his glory, power and kingdom, forever, amen. According to the rabbinic sources, this doxological acknowledgment of the kingdom and glory of God was in regular usage in the temple at the time of Jesus, and it was attributed to a much earlier time. It was traditionally believed that these words of praise were spoken by father Jacob to his sons shortly before his death.[2] Thus the extended ending of the Lord's Prayer, "for thine is the kingdom, and the power, and the glory, forever, amen," would probably have been recognized by several of Jesus' listeners as a traditional sign

---

1. Strack and Billerbeck, *Kommentar zum Neuen Testament*, 1:423, citing Mishnah, *Yoma* 6:2, and others.

2. Ibid.

of great sanctity and solemnity usually associated with the holiest of temple rituals on the Day of Atonement.

The stated purpose of Jesus' instruction about prayer is to show his followers how *not* to be "seen of men" or "heard for their much speaking," but how to be seen and heard of God. This is the cry of ages, the prayer that God will hear the words that we speak ("Then hear thou in heaven, " 1 Kings 8:32, 34, 36, 39, 43, 45, 49, from the dedicatory prayer of the Temple of Solomon).

The disciples were then invited to follow suit: "After this manner therefore pray ye" (3 Nephi 13:9–13).

The law of forgiveness is twice reiterated (see 3 Nephi 13:11, 14–15) to emphasize the fact that, under the new law, requests for forgiveness of sin and deliverance will not be granted unless the disciples forgive one another and hold no hard feelings or unforgiving attitudes toward others.

29. Fasting, washing, and anointing. A new order of fasting is then taught. In addition to requiring a secret inward righteousness in fasting, true fasting is to be accompanied with anointing the head and washing the face (see 3 Nephi 13:17). Washing the face, the head, the feet, the hands, or other parts of the body is symbolic of becoming completely clean (see John 13:9–10), "clean every whit" (John 13:10). The concept is similar to the desire to become clean from the blood and sins that one encounters in this world (cf. 2 Nephi 9:44). When a disciple seeks the Lord in true fasting and prayer in such a condition of purity, the Lord will see and reward him openly in heaven.

On three occasions in this section of the Sermon, the disciple is promised that the Lord will see him and reward him (see 3 Nephi 13:4, 6, 18). Clearly, the desire of the disciple is for God alone to hear the words of his cries and for him alone to notice and recognize his deeds. Moreover, the pattern of repeating things three times, or grouping things in clusters of three, has been identified as a dominant characteristic of the Sermon on the Mount.[1]

30. A requirement of consecration. The final affirmative requirement advanced in the Sermon is that of singleness of heart in serving God and not Mammon: "Lay not up for yourselves treasures upon earth, where moth and rust doth corrupt, and thieves break through and steal; but lay up for yourselves treasures in heaven, where neither moth nor rust doth corrupt, and where thieves do not break through nor steal. For where your treasure is, there will your heart be also. The light of the body is the eye; if, therefore, thine eye be single, thy whole body shall be full of light. . . . No man can serve two masters; for either he will hate the one and love the other, or else he will hold to the one and despise the other. Ye cannot serve God and Mammon" (3 Nephi 13:19-22, 24).

I view this instruction as tantamount to requiring one to consecrate all that one has and is to the Lord. Jesus commands the disciple, "Lay not up for yourselves treasures upon earth, . . . but lay up for yourselves treasures in heaven." The hearer is also required to have an eye "single" (*haplous*) to the glory of God, which refers not only to "singlemindedness" and "wholehearted dedication," but also to being pure in the sense of being "ready for sacrifice"[2] and being "unbegrudgingly generous"[3] toward the kingdom. The duty is to serve a single master: "Ye cannot serve God and Mammon." Indeed, the Sermon on the Mount presupposes a community that is "prepared to take respon-

---

1. Dale C. Allison, Jr., "The Structure of the Sermon on the Mount," *Journal of Biblical Literature* 106 (1987): 423-45; see also Matthew 7:2, discussed above, and the threefold ask-seek-knock discussed below.

2. *TDNT* 1:386; Strack and Billerbeck, *Kommentar zum Neuen Testament,* 1:431-32.

3. Henry J. Cadbury, "The Single Eye," *Harvard Theological Review* 47 (1954): 71.

sibility for the consequences of the teaching of Jesus, even if it means their lives."[1] By total devotion to God, disciples are promised that their "whole body shall be full of light" (3 Nephi 13:22). This assumes that further light and a fullness of light is what the righteous should continually seek.

31. Care promised for the twelve disciples. At this point in the Sermon at the Temple, Jesus turns to the twelve whom he had ordained and promises them that the Lord will take care of their needs. They are promised that they shall have sufficient for their needs, just as the Lord's Prayer in the Sermon on the Mount requests: "Give us this day bread 'sufficient for our needs' (*epiousion*)."[2] As the Lord's anointed, they need not worry about what they shall eat or drink, for they shall have sufficient for their needs. The promise of food and drink may also foreshadow the eucharist, another ritual aspect of the Sermon at the Temple focused on especially in the administration of the sacrament in 3 Nephi 18.[3]

32. Clothing (endowing) the disciples. Emphasis in the next section of the Sermon is upon the ordained disciple's clothing. They are promised that God will newly clothe them in glorious clothing. As the lilies of the field, so the chosen disciples will be clothed by God, even more gloriously than Solomon himself, whose temple was the most splendid of all (see 3 Nephi 13:25, 29–31).

---

1. Betz, *Essays on the Sermon on the Mount,* 21; see Matthew 5: 11–12.

2. This translation offered by R. ten Kate, "Geef üns heden ons 'dagelijks' brood," *Ned. Theol. Tijd.* 32 (1978): 125–39; see also *GELNT,* 296–97. The meaning of this cryptic word is widely debated and is by no means certain.

3. Cf. John 4, 6. Discussed also in connection with the miraculous feeding of the multitude in the forty-day literature and in 3 Nephi 20, in Hugh Nibley, "Christ among the Ruins," in *CWHN* 8:407–34.

The "clothing" of which Jesus speaks is richly symbolic. The Greek word for being clothed is *enduō* (*endumatos*, "raiment," in Matthew 6:25, 28; *endusesthe*, "put on," in Matthew 6:25). Jesus uses this word in Luke 24:49, shortly after his resurrection, when he tells his apostles, to remain in the city "until ye be *endued* with power from on high." It means "to endow." The Greek word *enduō* has two meanings, and both are pertinent to the endowment. First is "to dress, to clothe someone," or "to clothe oneself in, put on." The second is, figuratively, to take on "characteristics, virtues, intentions."[1] The meaning of the English word *endue* (or *indue* from the Latin) likewise "coincides nearly in signification with *endow*, that is, to put on, to furnish. . . . To put on something; to invest; to clothe,"[2] and Joseph Smith's diary uses these spellings interchangeably, as for example when Joseph prayed that all the elders might "receive an endument in thy house."[3]

Thus, in this section of the Sermon at the Temple, Jesus can be understood as promising more than garments that offer physical protection for the body (although garments do this, too); he speaks of garments that "endow" the disciples with powers and virtues more glorious than Solomon's. More is involved here than the promise of material well-being: "Is not the life more than meat, and the body than raiment?" (3 Nephi 13:25).

33. Preparing for the judgment. After the promise of this glorious endowment is given, the Savior turns his attention back to the multitude and to the presentation of information about the final judgment and how all may pass through

---

1. *GELNT*, 263.

2. Webster's *American Dictionary of the English Language* (1828).

3. Entry for Tuesday, 15 December 1835, in Dean Jessee, ed., *The Personal Writings of Joseph Smith* (Salt Lake City: Deseret Book, 1984), 105.

69

it. He first discloses the principles by which the final judgment will be administered: "Judge not, that ye be not judged. For with what judgment ye judge, ye shall be judged; and with what measure ye mete, it shall be measured to you again. And why beholdest thou the mote that is in thy brother's eye, but considerest not the beam that is in thine own eye? Or how wilt thou say to thy brother: Let me pull the mote out of thine eye—and behold, a beam is in thine own eye? Thou hypocrite, first cast the beam out of thine own eye; and then shalt thou see clearly to cast the mote out of thy brother's eye" (3 Nephi 14:1-5). Essentially no mortal can stand as a judge of his brother when he himself is flawed, and all people will find themselves judged at the bar of God by the same standard that they have used in judging others.

This particular concept of justice—namely, rewarding or punishing a person in a manner that matches his own being or conduct—is mentioned several times in the scriptures as the form of God's justice at the judgment day. For example, Alma 41:13-15 says that God will restore good to the good, evil to the evil, mercy to those who have been merciful. Similarly, forgiveness only comes through the atonement of Christ to those who have forgiven (see Matthew 6:15; 3 Nephi 13:15). Therefore, a primary concern of the true Christian should be to develop one's own character: To be pure ("cast the beam out of thine own eye"), to serve ("see clearly to cast the mote out of thy brother's eye"), to avoid hypocrisy, and to think and act toward others in the way that you would have God render judgment unto you. The judgment process is more reflective than it is projective.

34. Secrecy required. Next, the Lord requires that his hearers be willing to keep these holy things secret: "Give not that which is holy unto the dogs, neither cast ye your pearls before swine, lest they trample them under their feet, and turn again and rend you" (3 Nephi 14:6). "The original meaning [of this saying] is puzzling."[1] This saying seems badly out of place or hard to explain for most interpreters of the Sermon on the Mount,[2] for after demanding that the disciple should love his neighbor, even his enemy, it seems inconsistent for Jesus to call these people "dogs" and "swine" and to require his followers to withhold their pearls from them. The emphasis, however, is clearly on withholding certain things that are "holy" and protecting them as sacred. Drawing on Logion 93 in the *Gospel of Thomas*, Strecker identifies one possibility for "that which is holy" here as "gnostic secret knowledge."[3] The implication is that Jesus has given his hearers something more than what the recorded text reports, something they are required to keep sacred and secret—an implication consistent with some other interesting conclusions of Jeremias regarding the existence of sacred, secret teachings and practices in primitive Christianity.[4] Indeed, the *Didache* 9:5 associates this saying with a requirement of exclusivity, specifically the prohibition not to let anyone "eat or drink of the Eucharist with you except for those baptized in the name of the Lord" (see also *Didache* 14:1-2 connecting Matthew 5:23-25 and the observance of the sacrament).

This obligation of secrecy carries or implies harsh penalties and consequences. If it is violated, the pearls will be

---

1. Strecker, *Sermon on the Mount*, 146.

2. H. C. van Zyl, " 'n Moontlike verklaring vir Matteus 7:6 [A Possible Explanation of Matthew 7:6]," *Theol. Evang.* 15 (1982): 67-82, collapses this saying into Matthew 7:1-5 as a possible solution to the problem.

3. Strecker, *Sermon on the Mount*, 147.

4. Joachim Jeremias, *The Eucharistic Prayers of Jesus* (New York: Scribner's Sons, 1966), 125-37. P. G. Maxwell-Stuart, "Do Not Give What Is Holy to the Dogs," *Expository Times* 90 (1979): 341, argues that "dogs" has a nonliteral metaphorical sense of "those who are unbaptized and therefore impure, . . . without shame," and that "holy" might originally have meant "what is precious, what is valuable."

trampled, and the one who has disclosed the holy things will be torn to pieces. This reflects the method of punishment prescribed for covenant breakers in Psalm 50: "Those that have made a covenant with me, . . . consider this, ye that forget God, lest I tear you in pieces" (Psalms 50:5, 22). In a ritual context, a strict requirement of secrecy is most readily understandable, and of its seriousness the covenanters had been expressly forewarned when they were first charged with the prospects of becoming the salt of the earth, risking being "trodden under foot" (3 Nephi 12:13; Matthew 5:13).

Moreover, the Joseph Smith Translation confirms that Matthew 7:6 is exactly concerned with the requirement of keeping certain sacred things secret. It adds: "The mysteries of the kingdom ye shall keep within yourselves, . . . for the world cannot receive that which ye, yourselves, are not able to bear" (JST, Matthew 7:10–11). As Alma had said a century earlier, "It is given unto many to know the mysteries of God; nevertheless they are laid under a strict command that they shall not impart only according to the portion of his word which he doth grant" (Alma 12:9). Such a requirement of secrecy is a common feature of ritual initiations or temple ordinances.

35. A three-fold petition. Finally, the listeners are ready to approach the Father. They are told that if they will ask, seek, and knock (in other words, when a threefold petition is made), "it shall be opened unto you" (3 Nephi 14:7). This offer is open to all people (cf. Alma 12:9–11). Everyone that asks, having been brought to this point of entry, will receive and be received (see 3 Nephi 14:8). In my mind, it makes the best sense of Matthew 7:7 to understand it in a ceremonial context. Actual experience among Christians generally shows that the promise articulated here should not be understood as an absolute one: Many people ask, and seek, and knock; yet, in fact many of them do not find. Moreover, there is reason to believe that Jesus expected his

true followers to seek for something out of the ordinary: An early saying from Oxyrhynchus attributed to Jesus reads, "Let him who seeks not cease seeking until he finds, and when he finds, he will be astounded, and having been astounded, he will reign, and having reigned, he will rest."[1] It is crucial that a person come to the Father correctly (see 3 Nephi 14:21), and for all who seek and ask at this point in their progression—after believing and accepting the requirements in the Sermon that precede this invitation—for them it will be opened.

36. *Seeking a gift from the Father.* Who, then, will be there to open "it" unto the petitioner? The Father. "Or what man is there of you, who, if his son ask [for] bread, will give him a stone? Or if he ask [for] a fish, will he give him a serpent? . . . How much more shall your Father who is in heaven give good things to them that ask him?" (3 Nephi 14:9, 11). Asking for "bread" is the symbolic equivalent of asking for Jesus, who is the bread of life (see John 6:48). Asking for a fish, again, is figuratively asking for life through the atonement and salvation of Jesus. The promise is that those who properly ask for Jesus will not be stoned (suffer death), nor will they meet a serpent (Lucifer). Instead, the petitioner will receive good gifts from the Father (see 3 Nephi 14:11). The gift is eternal life, "the greatest of all the gifts of God" (D&C 14:7), descending below all things, rising above all heavens, and filling all things (see Ephesians 4:8-10, where *domata,* the Greek word for "gifts" in Matthew 7:11, also appears).

37. *Other people.* But one cannot enter into eternal life or heaven alone. In the final analysis, obedience to the law of charity is required to claim the blessings of the Lord, for

---

1. Joseph A. Fitzmyer, "The Oxyrhynchus Logoi of Jesus and the Coptic Gospel according to Thomas," in *Essays on the Semitic Background of the New Testament* (London: Chapman, 1971), 371.

without charity, the pure love of Christ, we are nothing (see 1 Corinthians 13:2). "Whoso is found possessed of [charity] at the last day, it shall be well with him" (Moroni 7:47). Thus, Jesus taught, "Therefore, all things whatsoever ye would that men should do to you, do ye even so to them" (3 Nephi 14:12).

Thus, all followers of the Lord Jesus Christ are responsible to see that other people are shown the way to salvation and eternal life and, where necessary, assisted in every way possible. In other words, Jesus may be commanding Christians not only to do things "to others" but "for others." The sense of the grammar can be read either way. The disciples are told that, whatever they would like others to do for them, they should do the same for others, again with reference being made to the law (of Moses) and the spirit of Elijah (the prophets). My conclusion is that Jesus intended here for his disciples to do more than merely engage in the deeds of human kindness normally associated with the Golden Rule. He would want them, above all, to be taught the gospel and be brought to salvation. So he admonishes them to do such things for others, implicitly to teach them the gospel and to perform for them, where necessary, any vicarious ordinances. As Boyd K. Packer has said, "Is it not Christlike for us to perform in the temples ordinances for and in behalf of those who cannot do them for themselves?"[1]

38. Entering through a narrow opening. The necessity of helping others through the gate arises because, as 3 Nephi 14:13-14 makes clear, there is only one gate and one narrow way that leads to life: "Enter ye in at the strait gate; for wide is the gate, and broad is the way, which leadeth to destruction, and many there be who go in thereat; because strait is the gate, and narrow is the way, which leadeth unto

---

1. "Covenants," *Ensign* 17 (May 1987): 24.

life, and few there be that find it." As 2 Nephi 31:17 indicates, that gate is exclusively the gate of repentance, baptism, remission of sins, and the gift of the Holy Ghost. Signposts and markers help guide people to the narrow gate, and instruction about the doctrine of the Two Ways — the path to life or the road to destruction — serves to remind the disciples that it is an undeviating path of truth that leads to life eternal.[1]

39. Bearing the fruit of the Tree of Life. Jesus next points to the imagery of the tree: "Every good tree bringeth forth good fruit; but a corrupt tree bringeth forth evil fruit" (3 Nephi 14:17). Having partaken of the Tree of Knowledge, man's life becomes a quest to find and righteously partake of the fruit of the Tree of Life and live forever. Echoes of temple and eschatological imagery are again discernible in the words of Jesus here.

These echoes come from several directions: First, these are no ordinary trees of which Jesus speaks: they are ultimate moral symbols: they either bear "evil" fruit (the Greek word is *ponerous*, "sick, wicked, worthless, degenerate, malicious") and are "corrupt" (*sapron*, meaning "decayed, rotten, evil, unwholesome"); or they are "good" (*agathon*, "fit, capable, of inner worth, moral, right"). Thus, Jesus speaks of eternal trees, symbolic of the final state of one's eternal character, determining whether one will either live or "be hewn down and cast into the fire" (3 Nephi 14:19).

Second, these good trees are trees of life. One only lives forever by partaking of the fruit of the Tree of Life (see Genesis 3:22). Accordingly, the tree is an important feature in the landscape of all temple literature.[2] It is, therefore,

---

1. The doctrine of the Two Ways was a salient teaching of the early Christians. See, e.g., Hugh Nibley, *The World and the Prophets* (Salt Lake City: Deseret Book and F.A.R.M.S., 1987), ch. 21, in *CWHN* 3:183–86, and Nibley, *Prophetic Book of Mormon*, in *CWHN* 8:462–63, 550–51.

2. John M. Lundquist, "The Common Temple Ideology of the Ancient

natural and logical that Jesus' thoughts should turn to the imagery of the Tree of Life immediately after he has described the path "which leadeth unto life" (3 Nephi 14:14). In an eternal perspective that path leads directly to the Tree of Life (see 1 Nephi 8:20, "I also beheld a straight and narrow path, which came along by the rod of iron, even to the tree by which I stood.")

Third, Jesus equates individual people with the Tree, for by partaking of the fruit of the Tree of Life, or by planting the seed of life in oneself, each disciple grows up into a tree of life, as the Prophet Alma describes (see Alma 32:41–42). Each good tree of life has a place in God's paradise, growing up unto eternal life and yielding much fruit—powerful imagery also present in the Old Testament Psalms (see Psalm 1:1–3) and in the earliest Christian hymns. "Blessed, O Lord, are they who are planted in Thy land, and who have a place in Thy Paradise; and who grow in the growth of Thy trees" (Odes of Solomon 11:18–24). In other allegories, there is only one tree, Jesus being the root and righteous people becoming the branches (see John 15:1–5; Jacob 5).

Fourth, another temple echo may be heard in the possibility that the cross is also, ironically, a symbol of a Tree of Life (see 1 Peter 2:24). Each person who is raised up in the form of the tree will have eternal life. Ritually, the early Christians prayed in the "cruciform" position, with their hands raised, "stetched out towards the Lord." This "extension," they said, "is the upright cross."[1] Originally this

Near East," in *The Temple in Antiquity: Ancient Records and Modern Perspectives*, ed. T. Madsen (Salt Lake City: Bookcraft and BYU Religious Studies Center, 1984), 53–76; and "Temple, Covenant, and Law in the Ancient Near East and in the Old Testament," in *Israel's Apostasy and Restoration*, ed. A. Gileadi (Grand Rapids, Michigan: Baker, 1988), 293–305.

1. *Odes of Solomon* 27:3; 35:7; 37:1; in OTP 2:759, 765–66. "The Odist refers to the early cruciform position for praying," James H. Char-

signified the passion of Christ and was a gesture used in confessing Christ at baptism; it imitated the cross, death, and a mystic unification and life with Christ.[1]

Those who do not become such a tree and bring forth good fruit, however, will be chopped down and thrown into the fire, for by their fruits they shall be known (see 3 Nephi 14:19-20). Evil trees that bring forth bad fruit are the "false prophets" who are sure to come. The Lord assures the disciples, however, that he has given them adequate knowledge so that they can test whether these purported prophets have come with truth and goodness: "Ye shall know them" (3 Nephi 14:20).

40. Entering into the presence of the Lord. Finally, there will be an encounter with the Lord himself: Some will say to him, "Lord, Lord," and they shall be allowed to "enter into the kingdom of heaven." But many, even good people of the world who have cast out devils and done wonderful works in the name of the Lord, will be turned away, for the Lord will have to acknowledge, "I never knew you, depart from me" (3 Nephi 14:22-23).

How is it that the Lord has not known them? The Hebrew word "know" (*yada*^{c}) has a broad range of meanings. One of them is covenantal:

"You only *have I known* of all the families on earth. Therefore I will punish you for all your iniquities." Amos' words [Amos 3:2] are no longer mysterious. Yahweh had

---

lesworth, *The Odes of Solomon* (Oxford: Oxford University Press, 1973), 125 n. 10. See also 1 Timothy 2:8: "I wish that men everywhere would raise holy hands." In the Greek tragedians, *hosioi cheires* are "hands which are ritually pure." Martin Dibelius and Hans Conzelmann, *The Pastoral Epistles* (Philadelphia: Fortress, 1972), 44.

1. D. Plooij, "The Attitude of the Outspread Hands ('Orante') in Early Christian Literature and Art," *Expository Times* 23 (1912): 199-203, 265-69. One early art work shows the figures "with the stigmata Christi in their hands." Ibid., 268.

recognized only Israel as his legitimate servants; only to them had he granted the covenant.[1]

Clearly, more than good works alone will be required, and the old covenant with Israel (see Hosea 13:4; Jeremiah 24:7), by which God knew (or recognized) Israel and by which the Israelites knew God, has now become new through the Sermon. Knowing more than simply the just and equitable principles of the noble men of the earth is required in order to enter into the kingdom of heaven. Knowing the Lord through making and keeping this covenant is crucial. Only those who are wise in this sense,[2] who know, remember, and do its requirements, will be recognized by the Lord at that day, raised up to see God and to inherit celestial glory (see 3 Nephi 15:1).

41. Lecture on the portion of God's covenant with Israel yet to be fulfilled. The Sermon at the Temple continues as Jesus reviews and recapitulates things he had said about the fulfillment of the law of Moses. Some of the people had not understood that all old things "had become new," apparently wondering how this could be, since the covenant promising that the Israelites (including the Nephites) would be gathered before the end had not yet been fulfilled. Jesus explained that the old *law* was ended, but that did not abrogate "things which are to come," especially the parts of the covenant that were "not all fulfilled" (3 Nephi 15:3–8).

---

1. Delbert R. Hillers, *Covenant: The History of a Biblical Idea* (Baltimore: Johns Hopkins University Press, 1969), 122. See, generally, Hillers' discussion of the use of the word *know* in connection with ancient Near Eastern treaty terminology, 120–24.

2. Most often in the words of Jesus, the wise man (*phronimos*) describes the person "who has grasped the eschatological condition of man (Mt. 7:24; 24:45; 25:2, 4, 8, 9; Lk. 12:42)," not the person who is intelligent or prudent in the practical worldly sense of the word "wise." Fitzmyer, *Essays on the Semitic Background of the New Testament*, 172 n. 21.

He reiterated that his new instructions were given by way of commandment and now constituted the "law and the prophets" (3 Nephi 15:10). Then he spoke to the disciples about their role as a light unto the people, about their relation to the other folds of Christ's sheep, and about the gathering of Israel in complete fulfillment of God's covenants with the House of Israel (see 3 Nephi 15:11–16:20).

42. Admonition to ponder. Turning again to the multitude, who now sat or stood "round about" Jesus (3 Nephi 17:1), he told them to go home and "ponder upon the things which [he had] said" (3 Nephi 17:3), for he knew they were weak and could not yet understand the full import and meaning of what he had said. This is such a typical reaction to the temple or other sacred teachings: They appear simple at first, and we think we understand—but we do not. Only through experience and diligent, prayerful contemplation over time are the mysteries of God unfolded to us (see Alma 12:9).

43. Healing the sick. Jesus was about to leave, but when he saw the tears in the eyes of the people looking steadfastly upon him and longing for him to tarry longer with them, Jesus invited the people to bring forward any who were sick, and he healed them (see 3 Nephi 17:5–9). They all bowed down around Jesus and worshipped him, and some went forward to wash his feet with their tears (see 3 Nephi 17:10). These reciprocal spiritual outpourings set other temple precedents: the prayer roll for the sick and the washing of feet are at home in the temple as well.

44. The parents and the children. Next, the people were all invited to bring their children forward and set them around Jesus; the multitude gave way so the children could come to the center of the throng, where they surrounded Jesus, and the parents were then told to kneel around that group of children. Jesus stood in the middle, with the children around him, and the parents kneeling around them (see 3 Nephi 17:11–13). Jesus himself then knelt and uttered a marvelous prayer. So great were the things they then *both* saw and heard that they cannot be written (see 3 Nephi 17:14–17). I suspect that the covenant of secrecy plays a role here, which explains in part why "no tongue can speak, neither can there be written by any man" what Jesus said and did.

I also imagine, although one cannot know for sure, that Jesus did more than pray, for it seems that he *did* things which the people *saw* just as he spoke words that they heard. This produced unspeakable joy. First the parents heard what Jesus prayed *for them*, the parents: "No one can conceive of the joy which filled our souls at the time we heard him pray *for us* unto the Father" (3 Nephi 17:17; italics added). The adults were overcome. Jesus asked them all to arise, and he blessed them and pronounced his joy to be full (see 3 Nephi 17:18–20). He then touched the children "one by one, and blessed them, and prayed unto the Father for them" (3 Nephi 17:21). This was done in the presence of God (Jesus), witnesses (the parents who "bore record of it," 3 Nephi 17:21), and angels (who came down and encircled the children with fire and ministered to them, 3 Nephi 17:24). In the end, Jesus turned to the parents and said, "Behold your little ones" (3 Nephi 17:23). It seems to me that Jesus is not just inviting the parents to look at their children and admire them. Although that simple reading is possible, I would suggest that he is saying, "Behold, *your* little ones"—they are *yours*. While it cannot be said exactly what transpired that afternoon, the children apparently now belonged to the parents in a way they had not belonged before.

45. The covenant memorialized and a new name given. Next, Jesus sent the disciples for some bread and wine, commanded the people to sit down on the ground, broke bread and blessed the wine, and gave it to his disciples and then to the multitude.[1] Jesus says that the bread is to be eaten "in remembrance of my body, which I have shown unto you" and as "a testimony" to remember him always; and the wine, as a "witness" of willingness to keep the commandments that he had given them that day (3 Nephi 18:1-14). The people also received a new name, the name of Christ (as in Mosiah 5:8-12), as they would be "baptized in [his] name" (3 Nephi 18:5, 11), and as they prepared to "take upon them the name of [God's] Son" (Moroni 4:3).

The covenant and ceremonial functions of the sacrament here are evident: The new words of these sacrament prayers would have sounded familiar to these people, for they strongly resemble the old words used by King Benjamin at the end of his coronation and covenant renewal speech when he put his people under covenant to obey God and their new king.[2] This is yet one more way all their old things had become marvelously new in this day with Jesus at Bountiful. Moreover, it is known for certain that these eucharistic words of Jesus became liturgical in Nephite religion; they became their sacrament prayers, spoken verbatim "according to the commandments of Christ" (Moroni 4:1) as the people continued to renew this ordinance for the next several hundred years. Although Latter-day Saints do not usually think of the sacrament in connection with the temple, this ordinance was kept holy and secret among early Christians, and it was regularly administered in the Kirtland Temple in 1836.

46. Continued worthiness required. Jesus' last instruc-

---

1. For further connections between this material and the forty-day literature, see Hugh W. Nibley, "Christ among the Ruins," in *CWHN* 8:407-34.

2. For a full discussion of the relations between the texts of Mosiah 5, 3 Nephi 18, and Moroni 4-5, see my article "The Nephite Sacrament Prayers: From Benjamin's Speech to Moroni 4-5," F.A.R.M.S. Paper, 1986.

tions in the Sermon at the Temple deal with the future. He told the people to watch and pray always in their families that they might remain blessed and faithful (see 3 Nephi 18:15–21). He also gave standards of worthiness to determine who should be allowed to participate in their covenant renewals (see 3 Nephi 18:22–33). In this way, their places of worship and their future ordinances would remain holy and be a continuing means of bringing salvation.

47. *Conferring the power to give the Holy Ghost.* Finally, Jesus "touched with his hand the disciples whom he had chosen, one by one" and gave them the power to bestow the gift of the Holy Ghost (3 Nephi 18:36–37). Through the events of the day, they had progressed from the lower to the higher priesthood. The words that Jesus spoke in this connection are recorded in Moroni 2:2. With this, the day being spent, a cloud overshadowed the multitude, like the cloud that covered the tabernacle of old and gave a sure sign of God's presence at his sanctuary (e.g., Exodus 40:34–38; Leviticus 16:2, 13; Numbers 9:15–22; Deuteronomy 31:15). Whereupon, Jesus ascended into heaven.

48. *From Sermon to ceremony.* Thus ended the first day. The incomparable Sermon at the Temple was over. It was a manifestation of divine will and presence never to be forgotten. From this experience come many things: teachings of practical ethical value; an understanding of that which was fulfilled and that which remained yet to be fulfilled; a comprehension of the continuity and transition from the old law to the new; knowledge and testimony of the resurrection and exaltation of Jesus Christ; commandments and covenants; and also a basis for religious ritual.

Out of such an experience would naturally flow sacred ceremonies, for it was typical and usual for the temple in Israel "to routinize the momentous, thus rendering it part and parcel of the ongoing religious experience of the individual Israelite and of the people, collectively."[1] Evidently, such also occurred among the Nephites. Several texts from the Sermon at the Temple are known to have been ritually intended and oriented. From the Sermon at the Temple came the Nephite liturgical prayers for baptism (see 3 Nephi 11:23-28), for the administration of the sacrament (see 3 Nephi 18:1-14; Moroni 4-5), for the bestowal of the gift of the Holy Ghost, and for the ordination of priests and teachers (see Moroni 2-3).

This gives reason to believe that more of the Sermon at the Temple, perhaps much more, was ritually understood and transmitted. The words of Jesus (as many as were permissible) were written down, apparently immediately, and checked by Jesus (see 3 Nephi 23:7-9) — further indication that the Nephite disciples gave sacred and meticulous regard to each element of the Sermon at the Temple. Not all is known to us, of course, for the people were taught secret things that were "unspeakable" and "not lawful to be written" (3 Nephi 26:18), and many things were "forbidden them that they should utter" (3 Nephi 28:14). But as much as possible, they went forth and established the Church of Jesus Christ, based upon these very "words of Jesus" (3 Nephi 28:34), words that profoundly put all things into perspective and coherence. These things point toward a view of the Sermon at the Temple as a sacred experience that was recorded, revered, repeated, and institutionalized, that could be ritually represented and reenacted for other audiences. It seems to me that something of this sort indeed occurred, for the disciples went forward to preach abroad not only words and ideas, but also dramatic events, demonstrating "things which they had both heard and seen" (3 Nephi 27:1).

---

1. Levine, *In the Presence of the Lord*, 52.

4

SOME PERSONAL REFLECTIONS

In the welter of opinions concerning Jesus' masterful Sermon transmitted by both Matthew and Mormon, I offer a view of the Sermon at the Temple as a profound temple-text. I realize that assembling this view has been assisted by looking at circumstantial evidence, contextual inferences, and comparative studies, and by reading the Sermon at the Temple in light of a Latter-day Saint's understanding of the temple. Nowhere does Jesus say to us, "I am presenting a temple experience here." He says only, "Who hath ears to hear, let him hear" (Matthew 13:9).

I also readily acknowledge that one can understand the Sermon in many other ways. There are many good interpretations of this rich and deeply spiritual text. Many elements present in the Sermon are basic to the first principles of the gospel and thus are certainly also relevant to general ethical exhortation, righteousness, and the covenants of baptism. For example, at baptism one covenants to care for the poor, to comfort those that mourn, and to keep God's commandments (Mosiah 18:8-10; see also Mosiah 5:3-8; Moroni 4:1-5:2), topics stressed also in the Sermon. So, individual teachings of the Sermon will apply in many gospel settings. Yet I know of no other single interpretation that

84

makes more consistent sense of the Sermon as a whole or gives more meaning to all its parts than does this one. No part is out of place or left out under this approach.

Moreover, although I cannot conclusively say through deductive logic that my view of the Sermon at the Temple is correct, I can say that I did not go into this text looking for this result. Whatever subtle bias or predisposition toward the temple may be involved, the pattern that emerges from this text is too natural for me to think that I have imposed it instrusively upon the data. After working for many years on the Sermon on the Mount and the Sermon at the Temple, all these things fell quite suddenly into place, without prodding or coercing. The experience was strong, as the echoes in the text became clearer voices for me. Finding a significant number of details compatible with this view scattered among the writings of various scholars then reinforced the experience.

I also realize now, better than ever before, how imprecise our tools and instruments are as we attempt to map the contours and main features of this rich spiritual landscape. As Jesus said to us, "I perceive that ye are weak" (3 Nephi 17:2). Nevertheless, he will bless us in our weakness, and, God willing, our "weak things" may "become strong" (Ether 12:27). I hope that the Spirit will guide all readers who take Jesus' advice to go home and ponder upon the things he said to the Nephites and "prepare [their] minds for the morrow" that he might come again (3 Nephi 17:3). To do this, more than dissecting analysis is called for. The meaning of the Sermon is reduced when it is subsumed under certain focal points only; the truth about God's mysteries is not likely to be found at the end of a syllogism or textual analysis.

Reading the Sermon in light of the temple can enhance our understanding of the Sermon. Equally, experiencing the Latter-day Saint temple in light of the Sermon enhances our

85

understanding of the temple. President Benson has promised that the Book of Mormon will give intellectual and spiritual unity to our lives. Perhaps this is one more example of how that promise can be fulfilled.

I hasten to add that people should also notice some differences between the Latter-day Saint temple and the Sermon. I do not think that the Nephite temple experience was exactly the same as today's — which itself changes somewhat from time to time. For example, the sequence in which the laws of obedience, sacrifice, chastity, consecration, and so forth are presented is not quite exactly the same in both, although they are very close. And the Sermon at the Temple mainly reports only the ordinances, laws, commandments, performances, and covenants; little background drama or creation narrative is given. Nevertheless, the essential elements appear to be there — certainly more than we had ever before thought present in the Book of Mormon, and, as for the rest, the presence of the Lord was drama enough.

If the Sermon at the Temple is a ritual text, one must next wonder the same about the Sermon on the Mount. I would not expect scholars unfamiliar with the Latter-day Saint temple to see — or even imagine — what I think is going on in the Sermon. Still, the number of New Testament scholars willing to recognize the importance of esoteric ordinances and cultic teachings among the early Christians is increasing. I think they should be able to discern readily a number of possible ritual elements in the Sermon on the Mount.

There are several examples: the use of macarisms (beatitudes) in ritual initiations as attested elsewhere as well; the requirement that a participant withdraw if he or she has aught against a brother; the instruction about how one is to swear one's oaths; the meaning of *teleios* as being fully introduced into the mysteries; the giving of an exemplary group prayer; connections between the Lord's Prayer and

John 17[1] (which connects it with the rituals of the Last Supper and the Upper Room); the promise of garments more glorious than Solomon's robes; the insistence upon secrecy; an asking, seeking, knocking, opening, receiving of a gift; entering into the Lord's presence, or rejecting, those who are good but lack a certain knowledge; "knowing" God (with its connotations in connection with covenant-making generally);[2] the sealing statement that Jesus taught with authority (see Matthew 7:29) in a manner somehow very different from the scribes and other teachers; the baptismal prelude to the Sermon on the Mount — the Father's voice speaking from heaven, a heavenly being descending out of heaven, and the expulsion of Satan (cf. Matthew 3–4); the venue of the mount as a new Sinai, a new Temple Mount;[3] the fact that a new covenant resulted, later witnessed by the cup of that new covenant (see Matthew 26:28; 1 Corinthians 11:25; 2 Corinthians 3:6); the recognition that the Sermon was directed only to a small group of disciples;[4] and the possible use of Sermon on the Mount materials as a cultic reminder in the earliest decades of Christianity in Jerusalem.[5] It requires little familiarity with esoteric texts and basic religious ritual to notice that such are the elements of which ceremony is readily and meaningfully made.

To me, the Sermon at the Temple in this way restores covenantal and sacred meaning to the Sermon on the

---

1. See W. O. Walker, "The Lord's Prayer in Matthew and John," *New Testament Studies* 28 (1982): 237–56, arguing that John 17 is a midrash on the Lord's Prayer.

2. Hillers, *Covenant*, 120–24.

3. See Davies, *Sermon on the Mount*, 31–32.

4. H. Burkhardt, "Die Bergpredigt — Eine allgemeine Handlungsanweisung?" *Theologische Beiträge* 15 (1984): 137–40.

5. Betz, *Essays on the Sermon on the Mount*, 1–16 (on the whole Sermon as an *epitome* of the gospel), 55–69 (on Matthew 6:1–18 as an early Jewish-Christian *didache*).

Mount—meaning which was lost or forgotten, as Nephi had prophesied in 1 Nephi 13:26. I infer that Jesus delivered the Sermon on the Mount to much the same effect in Palestine as in Bountiful as he gave his disciples the new order of the gospel, which they eventually accepted by way of oaths and covenants, with promises and penalties. In 1 Nephi 13, Nephi explained in some detail how the apostasy from early Christianity would occur. First Nephi 13:24–32 seems to identify *three* stages in this process—not just one.[1]

First, the Gentiles would take "away *from the gospel* of the Lamb many parts which are plain and most precious" (1 Nephi 13:26; italics added). This stage could have occurred simply by altering the *meaning* of the things taught by the Lord without necessarily changing the words themselves. This changing of understanding was the fundamental problem Nephi saw, for the things that would cause many to stumble were those things "taken away out of the gospel" (1 Nephi 13:29, 32).

Second, the Gentiles would next take away "many covenants of the Lord" (1 Nephi 13:26). We can note that this step, too, could be taken without deleting any words from the Bible as such. The knowledge and benefit of the covenants of God can be lost simply by neglecting the performance of ordinances, priesthood functions, or individual covenants. Then, once the understanding of a text like the Sermon on the Mount had been changed, the rest was merely paperwork. The words could even stay the same, yet they would already have lost their plain and precious meanings.

Only third did Nephi behold that "many plain and precious things" were consequently "taken away from the book" (1 Nephi 13:28). Apparently Nephi understood this step as a consequence of the first two, for 1 Nephi 13:28

---

1. For further discussion, see John W. Welch, "The Plain and Precious Things," F.A.R.M.S. Update, January 1987.

begins with the word "wherefore." Thus, things that were lost from the texts of the Bible were not necessarily a cause, but a result of the fact that, first, the gospel, and second, the covenants of the Lord had been lost or taken away.

Understanding this process helps us to see how the Book of Mormon corrects this situation. Containing the fulness of the gospel (see D&C 20:9), the Book of Mormon first gives a correct understanding of the divinity, the mission, and the atonement of Jesus Christ, along with the principles of faith and repentance, and teaches with unmistakable clarity other plain and precious parts of the plan of salvation. Second, it restores many covenants of the Lord. It provides us with the words of the baptismal prayer, along with instructions concerning the meaning and proper mode of baptism (see Mosiah 18; 3 Nephi 11; Moroni 6) and of confirmation (see Moroni 2). It preserves from ancient times the words of the sacrament prayers (see Moroni 4–5),[1] makes understandable the covenants of the Lord to the House of Israel, and teaches the necessity of priesthood authority and the manner of ordination (see, e.g., Moroni 3). It also restores an understanding of the covenantal context of the Sermon on the Mount.

Indeed, Nephi prophesied that "the records of [his] seed," or in other words the Book of Mormon, would be instrumental in making known "the plain and precious things which have been taken away" (1 Nephi 13:40–41), and one of the book's stated purposes is to make known "the covenants of the Lord" (Title Page). Lehi also prophesied that the Book of Mormon would bring people in the latter days "to the knowledge of my covenants, saith the Lord. And out of weakness he shall be made strong" (2 Nephi 3:12–13).

---

1. Discussed in detail in John W. Welch, "The Nephite Sacrament Prayers: From King Benjamin's Speech to Moroni 4–5," F.A.R.M.S. Paper, 1986.

For many years, however, the Book of Mormon has been taken lightly. People who harden their hearts "cast many things away which are written and esteem them as things of naught" (2 Nephi 33:2). This has been especially the case with respect to the Sermon on the Mount in 3 Nephi. In reality, though, what has seemed to many to be an embarrassing problem in the Book of Mormon is no naïve plagiarism but a scripture fully constituted and meaningfully contextualized. If Doctrine and Covenants 84:57 is instructive here, reminding us that the children of Zion are under condemnation until they "remember the new covenant, even the Book of Mormon," it is perhaps not the book's fault that we have not seen the full potential of this Sermon text before.

5

THE SERMON AT THE TEMPLE AND THE SERMON ON THE MOUNT: THE DIFFERENCES

I have presented in the preceding chapters an interpretation that, in my opinion, casts the Sermon at the Temple as a complex, subtle, original, systematic, coherent, and purposefully orchestrated text. Not all people, however, have seen this text so positively. In fact, most novice readers of the Book of Mormon peruse 3 Nephi 12–14 rather casually, perhaps viewing it as a block of foreign materials unrelated to the surrounding text and bluntly spliced into the narrative of 3 Nephi. The similarities between the Sermon on the Mount and the Sermon at the Temple have led many to view the Sermon at the Temple more as a liability than an asset to the Book of Mormon.

Ever since the publication of the Book of Mormon, one of the standard criticisms raised by those seeking to discredit the book has been the assertion that it plagiarizes the King James Version of the Bible, and the chief instance of alleged plagiarism is the Sermon on the Mount in 3 Nephi 12–14. Mark Twain quipped that the Book of Mormon contains passages "smouched from the New Testament, and no credit given."[1] Reverend M. T. Lamb, who characterized the

---

1. Samuel L. Clemens, *Roughing It*, 2 vols. (New York: Harper, 1913), 1:142.

Book of Mormon as "verbose, blundering and stupid,"[1] viewed 3 Nephi 11-18 as a mere duplication of the Sermon on the Mount "word for word," and saw "no excuse for this lack of originality and constant repetition of the Bible," for "we have all such passages already in the [Bible], and God *never does unnecessary things*."[2] "Careful examination proves it to be an unprincipled plagiarist."[3]

These criticisms, however, have been drawn prematurely. Until all the possibilities have been considered, passing judgment with such finality is hasty. Indeed, if the foregoing covenantal interpretation of the Sermon has merit to it, Jesus could have selected no more appropriate text than the Sermon on the Mount for use at the temple in Bountiful. I am aware of no more valuable contribution to our understanding of the Sermon on the Mount than the insights of the Sermon at the Temple. Instead of being a liability or an embarrassment to the historicity of the Book of Mormon, the text and context of the Sermon on the Mount in the Book of Mormon turn out, in my opinion, to be among its greatest strengths. Through the Sermon at the Temple, some of the things that have baffled New Testament scholars about the Sermon on the Mount become very plain and precious.

The case of critics like Mark Twain and Reverend Lamb gains most of its appeal by emphasizing the similarities and

---

1. M. T. Lamb, *The Golden Bible* (New York: Ward and Drummond, 1887), iii.

2. Ibid., 187-88 (italics in original). In response to a similar expression, B. H. Roberts countered, "I am led to believe that you have been so absorbed, perhaps, in tracing out the sameness in the expressions that you have failed to note the differences to which I allude, for you make the claim of strict identity between the Book of Mormon and King James' translation too strong." B. H. Roberts, "Bible Quotations in the Book of Mormon and Reasonableness of Nephi's Prophecies," *Improvement Era* 7 (1904): 181.

3. Ibid., 212.

discounting the differences between Matthew 5–7 and 3 Nephi 12–14. Under closer textual scrutiny, however, these differences turn out to be very significant. Accordingly, in this chapter, I will closely examine differences between the Sermon at the Temple and the Sermon on the Mount. While one can readily see that there are substantial similarities between 3 Nephi 12–14 and Matthew 5–7, the results presented here offer reasons to reject the claim that the Sermon at the Temple is simply a naïve, unprincipled plagiarism of the Sermon on the Mount.

While the differences between these two texts have long been cited by such writers as B. H. Roberts and Sidney B. Sperry to support the claim that the Sermon at the Temple is not a mindless copy of the Sermon on the Mount,[1] and while some commentators have sensed that the Sermon at the Temple is superior to the Sermon on the Mount in "sense and clearness,"[2] they have not thoroughly articulated the actual extent or nature of the differences. The following examination undertakes such an analysis. It examines every variance (for a complete comparison of the texts, see the appendix), and it concludes that there are enough important differences between the Sermon on the Mount and the Sermon at the Temple that the relationship between these texts cannot be attributed to a superficial, thoughtless, blind, or careless plagiarism. On the contrary, the differences are systematic, consistent, methodical, and in several cases quite deft.

---

1. Roberts, "Bible Quotations in the Book of Mormon," 184; Sidney B. Sperry, *Problems of the Book of Mormon* (Salt Lake City: Bookcraft, 1967), 104–6. James E. Talmage, *Jesus the Christ* (Salt Lake City: Deseret Book, 1976), 725, 729, sees a greater emphasis in the Sermon at the Temple than in the Sermon on the Mount on the adoration of Jesus, but otherwise considers the two sermons to be virtually identical, both containing "the same splendid array of ennobling precepts" and "the same wealth of effective comparison," p. 727.

2. Roberts, "Bible Quotations in the Book of Mormon," 191.

For purposes of discussion and testing, the following analyses will assume two things: first, that Jesus began in Bountiful with a speech that he had probably delivered several times in Palestine, as, for example, when he sent his disciples into the mission field (see JST, Matthew 7:1-2, 9, 11)[1] and again sometime before his ascension (see 3 Nephi 15:1); and second, that he modified that text for delivery to a Nephite audience in Bountiful after his resurrection. Each instance in which the Sermon at the Temple is different from the Sermon on the Mount, therefore, will be examined against this assumed context to determine if logical reasons can be found for the differences. The more rational and subtly sensible these differences are, the more respect one should reasonably have for the Sermon at the Temple and at the same time the less appropriate it becomes to speak disparagingly of the Sermon at the Temple as a plagiarism of the Sermon on the Mount.

Differences That Reflect A Post-resurrection Setting

Jesus appeared to the Nephites at the temple at Bountiful after his resurrection. Since some of the things he had said before his death were superseded by his atonement and resurrection, they needed to be modified in the Nephite setting to fit into a post-resurrection setting. For example,

---

1. I will not discuss in detail the differences between the Sermon at the Temple, Sermon on the Mount, and the Joseph Smith Translation. These three texts are set out in parallel columns in the appendix. For a discussion, see Robert A. Cloward, "The Sermon on the Mount in the JST and the Book of Mormon," in *The Joseph Smith Translation: The Restoration of Plain and Precious Things*, ed. M. Nyman and R. Millet (Provo: Religious Studies Center, 1985), 163-200. The fact that the Sermon at the Temple and the Joseph Smith Translation are not identical to each other shows, from one Latter-day Saint point of view, that Jesus delivered the Sermon several times, and thus one should not necessarily expect to find a single "correct" version of the text.

at the time of the Sermon on the Mount, the fulfillment of the law still lay in the future (see Matthew 5:18). But by the time of the Sermon at the Temple, the law of Moses had already been fulfilled, as Jesus had proclaimed out of the darkness at the time of his death (see 3 Nephi 9:17).

Thus, when Jesus spoke in Palestine, he had said, "One jot or one tittle *shall* in no wise pass from the law, till all be fulfilled" (Matthew 5:18; italics added), but in Bountiful, he affirmed that one jot or tittle *"hath not passed away* from the law, but . . . it *hath* all been fulfilled" (3 Nephi 12:18; italics added). Likewise, in summarizing the series of antitheticals in 3 Nephi 12:21–45, Jesus similarly drew them together in the Sermon at the Temple with the following conclusion: "Those things which were of old time, which were under the law, in me *are* all fulfilled. Old things *are* done away, and all things have become new" (3 Nephi 12:46–47; italics added). In light of the glorified state of the resurrected Jesus at the time of the Sermon at the Temple, he could accurately say, "I would that ye should be perfect even *as I*, or your Father who is in heaven is perfect" (3 Nephi 12:48; italics added). Furthermore, there was no need in Bountiful for Jesus to instruct the people to pray, "Thy kingdom come" (Matthew 6:10), a phrase missing from the Lord's Prayer in the Sermon at the Temple (see 3 Nephi 13:9–13), for God's Kingdom had already come both in heaven through Christ's victory over death and on earth that day in their midst.

These differences convey significant theological information. First, the Sermon at the Temple clarifies that all things under the law of Moses had been entirely fulfilled in Jesus' mortal life, death, atonement, and resurrection. The Sermon on the Mount, on the other hand, never addressed this important question of *when* the law would be fulfilled, but it left this key issue open, simply saying that nothing would pass from the law "till all be fulfilled" (Matthew

5:18). The issue of when that fulfillment became effective, as is well documented in the New Testament, deeply and tragically divided a number of the early Christian communities (see Acts 15; Galatians 5).[1] Second, the Sermon at the Temple speaks from a frame of reference in which Jesus had become glorified with God. Jesus had already ascended to the Father, and thus he could well command his listeners in Bountiful to be perfect as he or as God is perfect (see 3 Nephi 12:48).

A Nephite Setting

When Jesus addressed the Nephites at Bountiful, he spoke in terms they would understand. The change in setting from Palestine to Bountiful accounts for several differences between the Sermon on the Mount and the Sermon at the Temple. Instead of "farthing" (Matthew 5:26), Jesus mentions a "senine" (3 Nephi 12:26), a Nephite unit of exchange. Although this change might appear a superficial change or an artifice, there is subtle substance to it. Jesus undoubtedly had several meaningful reasons for mentioning the senine when he spoke to the Nephites.

First, it was not just one of many Nephite measures but was their basic measure of gold (see Alma 11:5-19). Through it one converted values of precious metals into the measurement "of every kind of grain" (Alma 11:7). Moreover, it was the smallest Nephite measure of gold (see Alma 11:8-10). Thus, when Jesus told the Nephites that they might be held in prison unable to pay "even one senine" (3 Nephi 12:26), he was referring to a relatively small amount, equal to one measure of grain. Furthermore, it was not just the smallness that Jesus had in mind, for otherwise he could better have spoken of a "leah" (Alma 11:17), their smallest

---

1. See Raymond E. Brown, *The Churches the Apostles Left Behind* (New York: Pauline, 1984).

measure of silver. The senine, however, was especially important because it was the amount paid to each Nephite judge for a day's service at law (see Alma 11:3). Evidently, the losing party in a law suit was liable to pay the judges one senine each, a burden that would give potential litigants all the more reason to "agree with thine adversary quickly while thou art in the way with him" (3 Nephi 12:25). One should note that the Greek phrase *en tē hodō*, "in the way," in Matthew 5:25, originally referred to the commencement of a law suit.[1]

Also, there is no mention of Jerusalem in 3 Nephi 12:35. Of course, no Nephite would be inclined to swear "by Jerusalem, . . . the city of the great King" (Matthew 5:35), since the Nephite view of Jerusalem was rather grim. But more than that, omitting this phrase may be closer to what Jesus originally said in Palestine as well. While Jerusalem was known anciently as "the city of the great king" (Psalm 48:2 — *tou basileos tou megalou* in the Septuagint), there is numismatic evidence that the precise phrase "great king" (*basileos megalou*) was a special political title in the Roman world that was not used in Palestine until after Jesus' death. This title was given to the client-king Herod Agrippa I as a result of a treaty (*orkia*) granting to him several territories in and around Galilee in A.D. 39 and 41, which he commemorated with coins in his name bearing this distinctive, honorific title.[2] Based on this information, it has

---

1. For example, Frank Zimmermann, *The Aramaic Origin of the Four Gospels* (New York: KTAV, 1979), 47. Strecker, *Sermon on the Mount*, 69, points out that the expression soon took on a broader meaning, however, than merely "the way to the courthouse."

2. The coins of Herod Agrippa I (37–44 A.D.) bearing the inscription *ORKIA BASILEOS MEGALOU AGRIPA* are catalogued in Ya'akov Meshorer, *Ancient Jewish Coinage* (Jerusalem: Amphora, 1982), 2:45, 47, 56, 246; see also Ernst W. Klimowsky, *On Ancient Palestinian and Other Coins, Their Symbolism and Metrology*, Numismatic Studies and Researches VII (Tel Aviv: Israel Numismatic Society, 1974), 105–6. For

been suggested that Jesus' saying about oaths (*orkoi*) may have originally contained no reference to "Jerusalem the city of the great King," since Herod Agrippa may not have been politically entitled to that title until after Jesus' ministry. While there is no way to be sure about this suggestion, especially since such words were also available to Jesus in Psalm 48:2, the absence of the phrase "the city of the great king" in the Sermon at the Temple would prove consistent with this obscure numismatic information.

There is no mention of rain in 3 Nephi 12:45, whereas Matthew 5:45 says that the Lord makes the sun rise and also the rain fall on the just and the unjust. It is unknown why the Sermon at the Temple does not mention rain in this verse. Perhaps this difference reflects less concern in Nephite lands over regular rain or different religious or cultural attitudes in Mesoamerica toward rainfall.

Finally, the Nephites had had no experience with the hypocrites of Matthew 6:2, who cast their alms with the sounding of (or into) trumpets, and thus Jesus did not speak to the Nephites of what such hypocrites "do," but what they "will do" (3 Nephi 13:2). For the Nephites, such behavior was hypothetical or figurative, not familiar.

An Audience Dependent upon Written Law

The Nephites relied heavily on the written law. Their ancestors treasured the Plates of Brass, also relying heavily upon those written records for specifications regarding the law of Moses and how they should keep it. Being cut off from most sources of oral or customary law, the Nephites saw the law primarily as a written body (see 1 Nephi 4:15–16) and viewed any change in the written law with deep

---

this information, I am indebted to Dennis C. Duling of Canisius College for his paper presented at the Society of Biblical Literature Annual Meeting in November 1988.

suspicion (see Mosiah 29:22–23). The Jews in Jerusalem in Jesus' day, on the other hand, had an extensive body of oral law to accompany the written Torah, and the oral law was very important in the pre-Talmudic period of Jewish legal history.

Accordingly, in the Sermon on the Mount, Jesus says repeatedly to the Jews, "Ye have *heard* that it was *said* . . . " (Matthew 5:21, 27, 33, 38, 43; italics added). To the Nephites, however, such a statement would not have carried as much weight as would a reference to the written law. Thus, in the Sermon at the Temple Jesus consistently cites the written law, saying, "Ye have heard that it hath been said by them of old time, and it is also written before you" (3 Nephi 12:21), "it is written by them of old time" (3 Nephi 12:27), "again it is written" (3 Nephi 12:33), "behold, it is written" (3 Nephi 12:38), "and behold it is written also" (3 Nephi 12:43).

An Explicit Covenant-making Setting

As has been explained extensively thus far, the Sermon at the Temple was delivered in a covenant-making context. Several significant differences between the two Sermons reveal and reflect this important dimension. In the Sermon at the Temple, the injunctions and instructions were given by Jesus as "commandments" (3 Nephi 12:20), and the people received them by entering into a covenant with God that they would always remember and keep those commandments that Jesus gave to them that day (see 3 Nephi 18:7, 10). Just as the children of Israel entered into a covenant to obey the law of Moses as it was delivered to them at Sinai, the Nephites at Bountiful received their new dispensation of law, superseding the old, as the Sermon at the Temple explains. Consistent with this setting, the Sermon at the Temple contains unique phrases that belong to the sphere of covenant-making.

99

First, Jesus' words in the Sermon at the Temple were given to the Nephites as commandments. No such designation appears in the Sermon on the Mount, and thus biblical scholars inconclusively debate whether Jesus' teachings in the Sermon on the Mount were intended as celestial ideals, as ethical or religious principles, or as social commentary. The Sermon at the Temple, however, leaves no doubt that the words Jesus spoke at Bountiful were intended to create binding obligations. Jesus issued laws of the gospel, which all those who entered into the covenant that day were to obey. The people were required to come unto Jesus and be saved by obedience to the "commandments which I have commanded you at this time" (3 Nephi 12:20).

Second, those who will be received into the kingdom of heaven are those who come unto Christ (see 3 Nephi 12:3, 20). The phrase "who come unto me" appears five times in the Sermon at the Temple (3 Nephi 12:3, 19, 20, and 23 twice), but it never occurs in the Sermon on the Mount. Coming unto Christ, according to the Sermon at the Temple, requires repentance and baptism (see, e.g., 3 Nephi 18:25, 32; 21:6; 30:2), and thus it is in essence a covenantal concept. Only those who "come unto [Christ] with full purpose of heart" through his prescribed ordinances will be received (3 Nephi 12:24; cf. 3 Nephi 14:21; 15:1). The presence of the phrase "come unto Christ" is thus consistent with the covenantal context of the Sermon at the Temple, and this connection is strengthened by the likelihood that the Hebrew phrase "come before the Lord" probably has cultic meanings of standing before his presence in the temple at Jerusalem.[1] Stephen D. Ricks suggests that the phrase "come unto me" in the Sermon at the Temple may be

---

1. John I. Durham, "Shalom and the Presence of God," in *Proclamation and Presence,* ed. John I. Durham and J. R. Porter (Richmond, Virginia: John Knox, 1970), 292, 290; see also Baruch A. Levine, *In the Presence of the Lord* (Leiden: Brill, 1974).

conceptually equivalent to the Old Testament expression "stand in the presence of the Lord," which is thought to be temple terminology. Along the same lines, John I. Durham presents evidence that the *shalom* described the complete blessedness that is "the gift of God, and can be received only in his Presence," and "the concept of the Presence of God was certainly of vital importance to the Old Testament cult."

Emphasis on the Desires of the Heart

Although the Sermon on the Mount already demands of its adherents an extraordinarily pure heart (see, e.g., Matthew 5:8, 28; 6:21), the Sermon at the Temple adds two more references to the heart. The first is expressly connected with the covenant-making process, requiring any person desiring to come to Christ to do so "with full purpose of heart" (3 Nephi 12:23-24; cf. 2 Nephi 31:13; Jacob 6:5; 3 Nephi 10:6; Acts 11:23). This instruction replaces the saying in the Sermon on the Mount about bringing one's gift to the temple altar (see Matthew 5:23).

The second such addition sharpens the instruction regarding adultery by issuing the following commandment: "Behold I give unto you a commandment, that ye suffer none of these things to enter into your heart" (3 Nephi 12:29; cf. Psalm 37:15). Likewise, the Sermon at the Temple prohibits any anger in the heart at all (see 3 Nephi 12:22), not allowing even justifiable anger as in the traditional Matthean view (see Matthew 5:22).

Undoubtedly, these statements about the heart would have been intensely poignant in the minds of the Nephites, since the only thing they knew about the new law at the time the Sermon at the Temple began was the fact that the old ritual law had been replaced by a new law of sacrifice requiring exclusively the sacrifice of "a broken heart and a contrite spirit" (3 Nephi 9:20). This added emphasis on the heart is therefore especially instructive to those Nephite listeners, given their pressing need to understand this new law of sacrifice.

A More Immediate Relation to God

In several passages in the Sermon at the Temple, subtle changes bring the divine influence more explicitly to the surface. When one is "filled" in the Sermon at the Temple, the beatitude is not left unspecified, as in the Sermon on the Mount, but it reads "filled with the Holy Ghost" (3 Nephi 12:6; see also JST). One suffers, not just "for righteousness' sake," but "for Jesus' name's sake" (3 Nephi 12:10; and JST). The murderer is in danger, not just of "the judgment," but of the judgment "of God" (3 Nephi 12:21–22; and JST). And when one comes to Christ after first being reconciled to his brother, Christ himself is the one who "will receive [him]" (3 Nephi 12:24). Such expressions give the Sermon at the Temple (and the JST) a somewhat more intimate, personal connection with the divine than what is conveyed in the Sermon on the Mount. This character is consistent with the Sermon at the Temple being delivered by Jesus in his divine and glorified state.

Absence of Unseemly Penalties

In two places, penalties mentioned in the Sermon on the Mount are conspicuously absent in the Sermon at the Temple. First, the Sermon on the Mount teaches that anyone who "shall break one of these least commandments, and shall teach men so, he shall be called the least in the kingdom of heaven" (Matthew 5:19), but the Sermon at the Temple mentions no such punishment or criticism. Second, where the Sermon on the Mount says, "If thy right eye offend thee, pluck it out, . . . and if thy right hand offend thee, cut it off" (Matthew 5:29–30), the Sermon at the Temple simply gives the commandment "that ye suffer none of these things to enter into your heart" (3 Nephi 12:29).

Interestingly, the Sermon on the Mount has been subjected to considerable criticism by commentators on account of these two passages. On the one hand, some have argued that the drastic punishment of one who breaks even the least commandment seems grossly disproportionate to the crime and, uncharacteristically, too legalistic for Jesus to have said. On the other hand, the suggestion of bodily mutilation seems wholly inconsistent with the extraordinary Jewish respect for the human body—an attitude that Jesus undoubtedly shared—and seems at odds with the other statement in the Sermon on the Mount that one should cast the beam from one's eye (but not cast away the eye). None of these problems arises, however, in the Sermon at the Temple. Indeed, the absence of these problematic passages here can even be used to support the idea that these two passages were not originally parts of the Sermon on the Mount, as some commentators have suspected.

Of course, penalties are not entirely absent from the Sermon at the Temple. The strict injunction to "give not that which is holy unto the dogs, neither cast ye your pearls before swine, lest they trample them under their feet and turn again and rend you" is present in both the Sermon at the Temple and the Sermon on the Mount (Matthew 7:6; 3 Nephi 14:6). While this passage has also presented great problems to interpreters of the Sermon on the Mount, who wonder why Jesus would say in one breath "love your enemies" (Matthew 5:44) and a few verses later call other human beings "swine" and "dogs,"[1] this situation can be

---

1. Albright and Mann say this applies to alien and heathen people. William F. Albright and Christopher S. Mann, *Matthew* (Garden City, New York: Doubleday, 1971), 84. Lachs links the Samaritans with the dogs and the Romans with the swine: "Who are the dogs and the swine in this passage? It is well known that they are both used as derogatory

103

explained quite naturally, as discussed above, in connection with a requirement of secrecy in a covenant-making context.

Holy and sacred things are not to be shared or broadcast indiscriminately, and this is on pain of severe penalties, as are typically mentioned in connection with oath-swearing and covenant-making in the ancient world. Thus, scholars may be correct in suggesting that the specific penalties mentioned in the Sermon on the Mount were not originally there (for the Sermon at the Temple presents those texts differently), but those commentators would go too far by concluding that penalties had no role in the personal teachings of Jesus at all.

A Church Organizational Setting

The Sermon on the Mount gives no clues about how its followers were organized ecclesiastically, or about their institutional positions or relationships. The Sermon on the Mount, for all that one knows about it from the Gospel of Matthew, could stand independently as a code of private conduct, quite apart from any religious society or organization. Nothing said expressly in or about the Sermon on the Mount tells us how early Christian communities used the Sermon on the Mount or how its parts related to the various officers and functionaries in that movement. Yet scholars such as Hans Dieter Betz have concluded that the Sermon must have occupied a prominent place in the religious and liturgical life of the early Jewish Christians in Jerusalem.[1]

Betz's proposition in general is more than confirmed in the Sermon at the Temple by the fact that it was delivered in connection with the establishment of a group of disciples

---

terms for the Gentiles." Samuel T. Lachs, *A Rabbinic Commentary on the New Testament* (New York: KTAV, 1987), 139.

1. Betz, *Essays on the Sermon on the Mount*, 1–16, 55–70.

who would lead the new church of Christ (see 3 Nephi 11:18–22; 18:36–37; 26:17–21). Several differences between the Sermon on the Mount and the Sermon at the Temple (often also with the JST) make this organizational setting explicit:

(1) At Bountiful, Jesus ordained and called priesthood leaders. Third Nephi 12 begins with two ecclesiastical beatitudes not found in the Sermon on the Mount: "Blessed are ye if ye shall give heed unto the words of these twelve whom I have chosen; . . . again, more blessed are they who shall believe in your words because that ye shall testify that ye have seen me, and that ye know that I am" (3 Nephi 12:1–2).

(2) All believers were instructed to enter into a covenant of baptism, becoming members of Christ's church (3 Nephi 18:5). As a result, to them it was given to be the salt of the earth: "*I give unto you to be* the salt of the earth" (3 Nephi 12:13; italics added), a transferral and casual connection unstated in the Sermon on the Mount's simple declaration, "*Ye are* the salt of the earth" (Matthew 5:13; italics added).

(3) Likewise, the two commissions, "I give unto you to be the light of this people" and "Let your light so shine before this people" (3 Nephi 12:14, 16), seem to refer most clearly to relationships over and among the believing covenant people (see 3 Nephi 12:2; 13:25; 15:12), who later in the Sermon clearly are called "the people of my church" (3 Nephi 18:5; cf. 3 Nephi 20:22; 27:24, 27). With similar language the Lord had also given covenant Israel its calling and mission: "I will also give thee for a light to the Gentiles" (Isaiah 49:6).

(4) Furthermore, the fact that the words in 3 Nephi 13:25–34 were addressed solely to "the twelve whom he had chosen" (3 Nephi 13:25) and the idea that the offended brother in 3 Nephi 12:22–23 had the power to judge ("whosoever is angry with his brother shall be in danger of *his*

judgment") are other places in the Sermon at the Temple where that text distinctively presupposes or discloses ecclesiatical or organizational elements.

A Greater Universality

Consistent with Jesus' open invitations to all mankind in the first parts of the text (see 3 Nephi 11:23; 12:2), the word "all" is introduced into the Sermon at the Temple five times in the beatitudes (3 Nephi 12:4, 6, 8, 9, 10). While this may seem a small addition, its repetition creates a crescendo of emphasis on the universality of the gospel and on the absolute desire of Jesus for all people to receive its blessings. In the Sermon at the Temple, "all" those present went forth and touched the Savior (3 Nephi 11:15-16), "all" bowed (3 Nephi 17:9-10), "all" came forth with their sick to be healed (3 Nephi 17:9), "all" saw, heard, and witnessed (3 Nephi 17:25; 18:24). The Sermon at the Temple is consistently emphatic that "all" participated, not just a small group of disciples (as in the Sermon on the Mount) who were separated from the multitudes (see Matthew 5:1).

The Absence of Anti-Pharisaical Elements

It has been argued that the Sermon on the Mount, in its present form in the Bible, has passed through the hands of an anti-Pharisaical community of early Christians who were struggling to separate themselves from, and who were having strained relations with, their mother Jewish faith and the established synagogues in Jerusalem.[1] Indeed, anti-Pharisaism can be seen as one of the main tendencies of Matthew, and hence its manifestations in the Sermon have been advanced as evidence of the Matthean composition of the Sermon on the Mount.

Interestingly, the places in which scholars think they

---

1. Ibid., 19.

see these anti-Pharisaical evidences in the Sermon on the Mount are not found in the Sermon at the Temple. Thus, the saying "except your righteousness shall exceed the righteousness of the scribes and Pharisees" (Matthew 5:20) is not present in 3 Nephi. A very different and important statement in 3 Nephi 12:19-20 about obedience and sacrifice appears instead. Likewise, the unflattering comparison between good men the world over and the publicans, both of whom love their friends (see Matthew 5:46-47), is wholly absent in 3 Nephi 12. Warnings against hypocrisy are present in both the Sermon at the Temple and the Sermon on the Mount (see Matthew 6:2, 5, 16; 7:5; 3 Nephi 13:2, 5, 16; 14:5), but these are not aimed specifically at the Pharisees.

The Absence of Possible Anti-Gentile Elements

Likewise, it has been argued that the Sermon on the Mount, as it stands in the Gospel of Matthew, has been redacted slightly by a Jewish Christian who held an anti-Gentile bias.[1] The evidence for this view comes from three passages. Whatever weight one may accord to such evidence in critical studies of the New Testament, in each of the three cases, the perceived anti-Gentile elements are unproblematical or absent in the Sermon at the Temple, as one would expect in a discourse delivered to a group of people who knew no Gentiles.

Accordingly, the references to publicans in Matthew 5:46-47 are absent in 3 Nephi 12, and the words "for after all these things do the Gentiles seek" (Matthew 6:32) do not appear in 3 Nephi 13:32. The problem of vain repetitions put up to God by the "heathens" (*ethnikoi*, Matthew 6:7), which is mentioned in the Sermon at the Temple, need not be a later anti-Gentile intrusion into the Sermon on the

---

1. Ibid., 21.

Mount. In any event, the problem of vain, repetitive apostate prayers was well known to the Nephites from Alma's shocking encounter with the practices of the Zoramites (see Alma 31:12–23).

The Absence of Alleged Anti-Pauline Elements

It has also been suggested that certain portions of the Sermon on the Mount are anti-Pauline.[1] Again, because of differences between the Sermon at the Temple and the Sermon on the Mount, either the purported anti-Pauline materials are lacking in the Sermon at the Temple or it is highly doubtful that the supposed anti-Pauline elements are in fact anti-Pauline.

The most likely deprecation of Paul in the Sermon on the Mount is the passage that condemns anyone who teaches people to ignore even the least of the commandments in the law of Moses—he will be called "the least in the kingdom of heaven" (Matthew 5:19). Paul is the obvious figure in early Christianity who taught and promoted the idea that Christians need not observe the law of Moses, and his ideas met with considerable hostility among both Jews and certain Christians. Since Paul was known as "the least" of the apostles (1 Corinthians 15:9), it seems quite plausible that early Christians would have seen in Matthew 5:19 a direct criticism of Paul's position, if not of Paul himself, for it is easier to believe this appellation was added to the Sermon on the Mount *after* Paul had called himself "the least" than to think he would have called himself that, knowing it was part of the pro-law tradition. If the text of the Sermon on the Mount solidified around the 50s when Paul's debate was raging, it is possible that Matthew 5:19

---

1. Ibid., 20–21. For reasons against seeing Matthew 7:15–23 as anti-Pauline, see David Hill, "False Prophets and Charismatics: Structure and Interpretation in Matthew 7:15–23," *Biblica* 57 (1976): 327–48.

was altered somewhat in light of that controversy (the crucial phrase is also absent in JST, Matthew 5:21). If that was the case, one would not expect to find Jesus using anti-Pauline words twenty years earlier in the Sermon at the Temple. In fact, no anti-Pauline elements can be suggested in the contrasting text of 3 Nephi 12:17–19.

Some have seen other passages in the Sermon on the Mount as anti-Pauline, but in those cases the evidence seems even weaker. The concern about destroying or fulfilling the law is too general to be identified exclusively with Paul. Concern over destroying the law, or the role of the law of Moses in the messianic age or in the world to come, was a general Jewish problem, not just an issue raised by Paul's views of salvation.[1] Questions posed to Jesus about tithing, ritual purity, healing on the Sabbath, and many other such things show that people in early Christianity were concerned with this precise issue from the beginning of Jesus' ministry. Concerns about how and when the law of Moses would be fulfilled was equally a Nephite issue from the time of Lehi and Nephi to the coming of Jesus at Bountiful (see, e.g., 2 Nephi 25:24–27; 3 Nephi 1:24; 15:2).

It is, therefore, fitting that Jesus would explain his relationship to the old law, both in the Sermon on the Mount and the Sermon at the Temple. Similarly, warnings against false prophets (see Matthew 7:15) need not refer covertly to Paul, but probably reflect long-standing Israelite concerns and rules (see Deuteronomy 18:20–22). Furthermore, the mere presence in the Sermon of the criticism against those who call "Lord, Lord" (*kurie, kurie*, Matthew 7:21) does not appear to be evidence that this condemnation was included as a polemic against Paul in a theological anti-*kurios* statement, as some have suggested,[2] for the same phrase appears

---

1. See, e.g., W. D. Davies, *Torah in the Messianic Age and/or the Age to Come* (Philadelphia: Society of Biblical Literature, 1952).

2. See, e.g., Betz, *Essays on the Sermon on the Mount*, 156–57.

in Luke 6:46, and Luke can scarcely be accused of being an anti-Pauline collaborator. To the same effect, regarding the assertion that advising people to build their house upon the rock (see Matthew 7:24) supported Peter (the rock) as opposed to Paul, see Luke 6:47–49.

While the Sermon on the Mount in its present form may have passed through the hands of an anti-Gentile, anti-Paul community, most traces of such influence are scant. The absence from the Sermon at the Temple of the chief bits of evidence of an anti-Pauline hand in the Sermon on the Mount supports the view that the Sermon at the Temple preserves a text based on a version that predates any such influences on the text.

Other Differences

A number of other differences between the Sermon on the Mount and the Sermon at the Temple are worth mentioning in passing. There seems to be a slightly greater emphasis in the Sermon at the Temple upon eschatological judgment. Futurity is stronger in the Sermon at the Temple than in the Sermon on the Mount: for example, "ye *shall* have great joy" (3 Nephi 12:12; italics added); or "the salt *shall* be thenceforth good for nothing" (3 Nephi 12:13; italics added).

The Sermon at the Temple seems slightly more personal, since "who" has been substituted for "which" on several occasions (see, e.g., 3 Nephi 12:6, 10, 45, 48; 13:1, 4, 6, 9), but it is unknown whether this first appeared on the original manuscript of the Book of Mormon or as a correction to the printer's manuscript. While these changes are very minor, they add to the overall intimacy of Jesus' words in the Sermon at the Temple. His audience at Bountiful is not a faceless crowd. Unlike the Sermon on the Mount, 3 Nephi even names some of the people who were there (see 3 Nephi 19:4).

The Sermon at the Temple achieves greater clarity by explicitly stating certain things that the Sermon on the Mount readily assumes: for example, "it" (3 Nephi 12:13); "nay" (3 Nephi 12:15); "wherein ye *will* take up your cross" (3 Nephi 12:30; italics added); "I say that I would that ye *should* do alms unto the poor" (3 Nephi 13:1; italics added); "even so *will* he clothe you, if ye are not of little faith" (3 Nephi 13:30; italics added). These changes strengthen the imperative force of Jesus' statements, especially those that change negative, self-evident statements into positive commands or promises.

Finally, several reasons may be suggested why Jesus dropped the petition "Give us this day our daily [*epiousion*] bread" (Matthew 6:11) in the Sermon at the Temple. Perhaps the petition did not fit the circumstances because Jesus knew he would spend the entire day with these people and would not take time for lunch. Perhaps it was omitted because Jesus wanted to supply a unique bread at the end of the day (see 3 Nephi 18:1). Perhaps it was dropped because Jesus is the bread of life, and the people had already received their true sustenance that day in the appearance of Jesus.

Unfortunately, the meaning of the word *epiousion* (daily? continual? sufficient? essential? for the future?) is obscure,[1] but one of the earliest interpretations of it (supported by the early fragmentary Gospel of the Hebrews) was eschatological: "*mahar* [the Hebrew that Jerome assumed stood behind the Greek *epiousion*] meant not only the next day but also the great Tomorrow, the final consummation. Accordingly, Jerome is saying, the 'bread for tomorrow' was not meant as earthly bread but as the bread of life" in an eschatological sense.[2] If the several scholars are correct who

---

1. W. Bauer, W. F. Arndt, and F. W. Gingrich, *A Greek-English Lexicon of the New Testament* (Chicago: University of Chicago Press, 1957), 296–97; *TDNT* 2:590–99.

2. Joachim Jeremias, *The Prayers of Jesus* (London: SCM, 1967), 100–101.

refer this petition "to the *coming* Kingdom and its feast,"[1] Jesus might have considered this petition unsuitable in the context of the Sermon at the Temple, since the kingdom had in one sense already come. His appearance at that time was a realized eschatological event. Assuming that this is the meaning of *epiousion*, this deletion would fall into the same category as the other differences, mentioned above, that reflect the post-resurrection setting of the Sermon at the Temple.

In sum, one can readily compare the texts of the Sermon on the Mount and the Sermon at the Temple. There are many differences. Although, to the casual observer, most of them seem insignificant or meddlesome, a closer examination shows that most are quite meaningful and subtle. The differences are consistent with the introduction of the Sermon into Nephite culture, with its covenant-making context, and with dating the text to a time before when the suspected factional alterations or additions were made to the Sermon on the Mount. All this, in my opinion, speaks highly for the Sermon at the Temple as an appropriate, well thought out, and pertinent text and supplies considerable evidence that the Sermon at the Temple was not simply plagiarized from the Sermon on the Mount.

Of course there are many similarities between the two texts, and in large sections no differences occur. These similarities are consistent with Jesus' open acknowledgement that he taught the Nephites "the things which I taught before I ascended to my Father" (3 Nephi 15:1). The Sermon at the Temple is, therefore, not only appropriately similar, but also meaningfully different from the Sermon on the Mount. The more I know of those differences, the more I am impressed that achieving this subtle balance was not something that just casually happened.

---

1. See references in *GELNT*, 297; *TDNT* 2:595.

6

THE COMMON
ISRAELITE BACKGROUND

The previous pages display many differences between the Sermon on the Mount and the Sermon at the Temple and show that all those variations were purposeful and consistent with the delivery of the Sermon in Bountiful. In further support of the assertion that the Sermon on the Mount appropriately appears in the Sermon at the Temple, one may wonder if Jesus did *not* change some things from the Sermon on the Mount that he should have changed in order to make the text understandable to the Nephites. Although it is impossible to know for sure how much of the Sermon at the Temple the Nephites readily recognized from their Old Testament and Israelite heritage (and 3 Nephi 15:2 makes it clear that they did not immediately understand everything that Jesus said), I conclude that there are few individual words or concepts in the Sermon at the Temple that should have been puzzling to the Nephites. There are no other words or phrases in the Sermon where something needed to be changed but was not.

Indeed, most of the words and phrases, images and ideas of the Sermon on the Mount are rather universal to all mankind. What person does not understand such basic concepts as the poor, mercy, peacemakers, salt, light, sun, wind, darkness, open, secret, treasure, heart, mote, beam, bread, serpent, tree, fruit, blossom, rock, sand, men, brother, love, hate, enemy, adversary, marriage, divorce, greet, day, tomorrow, throw, hand, pigs, dogs, grass, power, glory, rejoice, fields, barns, ask, seek, knock, listen, clothing, good, evil, sin, forgive, righteousness, obey, cut off, swear, kill, prophet, wide, narrow, parents, children, holy, stature, eye, call, judge, lamp, riches, pearls, fast, pray, law, debts, and so forth? There are some 383 Greek words in the total vocabulary of the Sermon on the Mount. Most are everyday words. The translation of these words is generally straightforward. Their meanings can hardly be mistaken, whether they are expressed in English, Latin, Greek, Aramaic, Nephite, or any other language.

Krister Stendahl has suggested one such translation problem in the way the Sermon at the Temple renders the fourth Beatitude. It reads, "Blessed are all they who do hunger and thirst after righteousness, for they shall be filled with the Holy Ghost." He remarked that it seemed unnatural to associate the Greek word *chortazō* in Matthew 5:6 ("physically filled") with a spiritual filling, since the New Testament Greek usually uses a different word, *pleroō*, when it speaks of being filled with the Spirit, and since *chortazō* appears in passages about actual feedings of multitudes, eating crumbs, and so on.[1]

The problem, however, is solved when we turn to the Old Testament backgrounds of the Sermon. The promise of Jesus, that those who hunger and thirst after "righteous-

---

1. Krister Stendahl, "The Sermon on the Mount and Third Nephi," in *Reflections on Mormonism*, ed. T. Madsen (Provo: Religious Studies Center, 1978), 142. Stendahl, an outside observer, offers several valuable insights into the Sermon at the Temple, but his explanations of them usually fall short. He notes well the emphasis on baptism, the ordination of the twelve, "coming unto Jesus," and the role of the commandments (ibid., 141–43). More is involved in 3 Nephi 11–18, however, as shown above, than the mere introduction of certain literary Johannine features.

ness" (*dikaiosunēn*) shall be filled (*chortasthesontai*), is closely related to the last two verses of Psalm 17 in the Greek Septuagint (the "LXX"), a rarely mentioned text that Stendahl apparently overlooked. The Psalm contrasts the filling (*echortasthesan*) of the stomach in uncleanliness with beholding the face of God in righteousness (*dikaiosunē*): "I shall be satisfied (*chortasthesomai*) when I awake with thy likeness" (Psalm 17:15). Here the word *chortazō* is used to describe one's being filled with the spirit and being satisfied by beholding the righteousness of God.

The distinctiveness of this use of *chortazō* in Psalm 17 and Matthew 5:6 only increases the likelihood that Jesus' New Testament audience would have recognized his allusion to these words in the Psalm, a passage that would have been quite familiar to them. It shows that the translation in the Sermon at the Temple does not commit an error by making explicit this particular understanding of *chortazō* as having reference to a spiritual filling by the Holy Ghost, such as comes when a person beholds the face of God in righteousness.[1]

Moreover, the text of the Sermon on the Mount is steeped in phraseology of early biblical literature. Although most Christians assume that Jesus' words were completely original, in fact many of the words and phrases in the Sermon on the Mount were taken directly from the Old Testament scriptures. These expressions would have had a familiar ring to his audience in Galilee and probably also to his listeners in Bountiful, who shared the Israelite scriptural heritage up to the time of Jeremiah. The following list shows the main biblical antecedents and precedents drawn upon by Jesus in the Sermon. Some are direct quotes; others, paraphrases or closely related expressions.

---

1. See also numerous references to the notion of being physically "filled with the spirit" in *Book of Mormon Critical Text*, 3 vols. (Provo: F.A.R.M.S., 1986), 3:1039 n. 297.

Old Testament	New Testament
"To comfort all that mourn" (Isaiah 61:2)	"Blessed are they that mourn: for they shall be comforted" (Matthew 5:4)
"The meek shall inherit the earth" (Psalm 37:11); "good tidings unto the meek" (Isaiah 61:1)	"Blessed are the meek: for they shall inherit the earth" (Matthew 5:5)
"The meek also shall increase their joy in the Lord, and the poor among men shall rejoice in the Holy One of Israel" (Isaiah 29:19)	"Blessed are the poor in spirit. . . . Blessed are the meek" (Matthew 5:3, 5)
"I shall be satisfied (chortasthesomai) . . . , I will behold thy face in righteousness (dikaiosunē)" (Psalm 17:15 LXX)	"Blessed are they which do hunger and thirst after righteousness (dikaiosunē): for they shall be filled (chortasthesontai) (Matthew 5:6)
"Who shall ascend into the hill [temple] of the Lord? or who shall stand in his holy place? He that hath clean hands, and a pure heart" (Psalm 24:3–4; see also Psalm 73:1)	"Blessed are the pure in heart: for they shall see God" (Matthew 5:8)
"They shall be called (klēthēsontai) the sons (huioi) of the living God" (Hosea 1:10 LXX)	"They shall be called (klēthēsontai) the children (huioi) of God" (Matthew 5:9)
"They mocked the messengers of God, and despised his words, and misused his prophets" (2 Chronicles 36:16)	"Men shall revile you, and persecute you, and shall say all manner of evil against you falsely . . . for so persecuted they the prophets which were before you" (Matthew 5:11–12)

116

"Trodden under foot" (Isaiah 18:7; 28:3; Lamentations 1:15; cf. Psalm 119:118)

"Trodden under foot" (Matthew 5:13)

"I will also give thee for a light to the Gentiles, that thou mayest be my salvation unto the end of the earth" (Isaiah 49:6; see also Isaiah 42:6)

"Ye are the light of the world" (Matthew 5:14); [ST] "I give unto you to be the light of this people" (3 Nephi 12:14)

"For thou wilt light my candle: the Lord my God will enlighten my darkness" (Psalm 18:28)

"Neither do men light a candle, and put it under a bushel" (Matthew 5:15)

"Thou shalt not kill" (Exodus 20:13)

"Thou shalt not kill" (Matthew 5:21)

"Thou shalt not commit adultery" (Exodus 20:14)

"Thou shalt not commit adultery" (Matthew 5:27)

"Lust not after her beauty in thine heart; neither let her take thee with her eyelids" (Proverbs 6:25)

"Whosoever looketh on a woman to lust after her hath committed adultery with her already in his heart" (Matthew 5:28)

"Seek not after your own heart and your own eyes, after which ye use to go a whoring" (Numbers 15:39)

"If thy right eye offend thee, pluck it out" (Matthew 5:29)

"Let him write her a bill of divorcement" (Deuteronomy 24:1)

"Let him give her a writing of divorcement" (Matthew 5:31)

"The Lord, the God of Israel, saith that he hateth putting away" (Malachi 2:16)

"Whosoever shall put away his wife, saving for the cause of fornication, causeth her to commit adultery" (Matthew 5:32)

"Thou shalt not bear false witness" (Exodus 20:16); "ye shall not swear by my name falsely" (Leviticus 19:12; see Numbers 30:2)

"Thou shalt not forswear thyself" (Matthew 5:33)

"Pay thy vows unto the most High" (Psalm 50:14)

"Perform unto the Lord thine oaths" (Matthew 5:33)

"If thou shalt forbear to vow, it shall be no sin in thee" (Deuteronomy 23:22)

"Swear not at all" (Matthew 5:34)

"The heaven is my throne, and the earth is my footstool" (Isaiah 66:1)

"Neither by heaven; for it is God's throne: nor by the earth; for it is his footstool" (Matthew 5:34–35)

"Zion, . . . city of the great King" (Psalm 48:2)

"Jerusalem; . . . the city of the great King" (Matthew 5:35)

"Eye for eye, tooth for tooth" (Exodus 21:24; Leviticus 24:20; Deuteronomy 19:21)

"An eye for an eye, and a tooth for a tooth" (Matthew 5:38)

"I gave my back to the smiters (*rhapismata*, LXX), and my cheeks to them that plucked off the hair" (Isaiah 50:6)

"Whosoever shall smite (*rhapizei*) thee on thy right cheek, turn to him the other also" (Matthew 5:39)

"If thou at all take thy neighbor's raiment to pledge, thou shalt deliver it unto him by [sundown]" (Exodus 22:26)

"If any man will sue thee . . . and take away thy coat, let him have thy cloke also" (Matthew 5:40)

"[Thou] shalt surely lend him sufficient for his need" (Deuteronomy 15:8)

"From him that would borrow of thee turn not thou away" (Matthew 5:42)

"Love thy neighbour" (Leviticus 19:18); "in that thou lovest thine enemies, and hatest thy friends!" (2 Samuel 19:6)

"Love thy neighbour and hate thine enemy" (Matthew 5:43)

"If thou meet thine enemy's ox or his ass going astray, thou shalt surely bring it back to him again" (Exodus 23:4); "if thine enemy be hungry, give him bread to eat; and if he be thirsty, give him water to drink" (Proverbs 25:21)

"Love your enemies, bless them that curse you, do good to them that hate you" (Matthew 5:44)

"Ye are the children of the Lord your God" (Deuteronomy 14:1)

"That ye may be the children of your Father" (Matthew 5:45)

"Ye shall be holy: for I the Lord your God am holy" (Leviticus 19:2); "thou shalt be perfect" (Deuteronomy 18:13)

"Be ye therefore perfect, even as your Father which is in heaven is perfect" (Matthew 5:48)

"He went in therefore, and shut the door upon them twain, and prayed unto the Lord" (2 Kings 4:33; cf. Isaiah 26:20)

"When thou prayest, enter into thy closet, and when thou hast shut thy door, pray to thy Father" (Matthew 6:6)

"I shall sanctify [hallow] my great name" (Ezekiel 36:23)

"Hallowed be thy name" (Matthew 6:9)

"This is the bread which the Lord hath given you to eat" (Exodus 16:16)

"Give us this day our daily bread" (Matthew 6:11)

"Thine, O Lord, is the greatness, and the power, and the glory, and the victory, and the majesty: for all that is in the heaven and in the earth is thine; thine is the kingdom, O Lord, and thou art exalted as head above all" (1 Chronicles 29:11)

"Thine is the kingdom, and the power, and the glory, for ever" (Matthew 6:13)

"Is it such a fast that I have chosen? a day for a man to afflict his soul? is it to bow down his head as a bulrush, and to spread sackcloth and ashes under him? wilt thou call this a fast, and an acceptable day to the Lord?" (Isaiah 58:5)

"When ye fast, be not . . . of a sad countenance. . . . When thou fastest, anoint thine head, and wash thy face" (Matthew 6:16-17)

"If a thief be found breaking up" (Exodus 22:2)

"Where thieves break through and steal" (Matthew 6:19)

"The spirit of man is the candle of the Lord" (Proverbs 20:27)

"The light of the body is the eye" (Matthew 6:22)

"Delight thyself also in the Lord; and he shall give thee the desires of thine heart" (Psalm 37:4)

"Seek ye first the kingdom of God, and his righteousness; and all these things shall be added unto you" (Matthew 6:33)

"Gather [manna at] a certain rate every day" (Exodus 16:4)

"Take . . . no thought for the morrow" (Matthew 6:34)

"Holy men . . . : neither shall ye eat flesh that is torn of beasts . . . ; ye shall cast it to the dogs" (Exodus 22:31)

"Give not that which is holy to the dogs, neither cast ye your pearls before swine" (Matthew 7:6)

"Ye shall seek me, and find me" (Jeremiah 29:13)

"Seek, and ye shall find" (Matthew 7:7)

The Two Ways (see Deuteronomy 11:26; 30:15; Jeremiah 21:8; Proverbs 28:6, 18)

The Two Ways (see Matthew 7:13-14)

"The prophet, which shall presume to speak [what] I have not commanded him to speak, . . . shall die" (Deuteronomy 18:20)

"Beware of false prophets" (Matthew 7:15)

"Her princes in the midst thereof are like wolves ravening the prey" (Ezekiel 22:27)

"Inwardly they are ravening wolves" (Matthew 7:15)

"The Lord alone shall be exalted in that day" (Isaiah 2:11, 17)

"In that day" (Matthew 7:22)

"[They] prophesy lies in my name" (Jeremiah 14:14; cf. 27:15)

"Have we not prophesied in thy name" (Matthew 7:22)

"Depart from me, all ye workers of iniquity" (Psalm 6:8)

"Depart from me, ye that work iniquity" (Matthew 7:23)

"And one built up a wall, and, lo, others daubed it with untempered morter [sand]: . . . there shall be an overflowing shower; and ye, O great hailstones, shall fall; and a stormy wind shall rend it" (Ezekiel 13:10-11)

"A foolish man . . . built his house upon the sand: and the rain descended, and the floods came, and the winds blew, and beat upon that house, and it fell" (Matthew 7:26-27)

"A broken spirit: a broken and a contrite heart" (Psalm 51:17)

[ST] "Come unto me with a broken heart and a contrite spirit" (3 Nephi 12:19)

121

This list is undoubtedly incomplete, but it is striking—and I believe most readers will be as surprised as I was by the substantial number of phrases in the Sermon on the Mount that essentially repeat or allude to phrases in the Old Testament. Many other parallels can also be adduced from the Dead Sea Scrolls and other Jewish writings. Obviously, the lines of the Sermon "are not a spontaneous lyrical outbreak of prophecy, but a profound message founded on a complex network of biblical reminiscences and midrashic exegesis."[1]

My purpose in displaying these parallels and likely precedents is not to claim that Jesus quoted each of these Old Testament passages verbatim. Several of them are precise quotes; others only paraphrases or similar concepts. My point is simply to show that Jesus' words would not have sounded strange to either his Jewish or Nephite listeners. Their common Israelite and prophetic heritages would have prepared both audiences to understand and appreciate the messages in this Sermon, as Jesus transformed their understanding of the old laws into the new.

While we cannot know for sure how many of these Old Testament expressions were found on the Plates of Brass or how closely they were rendered by Jesus into the contemporary Nephite dialect, certainly many of these phrases were known to the Nephites (especially the passages in the Pentateuch and Isaiah). Accordingly, although the Sermon is often thought of as a uniquely "Christian" scripture, it is saturated with Israelite and Jewish elements.[2] Passages

---

1. D. Flusser, "Blessed Are the Poor in Spirit," *Israel Exploration Journal* 10 (1960): 13.

2. In further discussions of the thoroughly Jewish character of the Sermon on the Mount, others have convincingly found Jesus the Jew at virtually every turn in the Sermon on the Mount; see, e.g., Strack and Billerbeck, *Kommentar zum Neuen Testament*, 1:188–474; Lachs, *Rabbinic Commentary on the New Testament*; W. D. Davies, "Does the Sermon on the Mount Follow a Rabbinic Pattern?" in "My Odyssey in New Testament Interpretation," *Bible Review* 5 (1989): 15.

from the law, the prophets, and the Psalms; covenantal injunctions about giving to the poor (see Mosiah 4:16–25) and praying and fasting (see Omni 1:26; Mosiah 27:23; Alma 5:46); and specific references to wealth (see Jacob 2:12–19), the temple of Solomon (2 Nephi 5:16), and the "strait and narrow" (1 Nephi 8:20) were familiar territory to the Nephites.

An informed Israelite or a devout Nephite would have readily recognized that the Sermon took the threads of the old covenantal law and wove them into a splendid new tapestry. Once we are aware of this rich background of Israelite origins, we can hardly imagine a reaction more fitting than that of the Nephites: Their reaction was one of marvel and wonder at how all their old and familiar things had suddenly become new (see 3 Nephi 15:3).

It is not difficult to identify many ways in which the Nephites could well have recognized that Jesus presented ideas to them that they had known before but that now appeared in a new form or context. Their Israelite backgrounds had schooled and prepared them to recognize and finally receive the principles and ordinances of the gospel of Jesus Christ. Some of the places in the Sermon at the Temple where one can discern points of transforming continuity between the old and the new include the following:

(1) Whereas previously "the Lord descended upon [Mount Sinai] in fire" and tumult (Exodus 19:18), now he came peacefully as "a Man descending out of heaven" (3 Nephi 11:8).

(2) The old Hosanna Shout of Psalm 118 could only look forward to him "that cometh in the name of the Lord" (Psalm 118:26), but now it rang out to bless him who had finally come (see 3 Nephi 11:17). This long-awaited event must have broken forth into the lives of the people at Bountiful with the kind of unbelievable euphoria that so many people in the world experienced with the initial opening of

the Berlin Wall in 1989—they had never dared to dream that they would actually live to see it happen.

(3) To take the place of the old sanctification of the people and the ritual washing of their clothes (for widespread indications of ceremonial ablutions to remove impurity both from the worshippers and temple priests, see Exodus 19:14; Leviticus 13:58; 15:17; Psalms 24:4; 26:6; 73:13; 2 Samuel 12:20; 2 Chronicles 4:6; Ezekiel 16:9),[1] the Nephites were given an expanded understanding of the ordinance of baptism for the remission of sins.

(4) Radically upgrading the nature of witnesses, which under the old law could be stones (see Joshua 24:27) or the heavens and the earth (see Deuteronomy 4:26), now the Godhead itself stood as witnesses of the doctrine and covenants of Jesus Christ (see 3 Nephi 11:35).

(5) The old curses, that for centuries had been ritually invoked upon those who privily worked wickedness (see Deuteronomy 27:11-26), were now converted into glorious blessings upon those who secretly worked righteousness (see 3 Nephi 12:3-11; 13:4, 6, 18).

(6) The old view of creation had presented the words, "Let there be light," as a physical phenomenon, but now it became a personal creation, "Let your light so shine" (3 Nephi 12:16).

(7) The old law of sacrifice was explicitly replaced by that of the "broken heart and contrite spirit" (3 Nephi 12:18-19), and whereas previously the sacrificial animal was to be pure and without blemish (*haplous*), now the disciples themselves are to become "single" (*haplous*) to the glory of God (see 3 Nephi 13:22; Matthew 6:22).

---

1. See also Hugh Nibley, *The Message of the Joseph Smith Papyri* (Salt Lake City: Deseret Book, 1975), 93-96; Robert A. Wild, *Water in the Cultic Worship of Isis and Sarapis* (Leiden: Brill, 1981), 143-48; Thomas F. Torrance, "The Origins of Baptism," *Scottish Journal of Theology* 11 (1958): 158-71.

(8) Similarly, old commandments regarding murder, adultery, divorce, and oath-swearing were dramatically transfigured in the new order of Christ to promise results even more glorious than Solomon's temple of old.

(9) Finally, in the covenant at Sinai, the people covenanted to do "all the words which the Lord hath said" (Exodus 24:3), and the Lord promised in return to "bless thy bread, and thy water, and [to] take sickness away from the midst of" the people (Exodus 23:25). So, too, the Nephites newly covenanted with blessed bread and wine to do what the Lord had commanded (see 3 Nephi 18:10), and he healed all their sick (see 3 Nephi 17:9).

Over and over it is evident in the Sermon at the Temple that indeed "all things had become new" (3 Nephi 15:3) in a great and marvelous way.

Only a few passages require discussion in regard to the Nephites' ability to understand what Jesus was talking about. The first is whether the Nephites would have understood the word *mammon*. The ancient origins and etymology of this word are highly uncertain.[1] Around the time of Jesus, it was a frequently used Aramaic word in Palestine, meaning "wealth, property, profit, or money," appearing in the Targums, the Mishnah, the Talmud, and the Damascus Document.[2] It is unknown how far back in history the word was known or where it came from, and thus one cannot be certain about the nature of its occurrence in 3 Nephi. Aramaic is old enough that a Nephite word for money could have been "mammon," but without access to the original Nephite texts it is unclear if Jesus used this Aramaic word in the Sermon at the Temple, or if it was a

---

1. *TDNT*, 4:388–90.

2. Matthew Black, *An Aramaic Approach to the Gospels and Acts*, 3rd ed. (Oxford: Clarendon, 1967), 139–40; citing A. M. Honeyman, "The Etymology of Mammon," *Archivum Linguisticum* 4:60; *GELNT*, 491.

part of Nephite vocabulary, or whether Jesus used some closely comparable Nephite word for "wealth" that was simply translated as "Mammon." Nevertheless, the context makes it clear what Jesus is talking about. Similar things can be said of the Aramaic word *Raca*, whose antiquity and possible derivation from Hebrew is also uncertain but whose basic meaning is unmistakable in its context.

The second asks if the Nephites would have known where it was written, "Hate thine enemy"? One searches in vain in the Old Testament for exactly such a writing; and, indeed, in this particular instance Jesus does not say to the Nephites, "It is also written *before you*," as he did with the first law against murder. Thus the Nephites may have been left to wonder who *had* written such a thing. Several scholars have suggested that Matthew 5:43 refers to a text from the community at Qumran: God commands his sons to "love everything that he has chosen but to hate everything that he has rejected."[1] Thus Jesus' listeners in Palestine may have recognized in his words a veiled criticism of that specific sect. Another possibility is that Jesus was responding to some other contemporary "popular maxim or partisan rallying cry" glossing Leviticus 19:18.[2] The roots of Matthew 5:43, however, may run much earlier, for similar sentiments are found in 2 Samuel 19:6, which criticizes the king for having everything backwards "in that thou lovest thine enemies, and hatest thy friends." The implication is that one should hate one's enemies and love one's friends. In any event, whether or not the Nephites knew where such a saying was written, they would have had

---

1. *1QS* 1:3-4; Strecker, *Sermon on the Mount*, 87; mentioned also in S. Kent Brown, "The Dead Sea Scrolls: A Mormon Perspective," *BYU Studies* 23 (1983): 65.

2. O. J. F. Seitz, "Love Your Enemies," *New Testament Studies* 16 (1969): 51; on the possible historical settings of Matthew 5:43-44 and Luke 6:27-28, see pp. 39-54.

no difficulty understanding Jesus' meaning. They may have thought immediately of their own ongoing, painful problems with the Lamanites, a group that expressly taught their children to hate their enemies eternally (see Mosiah 10:17; Jacob 7:26).

Third are the "figs" and "grapes" mentioned in 3 Nephi 14:16. "Do men gather grapes [literally "bunches"] of thorns, or figs of thistles?" Thorns and thistles were present in the New World, but grapes and figs are slightly more questionable. John Sorenson points out that "certain grapes were present, but we do not know that they were used for food or drink,"[1] although he reports that this is now thought to be more likely. Still, we cannot be sure what a Nephite might have thought when he heard the words "figs" and "grapes." There are several possibilities: Certainly the words were known to the Nephites from the Hebrew records brought with them from Jerusalem, and thus these fruits may have been known to them simply as archaic terms; or perhaps the Nephites used these names for local fruits; or again, perhaps the word *staphulas* ("bunches," usually of grapes) was simply understood to mean bunches of some other kind of fruit. In any event, several varieties of figs and grapes existed in the New World (fig bark was used to make paper in Mesoamerica), and the context would have made it clear to Jesus' audience that he was talking about bunches of fruit gathered from trees.

Fourth is the "sanhedrin" mentioned in Matthew 5:22. Since the Greek word *synedrion* seems to have been first used in the days of Herod as a title for the Great Sanhedrin of Jerusalem,[2] one may wonder if the Nephites would have understood what Jesus meant when he said, "Whosoever is

---

1. John L. Sorenson, *An Ancient American Setting for the Book of Mormon* (Salt Lake City: Deseret Book, 1985), 1986 n. 70.

2. *TDNT*, 7:862.

angry with his brother shall be in danger of his judgment [*krisei*]. And whosoever shall say to his brother, Raca, shall be in danger of the council [*synedrion*]. But whosoever shall say, Thou fool, shall be in danger of hell fire." Commentators on Matthew sometimes assert that the Greek words "judgment" and "council" refer technically to local Jewish courts, the Small Sanhedrins and the Great Sanhedrin,[1] but the terminology is not so specific. Courts or councils of all kinds could be denoted. Strecker argues that "judgment" can be understood only "figuratively. . . . Jesus is thinking of the final judgment."[2] Alternatively, the "council" could allude to the council in heaven, which figures in God's judgments upon the world (see 1 Nephi 1:6-10),[3] or, as I have suggested above, to an apostolic council that judges mankind in this world or in the world to come (see 3 Nephi 27:27).[4] All these are concepts the Nephites would have readily understood.

These are the cases where a Nephite might have had difficulty readily understanding the Sermon at the Temple. Most of its common human experiences and life settings, such as thieves breaking in, or going a second mile, need not presuppose anything out of the ordinary in Nephite

---

1. See, e.g., Strecker, *Sermon on the Mount*, 65-67.

2. Ibid., 65, as the concluding reference to "hell fire" makes apparent.

3. Raymond E. Brown, "The Pre-Christian Semitic Concept of 'Mystery,'" *Catholic Biblical Quarterly* 20 (1958): 419 n. 10, includes the word *synedrion* among the terms used in "the vocabulary of the LXX to translate *sōd* where it is used of the heavenly assembly," citing, however, only Proverbs 3:32 and Jeremiah 15:17. See, generally, E. Theodore Mullen, Jr., *The Assembly of the Gods* (Chico, California: Scholars, 1980); John W. Welch, "The Calling of a Prophet," in *First Nephi: The Doctrinal Foundation*, ed. M. Nyman and C. Tate (Provo: Religious Studies Center, Brigham Young University, 1988), 35-54.

4. On the use of the word *synedrion* in early Christianity to refer to a council of apostles, see *TDNT* 7:871. Ignatius spoke of a council of elders as the *topon* of the *synedrion* of the apostles and as "the council [*synedrion*] of God and the council [*synedrion*] of the apostles."

civilization. To my mind, this result is worth observing: In all the places where the two texts differ, good and sufficient reasons exist for the divergence; yet no further changes were probably needed in deference to the Nephite culture or audience, for which much of the newness of the Sermon was firmly grounded in familiar terrain.

7

JOSEPH SMITH AND THE SERMON AT THE TEMPLE

If the Sermon at the Temple is appropriately nuanced and subtly different from the Sermon on the Mount, as the previous chapters suggest, then one might wonder how this occurred. Joseph Smith explained that it came by the gift and power of God as the text was translated one line after another.

Those who reject this explanation must at least credit Joseph Smith with high marks in keeping many factors in mind as he allegedly modified the Sermon on the Mount to fit it into a Nephite context. Given enough time and research, a reasonably intelligent person could probably work his way through the Sermon on the Mount in a similar fashion; and with a little luck, he might not overlook or mistake anything important.

Time and research, however, were not on Joseph Smith's side. The account of Jesus' ministry among the Nephites was translated before May 15, 1829, the translation having commenced several hundred pages earlier on April 7, 1829.[1]

---

1. The chronology of events in these months is discussed in John W. Welch, "How Long Did It Take Joseph Smith to Translate the Book of Mormon?" *Ensign* 18 (January 1988): 46; John W. Welch and Tim Rathbone, "The Translation of the Book of Mormon: Basic Historical Information" (Provo: F.A.R.M.S., 1986), 38–39.

At this pace, only about two days could have been spent on 3 Nephi 11–18.

Moreover, several historical accounts of the translation process make it unlikely that any flagrant copying occurred. While many often assume that Joseph covertly took out his copy of the King James Bible and worked from it when he came to the Isaiah and Sermon on the Mount materials in the Book of Mormon, the following testimonies of people who intimately assisted Joseph Smith in the transcription process and routinely watched him work give evidence that such a thing did not occur. Emma Smith, Martin Harris, Oliver Cowdery, David Whitmer, William Smith, Lucy Mack Smith, Elizabeth Anne Whitmer Cowdery Johnson, Michael Morse, Sarah Heller Conrad, Isaac Hale, Reuben Hale, and Joseph Knight, Sr., all left historical comments on what they knew of how Joseph worked when translating the Book of Mormon. None of their statements mentions anything about the use of a Bible or allows room for it.

In an interview in 1879, Emma Smith was asked and asserted the following:

> Q. Had he not a book or manuscript from which he read, or dictated to you?
> A. He had neither manuscript or book to read from.
> Q. Could he not have had, and you not know it?
> A. If he had anything of the kind he could not have concealed it from me.[1]

While this interview occurred fifty years after the events it reports, Emma still had a vivid memory of many details. Her recollection can probably be trusted even more regarding things that did *not* occur than in describing the particulars of things that did occur, especially where she would

---

1. "Last Testimony of Sister Emma," *Saints' Advocate*, vol. 2, no. 4 (Plano, Illinois, October 1879): 50-52; and *Saints' Herald*, vol. 26, no. 19 (Plano, Illinois, October 1, 1879): 290.

have been unforgettably surprised to see Joseph cribbing from the Bible. It is unknown, however, whether she was present when the Sermon at the Temple was translated, although she would have been somewhere in and around the cabin in Harmony, Pennsylvania, in the second week of May 1829, when Joseph and Oliver were working their way through this material.

David Whitmer and others corroborated Emma's description. For example, in 1881 the *Deseret News* published an article from Richmond, Missouri, about this Book of Mormon witness. It reports, "Mr. Whitmer emphatically asserts, as did Harris and Cowdery, that while Smith was dictating the translation he had NO MANUSCRIPT NOTES OR OTHER MEANS OF KNOWLEDGE save the seer-stone and the characters as shown on the plates, he being present and cognizant how it was done."[1]

In 1833, Oliver Cowdery described the work of that period. As he vividly recalled, "These were days never to be forgotten—to sit under the sound of a voice dictated by the inspiration of heaven. . . . Day after day, I continued, uninterrupted, to write from his mouth, as he translated . . . the Book of Mormon."[2] Oliver was present during all of the translation of the Sermon at the Temple. It seems highly unlikely to me that Joseph could have read from the Bible and Oliver not have known it; and if he knew it, not to have been irreparably disillusioned. Oliver had himself attempted to translate (see D&C 9), but had been unsuccessful. Certainly he thought that more was involved in the translation process than simply reading from the Bible and making a few modifications to the text. It seems to me that Oliver would have instantly doubted Joseph's ability to

---

1. *Deseret News*, November 10, 1881 (capitalization in original).

2. Oliver Cowdery, "Letter I," *LDS Messenger and Advocate* 1 (October 1834): 14.

translate if he ever caught him using the Bible or suspected him of relying directly on it as he translated. Oliver and Joseph were in close proximity to each other, and the use of the interpreters would have made it very awkward for Joseph to put a large Bible anywhere into the picture without Oliver becoming aware of it.

It is possible, one may counter, that Joseph sat behind a curtain or blanket while he was translating, as is commonly imagined. But the only reports, so far as I know, that mention such a thing are from Professor Charles Anthon and Reverend John A. Clark.[1] Both of these hostile sources, even if we can trust them on this point, depend on information given to them by Martin Harris, who was scribe only in 1827–28. None of the scribes in 1829, however, ever mentions the use of a curtain while they were present. I think their silence is significant. All other factors indicate that Joseph was quite open with the translation process when Oliver and the others at the Whitmer farm were present and assisting.

It appears that Joseph used the curtain only at first and perhaps because he rightly did not trust Martin Harris as much as the others (see D&C 10:7, which calls Martin Harris "a wicked man" who "has sought to destroy" Joseph's gift of translation). Oliver Cowdery, on the other hand, had used the interpreters; and the Lord, who had appeared to Oliver early in 1829 testifying of "the truth of the work" and calling him to "write for [Joseph] and translate," had already shown him the plates in a vision.[2] With

---

1. See sources in Milton V. Backman, Jr., *Eyewitness Accounts of the Restoration* (Salt Lake City: Deseret Book, 1986), 213, 218; see also Royal Skousen, "Towards a Critical Text of the Book of Mormon," paper resulting from the Fourteenth Annual Deseret Language and Linguistics Symposium, Brigham Young University, 1988, p. 12 n. 26.

2. Joseph Smith, History, 1832, in Jessee, *Personal Writings of Joseph Smith*, 8; and in Dean C. Jessee, ed., *The Papers of Joseph Smith: Volume 1, Autobiographical and Historical Writings* (Salt Lake City: Deseret Book, 1989), 1:10.

such a divine endorsement for Oliver, Joseph would have had little need to use a curtain when Oliver was present. Indeed, Emma's testimony describes a similar situation, wherein she "frequently wrote day after day, often sitting at the table close by him, he sitting with his face buried in his hat, with the stone in it, and dictating hour after hour with nothing between us."[1] The recollection of Oliver's wife, Elizabeth Anne Whitmer Cowdery Johnson, written in 1870, also denies that a curtain was used while she was present during the final stages of translating at the Whitmer farm in Fayette:

> I often sat by and saw and heard them translate and write for hours together. Joseph never had a curtain drawn between him and his scribe while he was translating. He would place the director in his hat, and then place his face in his hat, so as to exclude the light, and then [dictate?] to his scribe the words [he said] as they appeared before [him?].[2]

At this time in Fayette, according to our best estimates,[3] Joseph translated the Small Plates of Nephi, which contain several sections of Isaiah material (see 1 Nephi 20-21; 2 Nephi 7-8, 12-24). So if Joseph simply cribbed from the Bible when he came to such sections, one must seriously wonder how he did it.

Thus, while the theory in question — that Joseph used his family Bible in translating the Book of Mormon — may appear to solve one problem, it only creates another. The idea that Joseph relied directly and heavily on his Bible may

---

1. "Last Testimony of Sister Emma," *Saints' Advocate*, 51.

2. Copy contained on the obverse of letter of William E. McLellin to "My Dear Friends," Independence, Missouri, February 1870, RLDS Archives P13 f191. Question marks indicate illegible words.

3. Welch and Rathbone, "The Translation of the Book of Mormon," 33-37.

ease the minds of those who resist seeing any divine power at work in the translation process, but it creates a different concern, namely that the historical accounts give no impression whatever that Joseph turned to the Bible when dictating the text of the Sermon at the Temple.

Additional considerations also make the claim of such plagiarism improbable. For example, Hugh Nibley has cogently argued that it is counterintuitive for one to imagine that Joseph would have included long passages in the Book of Mormon, closely resembling several chapters from Isaiah as well as the Sermon on the Mount, if he did not need to. He would not have been so stupid as to copy unnecessarily and thereby create an obvious problem for the Book of Mormon: "It is hard to see why a deceiver would strew the broadest clues to his pilfering all through a record he claimed was his own."[1]

While Roberts, Sperry, and others have conjectured that Joseph made direct use of his King James Bible in order to make the difficult translation job easier, they advance this theory as an assumption.[2] While the idea has some attractiveness and convenience, I am less inclined toward it today

---

1. Hugh W. Nibley, *Since Cumorah* (Salt Lake City: Deseret Book, 1967), 127; reprinted in *CWHN* 7:111.

2. Roberts, "Bible Quotations in the Book of Mormon," 181, says, "This is but a conjecture," but on page 192 he is more certain, "How are these differences to be accounted for? They unquestionably arise from the fact that the Prophet compared the King James' translation with the parallel passages in the Nephite records, and when he found the sense of the passage on the Nephite plates superior to that in the English version he made such changes as would give the superior sense and clearness." See also B. H. Roberts, *New Witnesses of God*, 3 vols. (Salt Lake City: Deseret Book, 1909), 3:441; Sidney B. Sperry, *Book of Mormon Compendium* (Salt Lake City: Bookcraft, 1967), 507; H. Grant Vest, "The Problem of Isaiah in the Book of Mormon," unpublished master's thesis (Provo: Brigham Young University, 1938), 3; Stanley R. Larson, "A Study of Some Textual Variations in the Book of Mormon," unpublished master's thesis (Provo: Brigham Young University, 1974), 246–47; *Book of Mormon Critical Text*, 1:ix.

than they were, or than I was ten years ago. It is neither a necessary nor an exclusive explanation. Other logical possibilities exist. For instance, although very little is known about the process of translating the Book of Mormon, for one who believes that Joseph Smith received *any* part of the book through the gift and power of God, it is a relatively small step from there to believe that the Sermon at the Temple was similarly translated and dictated under the direction of divine inspiration; that is, that God projected a text similar to the biblical text through Joseph Smith, or the power of God brought that text especially to his memory as those words were appropriate and helpful.

While there is no evidence that Joseph could recite verbatim long sections of Isaiah and Matthew, one may certainly assume that he had read or heard those chapters several times around the family hearth. This would make it possible for the powers of inspiration to draw these words out of his memory and put them extraordinarily at his disposal, causing him to recall them, even though they would have been buried too deep in his brain to be remembered voluntarily. As B. H. Roberts has said, "The English interpretation was a reflex from the Prophet's mind," and not "an arbitrary piece of mechanical work."[1] As Joseph studied the translation out in his mind (see D&C 9:8), the words he then thought and spoke rang true to him. I would think this occurred as the translation flowed forth, independent of immediate input but also reflexive of Joseph's vocabulary and prior knowledge, reinforced by his inspired subconscious recall of the parallel texts in the Bible.

Yet even if the claim of simple plagiarism is set aside, the question may still arise: Why, in any event, is the English translation of the Sermon at the Temple so pervasively sim-

---

1. B. H. Roberts, "Translation of the Book of Mormon," *Improvement Era* 9 (1906): 433.

ilar to the style and language of the King James rendition of Matthew 5-7? As general Christian commitment to the King James translation wanes, and as the number of years between modern readers and the time of Joseph Smith widens, the oddities of King James language grow more glaring and the force of this question increases.

But for people in 1830, the question was less obvious or bothersome than for us today. This was also not an issue for M. T. Lamb, who wrote in 1887 that the King James Version miraculously preserved the exact words of Jesus, penned by Matthew, who "remembered the exact words of the Saviour, and wrote just as they were first spoken."[1]

B. H. Roberts thus concluded that the stylistic similarity between the Sermon at the Temple and the Sermon on the Mount was simply due to Joseph's language. "While Joseph Smith obtained the facts and ideas from the Nephite characters through the inspiration of God, he was left to express those facts and ideas, in the main, in such language as he could command."[2] As Joseph translated, the Lord spoke to him "after the manner of [his] language," as he speaks to all men, "that they might come to understanding" (D&C 1:24). Where the King James English would best communicate the thought of a passage to Joseph Smith, that would be the preferred rendition.

Hugh Nibley has further suggested several other reasons that made the use of King James style important, if not necessary. One reason was Joseph's audience:

> When Jesus and the Apostles and, for that matter, the Angel Gabriel quote the [Hebrew] scriptures in the New Testament, do they recite from some mysterious Urtext? Do they quote the prophets of old in the ultimate original? . . . No, they do not. They quote the Septuagint, a

---

1. Lamb, *The Golden Bible*, 19.
2. Roberts, "Bible Quotations in the Book of Mormon," 181.

Greek version of the Old Testament prepared in the third century B.C. Why so? Because that happened to be the received standard version of the Bible accepted by the readers of the Greek New Testament.[1]

Another reason for the use of the style of the King James Version was the nature of the record: "The scriptures were probably in old-fashioned language the day they were written down."[2] Furthermore, "by frankly using that idiom, the Book of Mormon avoids the necessity of having to be redone into 'modern English' every thirty or forty years."[3] To such points, other explanations may be added, but these seem sufficient. The King James idiom yields a good translation of both the Sermon on the Mount and the Sermon at the Temple. In fact, a study of the Greek vocabulary used in Matthew 5–7 will show that in most cases, the traditional English translation is rather straightforward. The syntax of most of the sentences is relatively simple; the expressions are direct; most of the words and phrases have obvious and adequate primary choices in English as their translation (although their meaning and implications still remain profound).

Points such as these may sufficiently justify the similarities between the English Sermon at the Temple and the King's English in the Sermon on the Mount, but they do not explain the origins of the overwhelming preponderance of identical phraseology in these two translations. Something more than mere vocabulary, the needs of the audience, or the adequacy of the meaning is necessary to account for the nearly identical correspondence of expressions between

---

1. Hugh W. Nibley, "Literary Style Used in the Book of Mormon Insured Accurate Translation," in *The Prophetic Book of Mormon* (Salt Lake City: Deseret Book, 1989), *CWHN* 8:215.

2. Ibid., 218.

3. Ibid.

these two texts. For example, if a person were to undertake the task of translating an ancient text that had already been translated by another, and if one assumed that this person had no familiarity with the first translation, there is no chance that the second translation would ever turn out word for word the same as the first. Something more is necessary to account for the similarities between the Sermon on the Mount and the Sermon at the Temple. That shortfall, in my opinion, is made up in two ways: First, the problem with our hypothetical translator is that it assumes something that is not in evidence regarding Joseph Smith and the Sermon on the Mount, for Joseph *was* familiar with the King James translation. Second, the model inadequately assumes a normal translation process, rather than one impelled and activated by inspiration.

This last point naturally invites further reflection about a persistent question regarding the Book of Mormon, namely, what kind of a translation is it? There are several possibilities, and it exceeds anyone's ability at the present time to say which is correct.[1] Joseph Smith himself declined to comment very much, saying that "it was not expedient for him" to give "all the particulars,"[2] although in private

---

1. For general discussions of the mechanics of the translation process, see Richard L. Anderson, "By the Gift and Power of God," *Ensign* 7 (September 1977): 79-85; James E. Lancaster, " 'By the Gift and Power of God': The Method of Translation of the Book of Mormon," *Saints' Herald* 109 (Nov. 15, 1962): 798-802, 806, 817; Stephen D. Ricks, "Joseph Smith's Means and Methods of Translating the Book of Mormon," F.A.R.M.S. Paper, 1984. For other views to the effect that the translation was not a literal process, see Ed Ashment, "The Book of Mormon—A Literal Translation?" *Sunstone* 5:2 (March-April 1980): 10-14; Blake T. Ostler, "The Book of Mormon as a Modern Expansion of an Ancient Source," *Dialogue* 20 (Spring 1987): 66-123. For comments on Ostler, see Stephen E. Robinson, "The 'Expanded' Book of Mormon?" in *Second Nephi: The Doctrinal Structure*, ed. M. Nyman and C. Tate (Provo: Religious Studies Center, 1989), 391-414.

2. *History of the Church* 1:220

he apparently explained the process somewhat to David Whitmer and others.

Several factors indicate that it was quite a precise translation. The range of opinion, however, varies. Some commentators on one extreme have suggested (position 1) that it was a grammatically literal translation, a verbatim word-for-word, form-for-form rendition. This seems, however, to leave little room for the fact that Joseph had to take the matter and "study it out in [his] mind" (D&C 9:8) in order to translate the text "after the manner of [his] language" (D&C 1:24). As the discussion in chapter 8 below will show regarding minute grammatical comparisons of 3 Nephi 12–14 with the Greek manuscripts of the Sermon on the Mount, I do not imagine that Joseph's translation process produced this kind of literal translation.

On the other hand, such things as the presence of chiasmus in the Book of Mormon,[1] the precise nature of the book's internal quotations (see, e.g., Alma 36:22 quoting exactly from 1 Nephi 1:8; Helaman 14:12 quoting verbatim from Mosiah 3:8), its consistent use of technical legal terminology,[2] and many other instances of remarkable textual complexity indicate that most of the time the translation was probably not a very loose one either. Consequently, neither does it appear, as some have propounded on the other extreme, that the English translation has only (position 2) casual verbal connections with or, even more so, only (position 3) infrequent thematic intersections with the underlying record.

Accordingly, it seems to me that Joseph's English translation, while being more expressive than a mechanically

---

1. See several of my works on this topic, e.g., John W. Welch, "Chiasmus in the Book of Mormon," *BYU Studies* 10 (1969): 69–84.

2. See, e.g., "Statutes, Judgments, Ordinances and Commandments," F.A.R.M.S. Update, June 1988.

literal rendition, still (position 4) corresponded in some way, point-by-point, with the ancient writing that was being translated. Many of the textual details discussed in this study strongly suggest that the meaning of something on the plates gave rise to each element of meaning in the translation, although one cannot know in all cases how close that relationship or connection was. David Whitmer described how the characters from the plates would appear to Joseph on a parchment with the corresponding English translation below them. Whitmer once explained, "Frequently one character would make two lines of manuscript, while others made but a word or two words."[1] If this is an accurate statement, it confirms that the translation was rather strict, character for character, although sometimes several English words were required to express the meaning of a single inscription. So, for example, two simple characters might be translated into English as "the interpretation of languages" and two others as "the Book of Mormon," as Frederick G. Williams once wrote in Kirtland.[2]

With regard to the translation of the Sermon at the Temple, this would confirm, as the presence of consistently meaningful details has indicated above, that the English Book of Mormon reflects rather strictly the meaningful details in the record of Nephi, as the following two examples will further illustrate.

First, the account in 3 Nephi 17:5–10 of Jesus healing the sick is a beautiful five-part literary composition. It seems natural to ascribe its elegant and coherent structure to the ancient text, for it was written with care and reflection:

(A) It begins with three references to the eyes, as Jesus casts "his eyes round about again on the multitude," as he sees that their eyes are in tears, and as they look longingly

---

1. *Deseret News*, November 10, 1881.
2. See "Did Lehi Land in Chile" (F.A.R.M.S. Update, July 1988).

upon him hopeful that he will tarry with them longer (3 Nephi 17:5).

(B) Jesus next speaks to the people in balanced words that sincerely invite reciprocation (3 Nephi 17:6–7):

> Behold, my *bowels are filled*
> with *compassion* towards you.
>> Have ye any sick among you?
>> *Bring them hither.*
>>> Have ye any that are lame, or blind, or halt, or maimed,
>>> or leprous, or . . . withered, or . . . deaf, or . . . afflicted in any manner?
>> *Bring them hither*
>> and I will heal them,
> for I have *compassion* upon you;
> my *bowels are filled* with mercy.

(C) Jesus then draws himself close to the people through a series of intimate "I-you" statements. Here, too, are five parts, the symbolic number of mercy. These lines emotively and mercifully affirm God's personal relationship to mankind (3 Nephi 17:8):

> *I* perceive that *ye* desire
> that *I* should show unto *you*
> what *I* have done unto *your* brethren at Jerusalem,
> for *I* see that *your* faith is sufficient
> that *I* should heal *you.*

(B') The people then bring forth their sick to be healed. The "one" at the beginning of this verse is found in the throng coming forward with "one accord," but at the end it is in the individual acts of love as Jesus healed "every one" (3 Nephi 17:9):

> All the multitude, with *one* accord, did go forth
>> with their sick and their afflicted, and their lame,
>> and with their blind, . . . dumb, and . . . afflicted . . . ;
> and he did heal them every *one* as they were brought forth.

(A') Finally, the account concludes with three references to the feet, as the entire multitude bowed down at Jesus' feet, and many came forward to kiss his feet and "did bathe his feet with their tears" (3 Nephi 17:10). Mentioning the feet three times in this verse echoes the threefold emphasis placed on the eyes at the beginning of this pericope, thus conveying a sense of how completely these people were engrossed with their Savior, from head to foot. Moreover, in the end, their bathing his feet with their tears brings the account full circle back to the tears in their eyes, thus tying the episode together intimately and artistically. There is certainly nothing clumsy or out of place in the composition or translation of this record.

Second, Joseph's translation process produced a text that interestingly agrees with what appears to be the Aramaic words that Jesus originally spoke in Matthew 5:10. The Sermon at the Temple comes closer to the likely original intent of Jesus in this case than does the ancient Greek of the Sermon on the Mount. It is commonly assumed that Jesus usually spoke to his disciples in Aramaic (when and by whom the Sermon on the Mount was soon translated into Greek is unknown). When Jesus spoke to these fishermen and to the popular multitudes in Judea, he probably spoke to them in their local, native language. Accordingly, some scholars have worked hard, although not definitively, attempting to put the Greek of the New Testament back into what might have been the Aramaic of Jesus, to learn what that might tell us about his original intent.[1] In the Sermon on the Mount, several passages have been studied along these lines, but only a few have been detected where the Greek has likely misunderstood an underlying Aramaic

---

1. See, e.g., Black, *Aramaic Approach to the Gospels and Acts;* Joseph A. Fitzmyer, *Essays on the Semitic Background of the New Testament* (London: Geoffrey Chapman, 1971); Frank Zimmermann, *The Aramaic Origin of the Four Gospels* (New York: KTAV, 1979).

word or expression. In most cases, the nuances are very fine and the distinctions rather inconsequential.[1]

The case in Matthew 5:10 is an interesting example of this. Several scholars speculate that the Greek New Testament may have mistranslated the purported Aramaic original. Lachs argues that the word *saddiq* ("righteous one") was in the original form of Matthew 5:10, but that it was wrongly read as *sedeq* ("righteousness") and accordingly rendered into Greek as *dikaiosunē*.[2] Thus, the Greek reads "blessed are they which are persecuted for righteousness' sake." But this makes awkward sense compared with the Aramaic idea that one would be blessed for enduring persecution for the sake of the "Righteous One." The latter is far closer to the translation offered by the Sermon at the Temple: "Blessed are all they who are persecuted for *my name's sake*" (3 Nephi 12:10). Accordingly, Joseph's inspired translation in this detail finds significant independent support from biblical studies.

---

1. For example, Zimmermann argues that "bushel" is correct in Matthew 5, but was misunderstood by Luke and Mark (see Zimmermann, *Aramaic Origin of the Four Gospels*, 57); that "they shall see God" is in his opinion a theological impossibility and thus was a mistranslation of "they shall be seen of God" (ibid., 68–69); that in Aramaic the salt became "tasteless," not "foolish" (ibid., 70); that "rust" was a mistranslation of "eater" (i.e., a weevil?) (ibid., 71); that "body" and "life" in Matthew 6 should be translated more precisely as "soul" and "nourishment" (ibid., 37, 108); and that the wise man should be understood as building his house "with stone," not "upon" stone (ibid., 66). Objections can be raised quite readily to these conjectures.

2. Samuel T. Lachs, "Some Textual Observations on the Sermon on the Mount," *Jewish Quarterly Review* 69 (1978): 101–2. Strecker, *Sermon on the Mount*, 42, agrees that "righteousness" was a favorite word of Matthew, and thus indicates that Matthew introduced it into the text.

8

THE SERMON AT THE TEMPLE
AND THE GREEK
NEW TESTAMENT MANUSCRIPTS

The example of the probable Aramaic meaning of Matthew 5:10 and the similar Book of Mormon rendition in 3 Nephi 12:10 leads to yet a further area of textual study, namely the examination of the early Greek manuscripts of Matthew. What may they add to our understanding of the Sermon at the Temple?

Stanley R. Larson has recently published an article helping to identify places in the early Greek texts of the Sermon on the Mount where variants exist.[1] Although he advances this information for a diametrically opposed purpose,[2] his findings can be reexamined to show that the Book of Mormon has yielded a translation that communicates, in each case, the correct meaning of the ancient text. Conveying accurate and precise meaning, though not to the extent of

---

1. Stanley R. Larson, "The Sermon on the Mount: What Its Textual Transformation Discloses Concerning the Historicity of the Book of Mormon," *Trinity Journal* 7 (1986): 23–45.

2. He concludes that the Sermon at the Temple should be rejected as an historical text, not so much because it resembles the King James idiom of the Sermon on the Mount, but because it is like the Sermon on the Mount in places where it allegedly should not be. For the reasons discussed in this chapter, I have not found his evidence strong enough to support that conclusion.

reflecting minute variances in grammatical form, was evidently the burden of Joseph's translation.

Before turning to the particulars, the following general observations are worth bearing in mind. First, as Larson points out, there are forty-five places in the Sermon on the Mount where the early manuscripts vary in one way or another from each other. He examines the eleven cases that scholars consider to be "secure" (that is, where scholarly consensus agrees which reading most likely reflects the original Greek written by Matthew[1]) and that differ from the Textus Receptus (the Greek text from which the King James Version was translated). His purpose is to show that in these eleven cases the phrasing of the older Greek versions should have been (but was not) reflected by Joseph Smith in the Sermon at the Temple.

Parenthetically, eleven is a relatively low number of potential trouble spots. In fact, the early manuscripts of the Sermon on the Mount agree on the vast majority of their words, spellings, and conjugations; they differ noticeably from the received Greek text only in a few places. This high degree of confirmation of the Textus Receptus speaks generally in favor of the Sermon at the Temple, for one could

---

1. Of course, it is impossible to know exactly what the original copy of Matthew's Gospel was like. Thus, Larson is probably overconfident in undertaking "to establish what was originally written by Matthew, and eliminate any later additions and alterations," and then in concluding that, where the Book of Mormon differs, it must be in error. Ibid., 23. While Larson understands the inconclusiveness of textual criticism, many of his readers might not appreciate the indeterminacy of this discipline. Even though scholarly consensus may justifiably emerge in favor of a given reading for a disputed New Testament passage as scholars assimilate the biblical evidence that has survived from the second to the fifth centuries, scholars still disagree on many points and assign different degrees of certitude to their preferred readings. For the same reason, I do not claim to be able to prove them wrong, any more than they can prove they are right. The best one can do is examine the strength of the evidence and consider the weight it is being asked to bear.

not have wisely gambled on such confirmation a century and a half ago, before the earliest Greek New Testament manuscripts had been discovered. In the rush of manuscript discoveries in the late nineteenth and early twentieth centuries, many people expected that the earliest texts of the New Testament would prove radically different from the traditional manuscripts handed down through the ages, but the need to revise our texts significantly did not materialize.

Moreover, Larson assumes with many scholars (and I generally agree) that the older the manuscript, the closer it probably is to the original. Only time will tell, however, in how many cases this common assumption of textual criticism proves reliable, and so, for the time being, there is room to withhold judgment. As one scholar has written, "Often the *Textus Receptus* does preserve a text which represents the words of the original author where the older codices do not. The age of a manuscript should be no guide to the originality of its text."[1]

More than that, however, it is evident that most of these ancient textual variants in the Sermon on the Mount make no perceptible difference in the meaning of the text. Thus, in a roundabout way they confirm the correctness of the Book of Mormon translation, which in most of these cases renders the text into English quite acceptably. As the following case-by-case examination shows, the Sermon at the Temple never gives an incorrect translation, even though it may yet comport with the KJV. Moreover, a variety of secondary reasons give further support to the acceptability of the Book of Mormon's readings in each of these eleven cases, and in one additional instance (regarding Matthew 5:22), a vigorous case can be made that the Sermon at the Temple in fact conforms with the original manuscript tradition in

---

1. J. K. Elliott, "Can We Recover the Original New Testament?" *Theology* 77 (1974): 343.

the lone instance where the ancient textual variants do make a difference in meaning.

1. Matthew 5:27. "Ye have heard that it was said *by them of old time,* thou shalt not commit adultery." The best early manuscripts of this verse do not contain the words *tois archaiois* ("by them of old time"). They only read, "Ye have heard that it was said . . . " Textual purists are probably right that the phrase should be left out of our Greek texts of Matthew 5:27 today. But this does not mean that the KJV or the Sermon at the Temple are wrong to include it in Matthew 5:27 and 3 Nephi 12:27, for the meaning of this phrase is implicit in the Greek text, whether or not the words *tois archaiois* are written out. This is because the parallel sayings in Matthew 5:21 and 5:33 contain the phrase *tois archaiois,* so these words are understood in verse 27, just as they are understood in verses 38 and 43, where no Greek manuscript evinced a need to repeat the obvious either. In fact, this variant is insignificant enough that the United Bible Societies' Greek New Testament does not note it. Thus, the KJV and the Sermon at the Temple capture a correct meaning when they include the phrase "by them of old time" in verse 27.

It is also interesting to note that the Sermon at the Temple does not follow the KJV blindly on this point in any event. The phrase "by them of old time" does *not* appear in 3 Nephi 12:33, whereas it *does* appear in the Greek and KJV of Matthew 5:33. Thus, just as the Greek manuscripts sometimes include and other times exclude the words *tois archaiois* in the five "ye have heard" verses, so does the Sermon at the Temple. Neither the Sermon on the Mount nor the Sermon at the Temple needs to spell this phrase out each time in order to convey this meaning.

2. Matthew 5:30. The better Greek manuscripts read "lest your whole body go *off* (*apelthēi*) into hell," while other texts, including 3 Nephi 12:30, warn "lest your whole body *be cast* (*blēthēi*) into hell." These readings also present a distinction without a difference. There is no practical difference between these two idioms. The result is the same whether one's whole body "is cast" into hell or "goes off" into hell. So this variant, too, is not significant enough to have been noted in the United Bible Societies' Greek New Testament. Furthermore, it is evident that Jesus and his early apostles intended to convey no detectable difference in meaning between these two phrases, for they are used synonymously and concurrently in Mark 9:43, 45, and 47. Thus, they work as acceptable English equivalents in translation today.

Also, while the position of the prepositional phrase "into hell" shifts around in the various Greek manuscripts, in English this phrase can stand only at the end of the sentence. Thus, it is not possible to tell from the English translation of the Sermon at the Temple where the prepositional phrase was located in the underlying text; in other words, the English translation puts this prepositional phrase in the only place where English syntax will allow.

Moreover, although the textual evidence is on the side of "go to hell" in Matthew 5:30, it may be a quirk of fate that the oldest surviving manuscripts happened to have this reading. This observation receives some support from Matthew Black's argument that "cast into hell," preferred by the KJV, fits more comfortably into the alliteration of the Aramaic of this Markan (and Matthean) passage than does "go to hell."[1] Thus, Jesus may well have said "cast into hell" originally here in any event.

3. *Matthew 6:1.* The earlier texts begin, "Take heed that ye do not your *righteousness* before men"; later ones and the KJV read, "Take heed that ye do not your *alms* before

---

1. Black, *Aramaic Approach to the Gospels and Acts,* 171.

men."[1] Third Nephi 13:1 also talks about "alms." Has the Sermon at the Temple rendered a false translation? Again the answer is no, mainly because the "righteousness" discussed in Matthew 6:1–4 is unquestionably "almsgiving." All Greek manuscripts that read "righteousness" (*dikaiosunē*) in Matthew 6:1 still have "alms" (*eleēmosunē*) in Matthew 6:2. Since the "righteousness" referred to in Matthew 6:1 is clearly "almsgiving," it is not incorrect to translate *dikaiosunē* there as "almsgiving."[2]

For further clarification, the Sermon at the Temple begins 3 Nephi 13:1 with a sentence that is not present in the Sermon on the Mount: "Verily, verily, I say that I would that ye should do alms unto the poor" (3 Nephi 13:1). Since this text makes the topic of these verses explicitly clear, continuing with a reference to "righteousness" would have been awkward, although this could have been done and the reader still would have understood its meaning to be "righteous almsgiving."

Moreover, in Hebrew (and presumably in the Nephite language) there is not nearly so much difference between the two Semitic words "righteousness" (*zedeq*) and "almsgiving" (Syriac, *zedqthā*; Hebrew *zədāqāh*, which at Qumran meant "righteousness . . . justified by charity"),[3] as there is between the two Greek words *dikaiosunē* ("righteousness") and *eleēmosunē* ("generosity"). Indeed, one of the most important attributes of any person (including God)

---

1. J. Harold Greenlee, *Scribes, Scrolls, and Scripture* (Grand Rapids, Michigan: Eerdmans, 1969), 83, suggests that it is more likely that a text was changed from "righteousness" to "alms" than vice versa.

2. See also Walter Nagel, "Gerechtigkeit oder Almosen? (Mt 6:1)," *Vigiliae Christianae* 15 (1961): 141–45, which presents seven points justifying *eleēmosunē* as the better reading of Matthew 6:1.

3. Robert Eisenman, *Maccabees, Zadokites, Christians and Qumran* (Leiden: Brill, 1983), 110; see also Nagel, "Gerechtigkeit oder Almosen? (Mt 6:1)," 144; *Tobit* 14:10; and James H. Charlesworth, *Old Testament Pseudepigrapha*, 2 vols. (Garden City: Doubleday, 1983), 2:489 n. 64.

who is _zedeq_ is that he is charitable: he "gives freely, without regard for gain."[1] "The righteous (_zedeq_) sheweth mercy and giveth" (Psalms 37:21; see also Daniel 4:27 [Hebrew text 4:24]). If Jesus said in Hebrew, "Watch your _zedeq_," what did he mean? His message was about generosity, not just "righteousness" in some general sense. The Greek word _dikaiosunē_ (from _dikē_, "justice") is, therefore, not a satisfactory term to convey the full meaning of the Hebrew _zedeq_ or its Aramaic cognate, the languages Jesus spoke. "Doing alms," on the other hand, comes closer to conveying the meaning of "righteousness justified by charity." Assuming that Jesus said to the Nephites something like, "Watch your _zədāqāh_" (since he would not have spoken to the Nephites in Greek), Joseph Smith was most correct to translate this by reference to charitable "alms."

4. _Matthew 6:5._ The older Greek texts read "when you (_plural_) pray," but the later ones read "when you (_singular_) pray." The KJV and Sermon at the Temple both read "when _thou_ prayest." "Thou" in English is singular. Although the KJV may not grammatically reflect the older Greek texts, whether Jesus told his disciples not to behave in a certain way "when _you_ (plural) pray" or "when _you_ (singular) pray," the message in Matthew 6:5 is identical: Either way, his followers should not pray to be seen of men.

Moreover, Joseph Smith and his contemporaries were not rigid in their use of the words "thee," "thou," "you," and "ye." These singular and plural English forms are used interchangeably and side-by-side in a number of Book of Mormon texts (see, e.g., Alma 37:37, using "you," "thou," and "ye" all to refer to Helaman), and so one cannot suppose that Joseph Smith always used "ye" as a plural and "thou" as a singular, although this was generally the case. The only

---

1. R. Harris, G. Archer, and B. Waltke, _Theological Wordbook of the Old Testament_ (Chicago: Moody 1980), 753.

way to tell in English whether the pronoun "you" is meant to be singular or plural is to look at the context. Since Matthew 6:5-6 (3 Nephi 13:5-6) talks about *private* prayer, the sense of the text is more singular than plural. One does not go with a group, as in Matthew 6:7-13 where the texts are all in the plural, into one's closet to pray. Thus, again, the use of the singular in 3 Nephi 13:5 seems to convey the correct meaning.

These points about the pronouns in Matthew 6 may also indicate that the ancients were flexible in their use of singular and plural second person pronouns. It would be interesting to know more about the ancient distinctions between "you" (singular) and "you" (plural). On what occasions did the Greeks or Hebrews use one or the other in daily speech? Indeed, scholars have struggled to find any meaningful distinction between the singular and plural "you" forms in Deuteronomy, discovering that the differences (if any) are more formal than substantive.[1] Cazelles concludes, less than lucidly, that the *plural* was used in Deuteronomy to create a "more *personal* approach, . . . no more addressed in the singular but in the plural, to *each* Israelite who had to live a personal religion."[2] In other words, the plural form was used in Deuteronomy, according to Cazelles, to convey a stronger *singular* message. If he is right, in Israelite culture strict form was not determinative of meaning.

As Larson acknowledges, the plural and singular "thou" and "ye" appear indiscriminately throughout the verses in Matthew 6 immediately before and after Matthew 6:5. In such cases, many Bible translators do not demand of themselves rigid adherence to grammatical detail: "In many

---

1. See, e.g., Henri Cazelles, "Passages in the Singular within Discourse in the Plural of Dt 1-4," *Catholic Biblical Quarterly* 29 (1967): 207-19.

2. Ibid., 219; italics added.

languages, translators will use a plural in such cases, whether the noun used by the gospel writer is singular or plural, in order to make the plural meaning clear."[1]

5. *Matthew 6:12.* Here the textual issue is whether the Greek verb "to forgive" was originally written in the present tense, "as we *forgive,*" or in the past (aorist) tense, "as we *forgave.*" The better Greek manuscripts have this occurrence of the verb "forgive" in the aorist tense. Third Nephi 13:11 and the KJV have it in the present tense. From a textual point of view, there is a difference; but in terms of meaning and correct translation into English, the distinction does not matter.

The unambiguous meaning of this passage is clear either way: Forgiving others is a condition preceding being forgiven. Speaking on this very point, Moule comments, "The differences in the versions of this clause are a matter only of degree; for in either case, the petition is a conditioned one."[2] We cannot be forgiven until we have forgiven others. The sense of this condition is aorist whether the English reads "as we forgive" or "as we forgave."

It also would not have improved matters if Joseph Smith had rendered it "as we *have* forgiven our debtors." Since the ancient languages relevant to the Sermon on the Mount have a perfect tense as well as a simple past, to render this into English as "*have* forgiven" would have implied that the original text had put this verb into the *perfect* tense, which no text does. The other choice was to use the imperfect, but that would not have been idiomatic in English; we do not say, "forgive us our debts as we *forgave* our debtors." The translation given in the Sermon at the Temple and KJV is thus the best option available in English.

---

1. Paul Ellingworth, "Translating Parallel Passages in the Gospels," *Bible Translator* 34 (1983): 402–3.

2. C. F. D. Moule, *Essays in New Testament Interpretation* (Cambridge: Cambridge University Press, 1982), 279.

Furthermore, the writers of the Greek New Testament used this aorist tense on several occasions to translate the Semitic perfect, a tense used in Hebrew and Aramaic to convey a present tense meaning. Matthew Black comments on this point of grammar:

> As Wellhausen observed, . . . [the] Greek aorist [is] used with the force of a Semitic perfect: the latter [Semitic perfect] corresponds, not only to the aorist, but to the perfect and present tenses, in the latter use of present states or *general truths.* A similar instance is Mark 1:8, *ebaptisa,* the equivalent of a Semitic perfect, used either of a general truth or an immediately completed act. . . . The [aorist] tense of *ēgalliase* at Lk. 1:[44, 47] corresponds to a [Semitic] stative perfect, and *should be rendered by a present.*[1]

Thus the correct way to translate these Greek aorist verbs into English is with the present tense, just as the KJV and the Sermon at the Temple do. Black and others give several examples where the Gospel writers use the aorist in this way and where the aorist presupposes a continuing present condition.[2] For example, the voice of God at the baptism of Jesus (Matthew 3:17, only a few verses before the Sermon on the Mount) says, "This is my beloved Son in whom I *am well pleased (eudokēsa)*." This verb is an aorist, but one would not translate it "in whom I *was* well pleased." The meaning of this, or any other tense, is not determined strictly by its form, but "is established in part by the set of relations that tense enters into with its context."[3] Assuming that Joseph Smith had before him a

---

1. Black, *Aramaic Approach to the Gospels and Acts,* 128–29; italics added.

2. See D. A. Larson, *Exegetical Fallacies* (Grand Rapids, Michigan: Baker, 1984), 69–75.

3. Ibid., 73.

Nephite "stative perfect" verb in 3 Nephi 13:11, his most correct translation in this context into English would on all counts have been with a present tense verb, as is found in the Sermon at the Temple.

6. *Matthew 7:2.* The older texts of Matthew 7:2 read "and with what measure ye mete, it shall be *measured* to you" (*metrēthēsetai*), while the later ones used by the KJV add "and with what measure ye mete, it shall be *measured* to you *again*" (*antimetrēthēsetai*). Like the KJV, 3 Nephi 14:2 ends with the word "again." Since Luke 6:38 also has the word *antimetrēthēsetai* ("measured again"), New Testament scholars have generally concluded that the text of Matthew 7:2 was changed at some point to harmonize with Luke. Some have suggested that the threefold repetition of the Greek *en hōi metrōi metreite metrēthēsetai* has a cadence probably close to the Aramaic Jesus actually spoke.[1]

Behind the English word "again," however, stands only the Greek intensifying prefix *anti-*. With or without this prefix on the verb, the sentence means exactly the same thing. In either case, Jesus says that the standards a person uses to judge or to measure others will be used against the person who uses them. Since the idea that our standards will be used "in return, again, or back" against ourselves is present in the text either way, the difference between *metrēthēsetai* and *antimetrēthēsetai* is negligible. This variant was not considered significant enough to be noted in the United Bible Societies' Greek New Testament.

7. *Matthew 5:44.* Some texts say "love your enemies and pray for them which despitefully use you," while others add such words as "bless them that curse you, do good to them that hate you." The injunction to love one's enemies

---

1. There are similar expressions in *Wisdom of Solomon* 12:22 and Mishnah, *Sota* 1:7, but I have not compared them further. See Strack and Billerbeck, *Kommentar zum Neuen Testament*, 1:444.

is shorter in the earlier manuscripts; the later ones seem to have incorporated the additional words from Luke 6:27–28. Here the issue is a little different. Did Joseph have the shorter text on the plates and expand it in the translation process, or did the longer text appear there similar to the way Jesus had spoken in Luke 6:27–28? Either is possible. Jesus must have said something like "love your enemies" many times; he need not have said it exactly the same way every time.

These points seem to me to allow adequate room for the translation given in the Sermon at the Temple. For those who might see this point here to be more of a problem for the Book of Mormon than the other cases, one should be aware that the textual evidence is not as strong in this instance as it is in the other examples. Bezae Cantabrigiensis (D) and many other early Greek texts have longer and different versions of this saying. While D agrees with the Siniaticus and Vaticanus codices on most of these other points (e.g., Matthew 5:27; 5:30; 6:1; 6:4, 6, 18; 6:13), D does not agree with the generally accepted reading here, mainly because one normally assumes that the shorter version is the older, though this may not necessarily be so.

8–10. Matthew 6:4, 6, 18. Strong textual evidence supports the idea that Matthew 6:4, 6, and 18 originally said, "Your Father will reward you," not "Your Father will reward you *openly (en tōi phaneroi).*" The KJV and the Sermon at the Temple, however, read "openly." Again I think this conveys the only possible meaning of these verses, namely that God will openly reward the righteous with treasures in heaven on the judgment day. This understanding is sustained by the Greek verb for "reward." Here again it would help to know what the Aramaic or Hebrew may have been, but the Greek for "reward" is *apodidomi.* It has a wide variety of meanings, including "to give retribution, reward, or punishment." The verb *didomi* means to "give," and the prefix *apo* can mean, among other things, "out from." For example, in the word *apocalypse,* the prefix *apo* means "out from" that which is hidden. It is unclear what force the prefix *apo* has in the verb *apodidomi.* One sense it may convey, however, is the idea of being rewarded *apo,* "out from" the obscurity of the acts themselves, or openly. One does not need the phrase *en tōi phanerōi* in order to understand that "he who sees *in secret* will reward you *apo,* openly."

Some, however, have argued that the phrase *en tōi phanerōi* was mistakenly added to these verses in the Sermon on the Mount since it is inconsistent with the idea that one should do deeds of righteousness in secret so as *not* to be seen of men. But this argument assumes that the Sermon on the Mount primarily has a this-worldly orientation, which is not necessarily so. God will reward the righteous openly when the books are opened at the final judgment, and toward this end, the Sermon on the Mount admonishes the righteous to lay up treasures in heaven. Contemplating an open reward in heaven is even more consistent with the increased eschatological orientation of the Sermon at the Temple.

11. Matthew 6:13. Finally, there is the famous textual problem at the end of the Lord's Prayer in Matthew 6:13. Did the prayer originally include the doxology "For thine is the kingdom, and the power, and the glory, for ever. Amen"? This case raises a different sort of issue. In the ten cases discussed so far, the translations offered by the Sermon at the Temple and the KJV are not erroneous. Here the issue is simply whether one can assume, with Jeremias and others, that Jesus originally appended some ending to the Lord's Prayer, although it is not recorded in the earliest survivors of the Sermon on the Mount. This issue is unsettled among biblical scholars.[1]

---

1. For a recent debate regarding the long ending of the Lord's Prayer,

It is well known that the earlier Greek manuscripts have no doxology at the end of the Lord's Prayer; they end abruptly with "deliver us from evil." In this respect they resemble (and may have been changed to conform with) Luke 11:4, which also ends "but deliver us from evil." The Sermon at the Temple, along with later Greek manuscripts and the KJV conclude with the doxology. Whether the phrase was originally present in the text of Matthew cannot be known, although most textual critics find it easiest to believe that the phrase was introduced later into that text. For many circumstantial reasons, however, no one seems to doubt that Jesus probably pronounced a doxology at the end of his prayers; the only question is how early such a thing found its way into the text of the Gospel of Matthew.

The following circumstantial evidence makes it likely that Jesus ended his prayers in Jerusalem and Bountiful with a doxology. First, it would have been highly irregular at the time of Jesus to end a Jewish prayer without some words in praise of God. Jeremias states:

> It would be a completely erroneous conclusion to suppose that the Lord's Prayer was ever prayed without some closing words of praise to God; in Palestinian practice it was completely unthinkable that a prayer would end with the word "temptation." Now in Judiasm prayers were often concluded with a "seal," a sentence of praise freely formulated by the man who was praying.[1]

Second, Jeremias' point can be extended one step further into the temple. As pointed out above, a special acknowl-

---

see Andrew J. Bandstra, "The Original Form of the Lord's Prayer," *Calvin Theological Journal* 16 (1981): 15–37; Jacob van Bruggen, "The Lord's Prayer and Textual Criticism," *Calvin Theological Journal* 17 (1982): 78–87; Andrew J. Bandstra, "The Lord's Prayer and Textual Criticism: A Response," *Calvin Theological Journal* 17 (1982): 88–97.

1. Jeremias, *Prayers of Jesus,* 106.

edgment of the glory and kingdom of God was spoken in the temple of the Jews as a benediction on the Day of Atonement. The people bowed their knees, fell on their faces, and said, "Praised be the name of his glorious kingdom forever and eternally!" In the sacred matters in the temple, one did not simply answer "Amen."[1] It is all the more unlikely that a prayer at the temple would end without some form of doxology. This may be a factor in explaining why the prayer here at the temple includes the doxology, but the instruction given by Jesus on prayer out in the open in Luke 11 does not.

Third, the doxology in the KJV and Sermon at the Temple seems to have followed a traditional form, reflected in 1 Chronicles 29:10–13, as is widely observed.[2] The Nephites may have known such phraseology from their Israelite traditions, for it appears in an important blessing spoken by King David, and the Nephite records contained historical records of the Jews (see 1 Nephi 5:12), although it is unknown which ones. David's blessing reads: "Wherefore David blessed the Lord before all the congregation: and David said, Blessed be thou, Lord God of Israel our father, *for ever and ever.* Thine, O Lord, is the greatness, and the *power,* and the *glory,* and the victory, and the majesty: for all that is in the heaven and in the earth is thine; thine is the *kingdom*" (1 Chronicles 29:10–11).[3]

---

1. Strack and Billerbeck, *Kommentar zum Neuen Testament,* 1:423, citing Mishnah, *Yoma* 6:2, and others. Discussed above in chapter 3 concerning 3 Nephi 13:9–13.

2. Jeremias discusses this, as Larson too observes. See also John W. Welch, "The Lord's Prayers," *Ensign* 6 (January 1976): 15–17; Strack and Billerbeck, *Kommentar zum Neuen Testament,* 1:424.

3. Italics added. Note that "for ever and ever," which appears in the JST and which Larson claims is going "in a direction away from the original text" (Larson, "Sermon on the Mount," 39 n. 34), is close to this ancient blessing of David and is also the same as the typical ending of the Jewish temple benediction. Strack and Billerbeck, *Kommentar zum Neuen Testament,* 1:423, "*immer und ewig.*"

Fourth, while a minority, several early texts in Greek, Syriac, and Coptic, and in the *Didache* (ca. A.D. 100) also exist that include doxologies at the end of the Lord's Prayer. These indicate that the cultic use and acceptance of some doxology was apparently widespread at a very early time in Christianity.

Fifth, it can also be noted that the Lord's Prayer in the Sermon at the Temple differs in several other respects from the version of the prayer in the KJV, as discussed already above. The prayer in the Book of Mormon is longer than the version in Luke but agrees substantially with Matthew in wording, a felicitous result for the Sermon at the Temple in light of Jeremias' conclusion that "the Lucan version has preserved the oldest form with respect to *length*, but the Matthean text is more original with regard to *wording*."[1]

In sum, it is hard to see that the Sermon at the Temple can be faulted in these eleven cases. Unless one would require the Book of Mormon translation to be extremely literal, even to the point of being ungrammatical in English, Joseph Smith's translations are not erroneous. They do not miscommunicate the meaning of the text. Larson, it should be pointed out, claims to have ignored all the textual "variations that produce little or no difference in English translation," but readers must decide if his work lives up to that representation.[2]

---

1. Jeremias, *Prayers of Jesus*, 93 (italics in original).

2. Larson, "Sermon on the Mount," 25. Other examples exist that may be used for comparison. In Matthew 5:32, the early Greek manuscripts variously, but inconsequentially, read *"whoever," "each who,"* or *"whosoever"* shall divorce his wife. While Larson has not advanced this as one of his test cases, one may ask if the differences in his stated examples are not about as insignificant as these variants in Matthew 5:32. Similarly, when an alteration of two occurrences of a second person singular *sou* to the Lukan second person plural *humōn* exists in Matthew 6:21, "where *your* treasure is, there will *your* heart be also," Larson finds this is to be an insignificant textual difference. Larson, "Sermon on the Mount," 25. But his fourth example above seems to be no different.

Other issues could be raised in discussing and evaluating Larson's presentation of the textual variants in the Greek New Testament manuscripts, but they lead into wider fields of inquiry. What remains of these cases is not, however, that the Sermon at the Temple ever gives a false translation, but only the familiar complaint, already addressed above, that the Sermon at the Temple is very much like the KJV English. In other words, we are back to looking for places where the Sermon at the Temple could have optionally translated the text differently, in a way that might have improved on the meaning reflected in the Greek, but instead came out the same as the KJV.[1] But such points are nothing more than the general problem of similarity between the Sermon at the Temple and the KJV that has been obvious since the first day the Book of Mormon appeared.

12. Matthew 5:22. So far in this chapter, we have concentrated attention on passages in which the Sermon at the Temple and KJV lack strict formal textual support in the earliest Greek manuscripts. In one important passage, there is evidence that favors the Sermon at the Temple, and it deserves more notice and credit than it has been given.

The KJV of Matthew 5:22 reads, "Whosoever is angry with his brother *without a cause (eikē)* shall be in danger of the judgment." The Sermon at the Temple drops the

---

1. Larson suggests that "by them" would be better translated "to them"; that the *kai* ("also") in Matthew 6:12 should have been reflected in the English; that "in *(epi)* earth" in 6:10 (Printer's Ms) would have been better rendered as "on earth"; that the Sermon at the Temple "blindly follows" the KJV, which supplies "men" in italics (although this is clearly the meaning of the Greek); and that the Greek third person plurals ("they gather") could have been "better translated" as impersonals ("one gathers"). Larson, "Sermon on the Mount," 41–42. These do not seem to me to be candidates for serious translational blunders; moreover, it remains for Larson to show that the supposedly missing *kai* and the like were present in Jesus' Aramaic words. See also the discussion of the translation process at the end of chapter 7.

phrase "without a cause."[1] So do many of the better early manuscripts.[2]

This evidence favorable to the Sermon at the Temple has support from the sources named by Larson as being the most reliable. While lacking unanimous consensus in the early manuscripts (which is not unusual), the absence of the phrase "without a cause" from the Sermon on the Mount is evidenced by manuscripts p64, p67, Sinaiticus (original hand), Vaticanus, some minuscules, the Latin Vulgate (Jerome mentions that it was not found in the oldest manuscripts known to him), Justin, Tertullian, Origen, and others. Larson counts as compellingly original all readings that are supported by "the best Greek MSS — by the A.D. 200 p64 (where it is extant) and by at least the two oldest uncials, as well as some minuscules. In each case [he requires that] it also has some Latin, Syriac, Coptic, and early patristic support."[3] A check of the list of manuscripts supporting the Sermon at the Temple and the original absence of the phrase "without a cause" in Matthew 5:22 shows that this shorter reading meets Larson's criteria. Can it then be concluded that "the Book of Mormon *never* takes us to a verifiable text in antiquity"?[4]

Moreover, this textual difference in the Greek manuscripts of the Sermon on the Mount is the one that has the

---

1. This point was first published in John W. Welch, "A Book You Can Respect," *Ensign* 7 (September 1977): 45–48.

2. For a discussion of this text by a scholar who challenges many normal assumptions, see David A. Black, "Jesus on Anger: The Text of Matthew 5:22a Revisited," *Novum Testamentum* 30 (1988): 1–8. While acknowledging that "the shorter text undoubtedly has impressive manuscript support," Black presents reasons why the longer reading "should at least be reconsidered in scholarly discussions of this passage." Ibid., 5; cf. 2. His points, however, have not emerged persuasive enough to shift the balance of scholarly opinion in favor of including the word *eikē*.

3. Larson, "Sermon on the Mount," 43.

4. Ibid.; italics added.

most significant impact on meaning. It is much more severe to say, *"Whoever is angry* is in danger of the judgment," than to say, "Whoever is angry *without a cause* is in danger of the judgment." The first discourages all anger against a brother; the second permits brotherly anger as long as it is justifiable. The former is more like the demanding sayings of Jesus regarding committing adultery in one's heart (Matthew 5:28) and loving one's enemies (Matthew 5:43), neither of which offers the disciple a convenient loophole of self-justification or rationalization. Indeed, the word *eikē* in Matthew 5:22 may reflect a Semitic idiom that does not invite allowance for " 'just' anger in certain circumstances" at all, but "is original and echoes some Aramaic phrase, condemning anger as sinful in any case" and "as alluding to . . . the harbouring of angry feelings for any length of time."[1] In light of Wernberg-Moeller's interpretation of the underlying idiom, the original sense of Matthew 5:22 is accurately reflected in the Sermon at the Temple whether *eikē* is included in the Greek saying or not.

In my estimation, this textual variant in favor of the Sermon at the Temple is very meaningful. It makes more of a difference than all of the other textual cases combined. The removal of "without a cause" has important moral, behavioral, psychological, and religious ramifications. From the vantage point of meticulously conservative or fundamentalist New Testament textual scholarship, one might have thought the Sermon at the Temple would have hit the textual nail on the head more often by yielding more cases like this one in 3 Nephi 12:22, but in the end, this appears to be the only place where a significant textual change from the KJV was in fact needed and delivered.

---

1. P. Wernberg-Moeller, "A Semitic Idiom in Matt. V. 22," *New Testament Studies* 3 (1956): 72–73.

9

THE SYNOPTIC QUESTION: DID MATTHEW COMPOSE THE SERMON ON THE MOUNT?

The presence of virtually all the Sermon on the Mount in the Sermon at the Temple, and therefore in the *ipsissima vox* or personal voice of Jesus, will certainly present yet a different set of improbabilities to the minds of many liberal New Testament scholars. It is widely accepted in New Testament scholarship that Matthew gave the Sermon on the Mount its final form (although there is no consensus about when Matthew worked, how much he wrote himself, or which words and phrases he drew from the variously existing pre-Matthean sources or traditions that scholars have hypothesized). Moreover, the early manuscripts of the New Testament are not all identical. Some contain the longer ending of the Gospel of Mark, while others cut it short. Some include the story of the woman caught in adultery in John 8, while others do not; or they position it somewhere else in the text.

The Book of Mormon, however, presents the reader with a version of the Sermon on the Mount that is substantially identical to the Sermon in the King James Bible and that places this text entirely in the mouth of Jesus in A.D. 34. The idea that Jesus was the author of the Sermon on the Mount, let alone of the covenant-oriented interpretation which the Sermon at the Temple gives to the Sermon, is not likely to find many ready-made adherents among the disciples of Q or other source-critical students of the New Testament. Without purporting to deal with all the complexities of the synoptic question, I will attempt to explain to a general audience some of the very legitimate issues raised by New Testament studies and how the Sermon at the Temple has tended to shape my thinking about these scholarly endeavors.

At the outset, it is worth pointing out that there are no words in the Sermon at the Temple that Jesus *could not* have said. As discussed in chapter 5, places where scholars have found the strongest traces of later redaction in the Sermon on the Mount are not in evidence in the Sermon at the Temple. Perhaps far more of the Sermon on the Mount was original with Jesus than New Testament scholarship has come to assume; it is certainly too aggressive to date the entire Sermon on the Mount by its latest line.

Moreover, all the themes of the Sermon on the Mount are consistent with the generally accepted characteristics of the very voice of Jesus, even judged very cautiously. Those characteristics of Jesus' personal words, as they have been identified by Joachim Jeremias,[1] are readily visible in the Sermon, namely (1) the use of parables (e.g., the salt, the light, the tree, the house on the rock), (2) the use of cryptic sayings or riddles (e.g., Matthew 5:17), (3) speaking of the reign or kingdom of God (e.g., 3 Nephi 11:33, 38; Matthew 5:3, 10; 6:33), (4) the use of "amen" or "verily" (over 30 times in the Sermon at the Temple), and (5) the word *Abba*, or *Father* (Matthew 6:9, and dozens of other times in the Book of Mormon text). One normally presumes that such

---

1. *New Testament Theology* (London: SCM, 1971), 29–37; see also John Strugnell, " 'Amen, I Say unto You' in the Sayings of Jesus and in Early Christian Literature," *Harvard Theological Review* 67 (1974): 177–90.

words attributed to Jesus in the New Testament are authentic, the *ipsissima vox* of Jesus.

For most New Testament scholars, however, the question of authorship in the Sermon on the Mount is likely to be a much greater stumbling block to the Sermon at the Temple than any manuscript or stylistic issue, for it is a very widely held opinion that Matthew wrote the Sermon on the Mount as we now know it, collecting together miscellaneous sayings of Jesus and putting them together into a more or less unified sermon. The presence of this material in the Sermon at the Temple, however, commits the believing Latter-day Saint to be dubious of such a claim. It seems unlikely for a person to believe that the resurrected Jesus actually delivered the sermon recorded in 3 Nephi 11–18 within a year after his crucifixion as he visited the Nephites and at the same time to hold that the Evangelist gave the Sermon its basic form and selected its content.

It is thus necessary to ask why many scholars have concluded that Matthew composed the Sermon on the Mount. Are their assumptions and reasons persuasive? The synoptic question, which has driven an enormous amount of New Testament research, cannot be casually dismissed or lightly ignored. How the Gospels were composed, when and why they were written, how they are similar to or different from each other, and what underlying sources they drew upon, are all intriguing questions. After a century of work, these still remain fascinating to many readers.

Over the years, a steady flow of journal articles and books have advanced various ingenious theories and have marshalled evidence for or against certain positions regarding the composition of the synoptic gospels. Any thoughtful and well-informed Latter-day Saint can derive a wealth of information from these studies about the subtlety of these sacred records that tell us so much about the mortal ministry of Jesus Christ. But not every proposed theory regarding the synoptic question is equally persuasive. All readers must evaluate and carefully consider the evidence presented. Covert biases and assumptions are sometimes at work, and despite the overwhelming popularity of a particular hypothesis today, it may likely fall into disfavor tomorrow. Surmising, extrapolating, following hunches, and outright guesswork fuel much of this research, foraging for tidbits of information gleaned here and there from among the textual records.

With regard to the composition of the Sermon on the Mount in particular, the assertion of Matthean authorship is not a simple one. It is difficult to attack in large part because it is not very focused. The reasons for seeing Matthew's hand in the text of the Sermon on the Mount are vague and broad. They can scarcely be negated because they can hardly be verified. The theory has spawned numerous books and dissertations, developing and applying the hypothesis, but the results are still far from conclusive. Consequently the discussion here will be brief. Only general attention to broad rationales can be given, and possible Latter-day Saint approaches or responses proposed. I advance these thoughts only as ruminations. Limited to the methods of critical biblical studies, I can no more purport to prove that Matthew did not write the Sermon on the Mount than others can show that he did.

First, not all scholars agree on any particular theory of Matthean composition of the Sermon on the Mount, for

> the Sermon on the Mount presents unusual complications in the matter of sources. . . . Of the Sermon's 111 verses, about 45 have no obvious parallels in Luke, 35 have loose parallels, and 31 have parallels which are close both in content and in phraseology. The curious feature of this evidence is [that] . . . the close parallels are unusually close, and the loose parallels are unusually loose![1]

---

1. McArthur, *Understanding the Sermon on the Mount*, 22.

With this array of mixed evidence, it is not surprising that nothing approaching unanimity exists over how much of the Sermon on the Mount Matthew wrote himself, or how much he took over from an existing pre-Matthean source or sources. For those who have concluded that Matthew had documents at his disposal from which he drew, there is even less consensus about where those records came from or for what purpose they were written or used in the earliest Christian communities. The trend in recent years has been toward seeing somewhat less Matthean influence in the composition of the Sermon on the Mount itself and toward dating large sections of the Sermon on the Mount back into the first decades of Jewish Christianity. Hans Dieter Betz, in particular, has recently advanced the theory that the Sermon on the Mount was a composite of pre-Matthean sources, embodying a set of cultic instructions that served the earliest Jewish-Christian community in Jerusalem as an epitome of the gospel of Jesus Christ, which Matthew later incorporated into his Gospel.[1] Obviously, the jury is still out on this issue.

I am attracted to several aspects of Betz's thesis for many reasons. One of them is the support I find for it in a simple examination of the vocabulary of the Sermon on the Mount. When one compares the Greek words in the Sermon on the Mount with those used by Matthew in the rest of his Gospel, some sharp contrasts emerge. Of the 383 basic vocabulary words in the Sermon on the Mount, I count 73 (or 19% of the total) that appear *only* in the Sermon (sometimes more

---

1. Betz, *Essays on the Sermon on the Mount*, 1–15, 55–76. Alfred Perry, "The Framework of the Sermon on the Mount," *Journal of Biblical Literature* 54 (1935): 103–15, similarly finds evidence that Matthew worked from a written source "that he regarded so highly that he used it for the foundation of his longer Sermon, even in preference to the Q discourse." On the conjectured existence of other pre-Matthean sources, see Strecker, *Sermon on the Mount*, 55–56, 63, 67–68, 72.

than once) and *never* elsewhere in the Gospel of Matthew (and often are *never* used again in the entire New Testament). In some cases, words used in the Sermon on the Mount, such as *doma* ("gift," Matthew 7:11; cf. Ephesians 4:8, quoting Psalm 68:18), appear un-Matthean, for on all nine other occasions outside the Sermon on the Mount when Matthew speaks of "gifts," he prefers to use the word *dōron* ("gift"), even where the context is similar to that of Matthew 7:11 (see, e.g., Matthew 2:11; 15:5). Only two words in the Sermon, *geennan* ("hell") and *grammateus* ("scribe"), are used by Matthew in greater preponderance than other New Testament writers, and in only one case, *rhapisei* ("smite," Matthew 5:39; 26:67), is Matthew the sole New Testament writer to use a Sermon on the Mount vocabulary word outside the Sermon.

Thus on the level of mere vocabulary, the Sermon on the Mount appears to be unlike Matthew's writings. Although this kind of word study is not conclusive of authorship, especially since the textual sample involved is statistically small, this result does seem to me to be indicative.[1] If Matthew's hand played a significant role in drafting, selecting, or reworking the contents of the Sermon on the Mount, it seems odd that nearly every fifth vocabulary word is one that Matthew never had occasion to use again in his Gospel.

Nevertheless, the issue is not cut and dried. I am confident that New Testament scholars are doing about the best they can with what they have. If it were not for my acceptance of the material contained in the Book of Mormon, I would readily agree with many of their conjectures. They have three synoptic Gospels — Matthew, Mark, and

---

1. Goulder comments that "word-counts can be used in a much more sophisticated way than is usual. . . . Over a longer passage, say the Sermon, such counting would be significant." M. D. Goulder, "The Beatitudes: A Source-Critical Study," *Novum Testamentum* 25 (1983): 211.

Luke—and it is entirely indeterminable in most passages which Gospel is the oldest or reflects the most accurate or original image of the historical Jesus. Sometimes Luke appears to give the better view, other times Mark, and still other times Matthew. Discussion and resolution of the problem, however, are prejudicially circumscribed by the documents permitted into consideration. For example, if the Gospel of Thomas, or another newly discovered text, were to be accepted as a very early source, it would have tremendous impact on the question of which sayings of Jesus in the synoptic Gospels people would accept as authentic.

History is always vulnerable to the inherent weaknesses of its records. For example, newspapers recently reported that a cannon mounted on a monument erected by the Daughters of the Utah Pioneers in Farmington, Utah, could not have been brought across the Plains, since its serial number and an 1864 date stamp indicate that it was cast in Richmond, Virginia, during the Civil War.[1] If this were the only information known about the famous pioneer cannon, we would be tempted to reject out of hand the mind-boggling stories about dragging a cannon all the way from Nauvoo to Salt Lake City in 1847 through the mud and over hundreds of trackless miles. In this case, however, the 1847 diary of Charles C. Rich removes any doubt: There was a cannon that his company fired regularly as the wagon train moved across the prairie, even though the Farmington monument may not have the right one. This serves as a sobering reminder of our inability to date historical details conclusively by relying solely on the earliest surviving artifact.

The question of which sayings of Jesus are authentic usually turns on certain assumptions people have made about which parts of the Gospel accounts were early or

---

1. *Deseret News* (August 5, 1989), B1.

which came later. For example, if a person holds to the premise that Jesus neither ordained apostles nor formally organized a church in Palestine, then it is a foregone conclusion that the person will strongly discount any sayings with ecclesiastical content in the Gospels as being later additions by someone belonging to the settled church later in the first century. Of course, such issues are complex and deeply interwoven with other historical and literary strands. My point is that the discussion of the Matthean composition of the Sermon on the Mount begins, and to a large extent ends, with the same sort of preassessment of source documents and their possible provenances.

These points are relevant to our discussion of the Sermon at the Temple. Most scholars are willing to change or modify their old opinions when new, credible evidence is discovered. My personal verdict is that the Sermon at the Temple constitutes such evidence. If it is admitted into evidence, then it becomes a major factor in settling the question of who wrote the Sermon on the Mount. The problem, of course, rests in determining whether the Book of Mormon should be allowed to contribute any primary evidence in this discussion. Of course, for Latter-day Saints who are convinced on their own grounds, the Sermon at the Temple will figure as one of the main determining documents in their discussion of the issue of who composed the Sermon, rather than as a text whose character is judged as a by-product of that discussion.

Others will likely reject the Sermon at the Temple and the Book of Mormon as such evidence, but that rejection will usually be made on other religious or theological grounds, not on the alleged Matthean authorship of the Sermon on the Mount. It would be circular, of course, to disallow the Sermon at the Temple as evidence against Matthean authorship by rejecting it simply on the ground that Matthew wrote the Sermon on the Mount, for that is the very question about which one seeks the further documentary evidence in the first place.

Limited to the sources in the New Testament, scholars advance several reasons for the proposition that Matthew wrote the Sermon on the Mount. I have not found any of them to be persuasive enough to discredit the Sermon at the Temple.

For example, many scholars assume that the sayings of Jesus started out short and simple and that they grew in complexity as they were collected, grouped, and handed down in lore and tradition until his followers canonized them. Hence, Jeremias reasons as follows: "The Sermon on the Plain [in Luke 6] is very much shorter than that on the mount, and from this we must [!] conclude that in the Lucan Sermon on the Plain we have an earlier form of the Sermon on the Mount."[1] This view receives some support from the fact that pithy sayings of Jesus were collected elsewhere by Matthew into single chapters (as in the Parable Sermon of Matthew 13), and thus one infers that the same thing occurred with the Sermon on the Mount.[2]

This inference is not compelling, however. What apparently happened in the case of Matthew 13 need not have happened for Matthew 5-7. Moreover, it seems more characteristic of movements as dynamic as early Christianity that they do not begin with a sputtering start. Great religious and philosophical movements typically begin with the monumental appearance of a figure who captures the spirit of his followers and galvanizes them into dedicated action. It seems more likely to me, as a hypothesis, that the words and discourses of Jesus started out profound and already well developed, than that they began as disjointed sayings or fragmented maxims. Day in and day out, Jesus spoke to

---

1. Jeremias, *Sermon on the Mount*, 15.
2. See, e.g., ibid., 13.

his disciples and to the multitudes who flocked to see him. I doubt that they came out to hear a string of oracular one-liners. What they heard were coherent sentences projecting a vision and world-view. The Sermon on the Mount would reflect such wisdom and perspective, making it just as likely that the abbreviated excerpts of it that are scattered elsewhere in the synoptic gospels are the derivatives.

One can hardly be unaware of the vast amount of effort that has been spent searching for Q and for the original words of Jesus.[1] In this quest some scholars will conclude that a saying in Mark or Luke was earlier than the parallel saying in Matthew. But this discipline is far from objective or certain. For example, many have often argued that Luke 6, the Sermon on the Plain, was earlier than the Sermon on the Mount and that Matthew used the Sermon on the Plain as one of his sources in compiling the Sermon on the Mount. It is also possible, however, that Luke 6 was dependent on the Sermon on the Mount. The debate tilts both ways. Some articles advance reasons for seeing the Matthean Beatitudes and Lord's Prayer or other formulations as bearing the characterisitics of being earlier sayings,[2] while a

---

1. For the present state of the art, see John S. Kloppenborg, Q Parallels: Synopsis, Critical Notes and Concordance (Sonoma, California: Polebridge, 1988).

2. Guelich, "The Matthean Beatitudes," 416–19; Michael D. Goulder, "The Composition of the Lord's Prayer," Journal of Theological Studies 14 (1963): 32–45; Ernest Lohmeyer, The Lord's Prayer, tr. J. Bowden (London: Collins, 1965), 27–28; Raymond E. Brown, "The Pater Noster as an Eschatological Prayer," in New Testament Essays (London: Geoffrey Chapman, 1965), 244. Erik Sjöberg, "Das Licht in dir. Zur Deutung von Matth. 6,22f Par.," Studia Theologica (Lund: Gleerup, 1952), 5:89, finds that there "can be no doubt that the Matthean formulation is the original" of Matthew 6:22, as compared with Luke 11: 35–36. D. Flusser, "Blessed are the Poor in Spirit," Israel Exploration Journal 10 (1960): 11, concludes that it is "certain that Matt. v, 3–5 faithfully preserves the saying of Jesus and that Luke vi, 20 is an abbreviation of the original text."

minority of others advance reasons for Lukan priority of the same material.[1] These arguments revolve around a number of assumptions about the kinds of words, expressions, themes, or issues that Jesus would most likely have used or that would have concerned him. Much of this is sophisticated, technical guesswork.

Many scholars have also often assumed that Jesus said something only once, or said it in only one form. Hence scholars launch prolonged odysseys, such as the one to ascertain the "original form" of the Beatitudes or of the Lord's Prayer. This quest, however, assumes that Jesus blessed his disciples using the words of the Beatitudes only once and taught his followers to pray using the words of the Lord's Prayer on only one occasion. If this assumption fails, then two different iterations (even though closely related to each other in form) could both be original sayings.

It should also be noted that the most persuasive evidence for the synoptic problem comes from parallel reports of events rather than sayings. In the case of singular events, which logically can be assumed to have happened only once, the differences in the accounts of Matthew, Mark, and Luke are very telling. But the same logic does not necessarily carry over into the reported speeches, all or parts of which could very well have been repeated more than once and not quite exactly the same each time.

Others argue that if the Sermon on the Mount had been in existence before the writing of the Gospel of Matthew, then Mark and Luke would also have used it. This, however, is an argument from silence. Mark's and Luke's purposes were different from Matthew's; they included different sorts of speeches and information. In Mark's case, there is

---

1. McEleney, "The Beatitudes of the Sermon on the Mount/Plain," 7–8; Robert A. Guelich, "The Antitheses of Matthew V 21–48: Tradition and/or Redactional?" *New Testament Studies* 22 (1976): 446–49.

reason to believe that he consciously chose not to include all that he knew of what Jesus had said.[1]

Certain passages in the Sermon on the Mount seem likely to postdate Jesus' lifetime, such as those that reflect anti-Pharisaical, anti-Gentile, or anti-Pauline sentiments, and possibly the designation of Jerusalem as the city of the Great King. These passages have been pointed to as sure signs of late composition of the Sermon on the Mount. Strecker, for example, argues that "Matthew does not reflect a historically faithful picture" because he distinguishes between the Pharisees and Scribes, when "in truth one cannot differentiate stringently between Scribes and Pharisees."[2] However, such verses alone may simply be later additions. They need not point to a late composition of the entire Sermon on the Mount. As discussed above, all of these elements, which may be strongly suspected of being late intrusions, are absent from the Sermon at the Temple.

Finally, some scholars point to the possible presence of Greek concepts in the Sermon on the Mount and argue that only Matthew could have inserted them. These points of possible Hellenistic influence are far from certain, however; and even if they are present in the Sermon on the Mount, it is equally possible that Jesus would have known them from his cultural surroundings. Nor must these ideas be understood exclusively as Hellenisms in any event. These are the kinds of arguments, generally speaking, that have been advanced supporting the theory of Matthean composition of the Sermon on the Mount.

In addition to the rebuttals made above, several affirmative reasons can be adduced for believing that the Sermon on the Mount was not written by Matthew but existed as

---

1. See the discussion of the *Secret Gospel of Mark*, in chapter 3, concerning 3 Nephi 12:48.

2. Strecker, *Sermon on the Mount*, 59.

a pre-Matthean source. For example, the Sermon on the Mount is in tension in places with the major themes of the Gospel of Matthew as a whole. Kingsbury, for example, finds that the Sermon presents Jesus as a conciliatory "teacher" and a new Moses, whereas "the driving force of the plot [of the Gospel of Matthew] is the element of conflict," culminating in this other direction in the passion narrative.[1] As discussed above, Betz and others have marshalled considerable evidence that the Sermon on the Mount is the kind of document used as a cultic text or to instruct or remind initiates of church rules, and it makes the most sense for the Sermon to have been used in that way before the time when the Gospel of Matthew was written.[2]

I would add that verbal and conceptual similarities between the epistle of James (which I believe to be early) and the Sermon further indicate that James knew the Sermon on the Mount when he wrote his letter. Compare, for example, James 5:12 with Matthew 5:33–37 on oaths; James 3:11–12 with Matthew 7:16–22 on knowing a fig tree or vine by its fruit; James 1:13 with Matthew 6:13 on being led into temptation; James 4:11 with Matthew 7:1–2 on judging a brother; and many other similarities.[3] Jeremias has also

---

1. Jack D. Kingsbury, "The Place, Structure, and Meaning of the Sermon on the Mount within Matthew," *Interpretation* 41 (1987): 132–33; he also points out that the depiction of the disciples in Matthew 5:11–12 and 7:15–23 has "no place in the picture the narrator paints of the disciples during the earthly ministry of Jesus." Ibid., 135. See Charles E. Carlston, "Interpreting the Gospel of Matthew," *Interpretation* 29 (1975): 3–12, for a more harmonious view of the unique traditional and ecclesiastical interests of Matthew. See, generally, C. J. A. Hickling, "Conflicting Motives in the Redaction of Matthew: Some Considerations on the Sermon on the Mount and Matthew 18:15–20," *Studia Evangelica* 7, in *Texte und Untersuchungen* 126 (1982): 247–60.

2. Betz, *Essays on the Sermon on the Mount*, 55–70; Davies, *Sermon on the Mount*, 105–6.

3. These are mentioned in John W. Welch, "Chiasmus in the New Testament," in *Chiasmus in Antiquity*, ed. J. Welch (Hildesheim: Ger-

noted that James and the Sermon on the Mount share the same character as "the classical example of an early Christian didache,"[1] and this rings true in light of the way the early Christian *Didache*, discovered in 1873, quotes extensively from the Sermon on the Mount. It seems quite evident that the epistle of James was consciously drawing on a known body of basic Christian teachings, already known and used in the church as persuasive, authoritative sayings. Thus it seems unlikely that James could have written as he did unless something like the Sermon on the Mount was already considered scriptural. In that case, is it possible that Matthew could have written the Sermon on the Mount late in the day and have pawned it off in James' community as an original? At the time Matthew wrote, people were still alive who remembered Jesus. One must ask how a totally new sermon of Jesus, compiled and advanced by Matthew, would ever have been accepted.

In sum, these brief comments on the synoptic question are not intended to be conclusive. By offering these thoughts, I acknowledge the vast amount of literature that exists concerning the question of authorship of the Sermon on the Mount. I find the questions fascinating and engaging, but most of them still remain questions. I know of no reason why Jesus could not have said all the things contained in the Sermon at the Temple or on the Mount, the many theories and treatises to the contrary notwithstanding.

---

stenberg, 1981), 212; see also the recent dissertation of Patrick John Hartin, University of Witwatersrand, Johannesburg, South Africa, on James and the Q Sermon on the Mount/Plain. John Gee has observed further connections between Matthew 5:48 (*teleios*) and James 1:4 (*teleion*); asking of God (James 1:5–6; Matthew 7:7–11); "blessed" (*makarios*) in James 1:12 and the Beatitudes; lust (James 1:14–15; Matthew 5:28); good gifts and perfect (*teleion*) offerings (James 1:16; Matthew 7:11); anger and insult (James 1:19–20; Matthew 5:22); doing the word (James 1:22–25; Matthew 7:21–27), and several others.

1. Jeremias, *Sermon on the Mount*, 22.

10

RESULTS AND CONCLUDING THOUGHTS

This study has surveyed the terrain of the temple-mount of the Sermon from several angles: textually, historically, linguistically, analytically, comparatively, religiously, and ritually. In my mind, the quest has borne good fruit. If the Sermon at the Temple is to be known by its fruits, the simple fact that the Sermon at the Temple lends itself rewardingly to such scrutiny should be a strong clue that much more remains to be said and thought about the Sermon on the Mount and the Sermon at the Temple.

Much more also lies ahead in thinking about the implications of this study on other areas of research. The Sermon on the Mount is a key scriptural text. How a person understands the Sermon on the Mount—when it was written, why it was given, and what it means—has a deep impact on how one interprets the entire ministry of Jesus, numerous texts of the New Testament, and many of the experiences of early Christianity. How one views the Sermon has equally far-reaching consequences for approaching the Book of Mormon—how it was translated, what it contains, and why it is important. Sooner or later, all roads in the gospel lead past this scriptural Mount.

Thus my interpretation will surely not be the last word

on the Sermon on the Mount or its ramifications. This interpretation is likely to evoke all kinds of responses — some positive and some negative. It would be a first were that not the case: Few interpretations of the Sermon have ever met with anything close to universal acceptance. I will be the first to acknowledge that important questions and historical uncertainties remain. In thinking about this text that for centuries has defied consensus in analysis and summation, however, I hope to have shown that there is room for a Latter-day Saint interpretation that places a premium on the background and contextualizing information about the Sermon provided by the Book of Mormon.

That information leads me to the conclusion that the Sermon at the Temple is a powerful and meaningful scripture. To a greater extent than has been suspected before, it contains the fulness of the gospel, both as an epitome of Jesus' teachings and as an implementation of his commandments by sacred temple covenant, for many elements of the new covenant Jesus brought to the temple at Bountiful are fundamentally comparable to the temple ceremony familiar to Latter-day Saints. All portions of the text — some more obviously than other — can be understood ritually. The Sermon on the Mount is a natural script for an initiation text, which means that it (like the parables of Jesus) may have had esoteric significance, as well as public levels of meaning, to early Christians. To see the Sermon on the Mount simply in the genre of commandments, or as ethical teachings, or again as making extraordinary apocalyptic demands, or as eschatology, is to see only parts of the whole. Through symbolic representation and covenantal ritual, however, one can journey conceptually and spiritually through the sum of its truths, from one's present condition on into the blessings of eternity.

In the end, my interpretation has not yet really answered the ultimate question, "What is the meaning of the Sermon on the Mount?" That remains for the reader to discover. What I have tried to supply is a map, a few tools, and the ability to recognize some major landmarks along the way. After all is said and done, as Harvey McArthur has written, "When the reader lifts his eyes from the details and ponders the over-all meaning of what he has read, he is still confronted by [the] basic questions"—what does Jesus mean, and how should I live?[1] For a Latter-day Saint, I suggest, the answer to these questions is the same as the answer to a similar question, "What is the meaning of the temple?" The answer to that central Latter-day Saint concern is sought through such things as repeated hearing, personal experience, meditation, contemplation, faith, repentance, obedience to sacred covenants, Christ-centered living, the integration of truth into the gospel and atonement of Jesus Christ, and a steadfast walk on an undeviating path toward the day of judgment and exaltation. The meaning of the Sermon will be found in similar ways.

In the course of this study, I have also explained why, in my opinion, the superficial label of plagiarism does not fit the Sermon at the Temple very well. I consider this an interesting secondary concern of this study. The Nephite text differs for sound reasons from the Sermon on the Mount. These differences are significant and often subtle and, along with many other factors, show that the Sermon on the Mount was not crudely spliced into the text of 3 Nephi. There is much more in the Sermon at the Temple than the theory of plagiarism can account for. Nor is the Sermon at the Temple compromised by its similarity to the King James English or by critical studies of the New Testament. Instead, there are historical and philological reasons for believing that the Sermon at the Temple bears the hallmarks of an accurate and inspired translation of a

---

1. McArthur, *Understanding the Sermon on the Mount,* 15.

contemporaneous record of the words that Jesus spoke in A.D. 34 at the temple in Bountiful.

My main purpose in writing and sharing this study has been to enhance the respect and appreciation of Latter-day Saints for the Sermon at the Temple and, at the same time, to improve our understanding of the Sermon on the Mount. I realize that I have broken new ground, to say nothing of breaking stride with the preponderance of New Testament scholarly opinion by taking seriously the idea that Jesus was the author of the Sermon. I am also aware that not all the points I have advanced are equally persuasive or fully developed. I hope, however, that this uphill climb has been intelligently and engagingly conducted. After the trek, it seems clear enough to me that one should not dismiss this Mount on the basis of a few partial geological reports from the bottom. Hopefully, it will give all who make the ascent a clearer view from the top.

APPENDIX
A COLUMNAR COMPARISON
OF THE SERMON ON THE MOUNT
AND THE SERMON AT THE TEMPLE

Text that is bolded is unique to 3 Nephi
Text that is bolded and italicized is unique to Matthew
Text that is italicized is unique to the Joseph Smith Translation
<u>Text that is underlined is the same in 3 Nephi and the Joseph
Smith Translation and is not found in Matthew</u>

Book of Mormon 3 Nephi 12	King James Version Matthew 5	Joseph Smith Translation Matthew 5
1 And it came to pass that when Jesus had spoken these words unto Nephi, and to those who had been called, (now the number of them who had been called, and received power and authority to baptize, was twelve) and behold, he stretched forth his hand unto the multitude, and cried unto them, saying: Blessed are ye if ye shall give heed unto the words of these twelve whom I have chosen from among you to minister unto you, and to be your servants; and unto them I		

Book of Mormon 3 Nephi 12	King James Version Matthew 5	Joseph Smith Translation Matthew 5

have given power that they may baptize you with water; and after that ye are baptized with water, behold, I will baptize you with fire and with the Holy Ghost; therefore blessed are ye if ye shall believe in me and be baptized, after that ye have seen me and know that I am.

1 And seeing the multitudes, *he* went up into a mountain: and when he was set, his disciples came unto him:

1 And *Jesus*, seeing the multitudes, went up into a mountain; and when he was set *down*, his disciples came unto him;

2 And again, more blessed are they who shall believe in your words **because that** ye shall testify that ye have seen me, and **that** ye know that I am. Yea, blessed are they who shall believe in your words, and come down into the depths of humility and be baptized, for they shall be visited with fire and **with** the Holy Ghost, and shall receive a remission of their sins.

2 And he opened his mouth, and taught them, saying,

2 And he opened his mouth, and taught them, saying,

3 Blessed are they who shall believe on me; and again, more blessed are they who shall believe *on* your words, *when* ye shall testify that ye have seen me and that I am.

4 Yea, blessed are they who shall believe *on* your words, and come down into the depth of humility, and be baptized *in my name*; for they shall be visited with fire and the Holy Ghost, and shall receive a remission of their sins.

3 Yea, blessed are the poor in spirit who come unto me, for theirs is the kingdom of heaven.

3 Blessed are the poor in spirit: for theirs is the kingdom of heaven.

5 Yea, blessed are the poor in spirit, who come unto me; for theirs is the kingdom of heaven.

4 And again, blessed are **all** they that mourn, for they shall be comforted.

4 Blessed are they that mourn: for they shall be comforted.

6 And again, blessed are they that mourn; for they shall be comforted.

5 And blessed are the meek, for they shall inherit the earth.

5 Blessed are the meek: for they shall inherit the earth.

7 And blessed are the meek; for they shall inherit the earth.

6 And blessed are all they **who** do hunger and thirst after righteousness, for they shall be filled with the Holy Ghost.

6 Blessed are they **which** do hunger and thirst after righteousness: for they shall be filled.

8 And blessed are all they that do hunger and thirst after righteousness; for they shall be filled with the Holy Ghost.

APPENDIX

Book of Mormon 3 Nephi 12	King James Version Matthew 5	Joseph Smith Translation Matthew 5

7 And blessed are the merciful, for they shall obtain mercy.

8 And blessed are all the pure in heart, for they shall see God.

9 And blessed are all the peacemakers, for they shall be called the children of God.

10 And blessed are all they who are persecuted for my name's sake, for theirs is the kingdom of heaven.

11 And blessed are ye when men shall revile you and persecute, and shall say all manner of evil against you falsely, for my sake;

12 For ye shall have great joy and be exceedingly glad, for great shall be your reward in heaven; for so persecuted they the prophets who were before you.

13 Verily, verily, I say unto you, I give unto you to be the salt of the earth; but if the salt shall lose its savor wherewith shall the earth be salted? The salt shall be thenceforth good for nothing, but to be cast out and to be trodden under foot of men.

14 Verily, verily, I say unto you, I give unto you to be the light of this people. A city that is set on a hill cannot be hid.

7 Blessed are the merciful: for they shall obtain mercy.

8 Blessed are the pure in heart: for they shall see God.

9 Blessed are the peacemakers: for they shall be called the children of God.

10 Blessed are they which are persecuted for righteousness' sake: for theirs is the kingdom of heaven.

11 Blessed are ye, when men shall revile you, and persecute you, and shall say all manner of evil against you falsely, for my sake.

12 Rejoice, and be exceeding glad: for great is your reward in heaven: for so persecuted they the prophets which were before you.

13 Ye are the salt of the earth: but if the salt have lost his savour, wherewith shall it be salted? it is thenceforth good for nothing, but to be cast out, and to be trodden under foot of men.

14 Ye are the light of the world. A city that is set on an hill cannot be hid.

9 And blessed are the merciful; for they shall obtain mercy.

10 And blessed are all the pure in heart; for they shall see God.

11 And blessed are all the peacemakers; for they shall be called the children of God.

12 Blessed are all they that are persecuted for my name's sake; for theirs is the kingdom of heaven.

13 And blessed are ye when men shall revile you, and persecute you, and shall say all manner of evil against you falsely, for my sake.

14 For ye shall have great joy, and be exceeding glad; for great shall be your reward in heaven; for so persecuted they the prophets which were before you.

15 Verily, verily, I say unto you, I give unto you to be the salt of the earth; but if the salt shall lose its savor, wherewith shall the earth be salted? the salt shall thenceforth be good for nothing, but to be cast out, and to be trodden under foot of men.

16 Verily, verily, I say unto you, I give unto you to be the light of the world; a city that is set on a hill cannot be hid.

185

Book of Mormon 3 Nephi 12	King James Version Matthew 5	Joseph Smith Translation Matthew 5
15 <u>Behold</u>, do men light a candle and put it under a bushel? <u>Nay</u>, but on a candlestick, and it giveth light <u>to</u> all that are in the house;	15 *Neither* do men light a candle, and put it under a bushel, but on a candlestick; and it giveth light **unto** all that are in the house.	17 <u>Behold</u>, do men light a candle and put it under a bushel? <u>Nay</u>, but on a candlestick; and it giveth light <u>to</u> all that are in the house.
16 <u>Therefore</u> let your light so shine before <u>this</u> **people**, that they may see your good works and glorify your Father <u>who</u> is in heaven.	16 Let your light so shine before **men**, that they may see your good works, and glorify your Father **which** is in heaven.	18 <u>Therefore</u>, let your light so shine before <u>this</u> *world*, that they may see your good works, and glorify your Father <u>who</u> is in heaven.
17 Think not that I am come to destroy the law or the prophets. I am not come to destroy but to fulfil;	17 Think not that I am come to destroy the law, or the prophets: I am not come to destroy, but to fulfil.	19 Think not that I am come to destroy the law, or the prophets; I am not come to destroy, but to fulfill.
18 For verily I say unto you, one jot **nor** one tittle **hath not passed away** from the law, **but in me it hath** all **been** fulfilled.	18 For verily I say unto you, *Till* heaven and earth pass, one jot or one tittle shall in no wise pass from the law, *till* all be fulfilled.	20 For verily I say unto you, Heaven and earth *must* pass away, *but* one jot or one tittle shall in no wise pass from the law, *until* all be fulfilled.
19 **And behold, I have given you the law and the** commandments **of my Father, that ye shall believe in me, and that ye shall repent of your sins, and come unto me with a broken heart and a contrite spirit. Behold, ye have the commandments before you, and the law is fulfilled.**	19 Whosoever therefore shall break one of these least commandments, and shall teach men so, he shall **be called the least** in the kingdom of heaven: but whosoever shall do and teach **them**, the same shall be called great in the kingdom of heaven.	21 Whosoever, therefore, shall break one of these least commandments, and shall teach men so *to do*, he shall *in no wise be saved* in the kingdom of heaven; but whosoever shall do and teach *these commandments of the law until it be fulfilled*, the same shall be called great, and *shall be saved* in the kingdom of heaven.
20 **Therefore come unto me and be ye saved**; for **verily** I say unto you, that except **ye shall keep my commandments, which I have commanded you at this time**, ye shall in no case enter into the kingdom of heaven.	20 For I say unto you, That except your righteousness shall exceed *the righteousness* of the scribes and Pharisees, ye shall in no case enter into the kingdom of heaven.	22 For I say unto you, Except your righteousness shall exceed *that* of the scribes and Pharisees, ye shall in no case enter into the kingdom of heaven.

186

APPENDIX

Book of Mormon 3 Nephi 12	King James Version Matthew 5	Joseph Smith Translation Matthew 5
21 Ye have heard that it <u>hath been</u> said by them of old time, **and it is also written before you**, <u>that</u> thou shalt not kill, and whosoever shall kill shall be in danger of the judgment <u>of God;</u>	21 Ye have heard that it *was* said by them of old time, Thou shalt not kill; and whosoever shall kill shall be in danger of the judgment:	23 Ye have heard that it <u>hath been</u> said by them of old time <u>that</u>, Thou shalt not kill; and whosoever shall kill, shall be in danger of the judgment <u>of God</u>.
22 But I say unto you, that whosoever is angry with his brother shall be in danger of <u>his</u> judgment. And whosoever shall say to his brother, Raca, shall be in danger of the council; <u>and</u> whosoever shall say, Thou fool, shall be in danger of hell fire.	22 But I say unto you, That whosoever is angry with his brother *without a cause* shall be in danger of *the* judgment: and whosoever shall say to his brother, Raca, shall be in danger of the council: *but* whosoever shall say, Thou fool, shall be in danger of hell fire.	24 But I say unto you, that whosoever is angry with his brother, shall be in danger of <u>his</u> judgment; and whosoever shall say to his brother, Raca, *or Rabcha*, shall be in danger of the council; *and* whosoever shall say to *his brother*, Thou fool, shall be in danger of hell fire.
23 Therefore, if <u>ye shall come unto me, or shall desire to come unto me</u>, and rememberest that thy brother hath <u>aught</u> against thee—	23 Therefore if thou bring thy gift to the altar, and there rememberest that thy brother hath ought against thee;	25 Therefore, If <u>ye shall come unto me, or shall desire to come unto me</u>, *or if thou* bring thy gift to the alter, and there rememberest that thy brother hath <u>aught</u> against thee,
24 Go thy way <u>unto thy brother, and</u> first be reconciled to thy brother, and then come **unto me with full purpose of heart, and I will receive you.**	24 Leave *there* thy gift before the altar, and go thy way; first be reconciled to thy brother, and then come and offer thy gift.	26 Leave *thou* thy gift before the alter, and go thy way <u>unto thy brother, and</u> first be reconciled to thy brother, and then come and offer thy gift.
25 Agree with thine adversary quickly while thou art in the way with him, lest at any time **he shall get thee**, and thou **shalt** be cast into prison.	25 Agree with thine adversary quickly, whiles thou art in the way with him; lest at any time *the* adversary deliver thee to the judge, and the judge deliver thee to the officer, and thou be cast into prison.	27 Agree with thine adversary quickly, while thou art in the way with him; lest at any time *thine* adversary deliver thee to the judge, and the judge deliver thee to the officer, and thou be cast into prison.

Book of Mormon 3 Nephi 12	King James Version Matthew 5	Joseph Smith Translation Matthew 5
26 Verily, **verily**, I say unto thee, thou shalt by no means come out thence <u>until</u> thou hast paid the uttermost **senine. And while ye are in prison can ye pay even one senine? Verily, verily, I say unto you, Nay.**	26 Verily I say unto thee, Thou shalt by no means come out thence, ***till*** thou hast paid the uttermost farthing.	28 Verily I say unto thee, thou shalt by no means come out thence, <u>until</u> thou hast paid the uttermost farthing.
27 <u>Behold</u>, it <u>is written</u> by them of old time, <u>that</u> thou shalt not commit adultery;	27 ***Ye have heard that*** it *was* said by them of old time, Thou shalt not commit adultery:	29 <u>Behold</u>, it <u>is written</u> by them of old time, <u>that</u> thou shalt not commit adultery.
28 But I say unto you, that whosoever looketh on a woman, to lust after her, hath committed adultery already in his heart.	28 But I say unto you, That whosoever looketh on a woman to lust after her hath committed adultery with her already in his heart.	30 But I say unto you, that whosoever looketh on a woman to lust after her, hath committed adultery with her already in his heart.
29 <u>Behold, I give unto you a commandment, that ye suffer none of these things to enter into your heart;</u>		31 <u>Behold, I give unto you a commandment, that ye suffer none of these things to enter into your heart, for it is better that ye should deny yourselves of these things, wherein ye will take up your cross, than that ye should be cast into hell.</u>
30 <u>For it is better that ye should deny yourselves of these things, wherein ye will take up your cross, than that ye should be cast into hell.</u>		
	29 ***And*** if thy right eye offend thee, pluck it out, and cast it from thee: for it is profitable for thee that one of thy members should perish, and not that thy whole body should be cast into hell.	32 *Wherefore*, if thy right eye offend thee, pluck it out and cast it from thee; for it is profitable for thee that one of thy members should perish, and not that thy whole body should be cast into hell.
	30 ***And*** if thy right hand offend thee, cut if off, and cast it from thee: for it is profitable for thee that one of thy members should perish, and not that thy whole body should be cast into hell.	33 *Or* if thy right hand offend thee, cut it off and cast it from thee; for it is profitable for thee that one of thy members should perish, and not that thy whole body should be cast into hell.

APPENDIX

Book of Mormon 3 Nephi 12	King James Version Matthew 5	Joseph Smith Translation Matthew 5
		34 *And now this I speak, a parable concerning your sins; wherefore, cast them from you, that ye may not be hewn down and cast into the fire.*
31 It hath been <u>written, that</u> whosoever shall put away his wife, let him give her a writing of divorcement.	31 It hath been **said**, Whosoever shall put away his wife, let him give her a writing of divorcement.	35 It hath been <u>written that</u>, Whosoever shall put away his wife, let him give her a writing of divorcement.
32 <u>Verily, verily</u>, I say unto you, that whosoever shall put away his wife, saving for the cause of fornication, causeth her to commit adultery; and **whoso** shall marry her **who** is divorced committeth adultery.	32 **But** I say unto you, That whosoever shall put away his wife, saving for the cause of fornication, causeth her to commit adultery : and whosoever shall marry her that is divorced committeth adultery.	36 <u>Verily, verily</u>, I say unto you, that whosoever shall put away his wife, saving for the cause of fornication, causeth her to commit adultery; and whosoever shall marry her that is divorced, committeth adultery.
33 **And** again it **is** <u>written</u>, thou shalt not forswear thyself, but shalt perform unto the Lord thine oaths;	33 Again, *ye have heard that* it hath been *said* by them of old time, Thou shalt not forswear thyself, but shalt perform unto the Lord thine oaths:	37 Again, it hath been <u>written</u> by them of old time, Thou shalt not forswear thyself, but shalt perform unto the Lord thine oaths.
34 But **verily, verily**, I say unto you, swear not at all; neither by heaven, for it is God's throne;	34 But I say unto you, Swear not at all; neither by heaven; for it is God's throne:	38 But I say unto you, Swear not at all; neither by heaven, for it is God's throne; nor by the earth, for it is his footstool; neither by Jerusalem, for it is the city of the great King; neither shalt thou swear by thy head, because thou canst not make one hair white or black.
35 Nor by the earth, for it is his footstool;	35 Nor by the earth; for it is his footstool: neither by Jerusalem; for it is the city of the great King.	
36 Neither shalt thou swear by thy head, because thou canst not make one hair **black or white**;	36 Neither shalt thou swear by thy head, because thou canst not make one hair white or black.	
37 But let your communication be Yea, yea; Nay, nay; for whatsoever **cometh of** more than these **is** evil.	37 But let your communication be, Yea, yea; Nay, nay: for whatsoever is more than these cometh of evil.	39 But let your communication be Yea, yea; Nay, nay; for whatsoever is more than these cometh of evil.

Book of Mormon 3 Nephi 12	King James Version Matthew 5	Joseph Smith Translation Matthew 5
38 **And behold**, it **is written**, an eye for an eye, and a tooth for a tooth;	38 Ye have heard that it hath been said, An eye for an eye, and a tooth for a tooth:	40 Ye have heard that it hath been said, An eye for an eye, and a tooth for a tooth.
39 But I say unto you, that ye **shall not resist** evil, but whosoever shall smite thee on thy right cheek, turn to him the other also;	39 But I say unto you, That ye resist not evil: but whosoever shall smite thee on thy right cheek, turn to him the other also.	41 But I say unto you that ye resist not evil; but whosoever shall smite thee on thy right cheek, turn to him the other also.
40 And if any man will sue thee at the law and take away thy coat, let him have thy cloak also;	40 And if any man will sue thee at the law, and take away thy coat, let him have thy cloke also.	42 And if any man will sue thee at the law, and take away thy coat, let him have *it; and if he sue thee again, let him have* thy cloak also.
41 And whosoever shall compel thee to go a mile, go with him twain.	41 And whosoever shall compel thee to go a mile, go with him twain.	43 And whosoever shall compel thee to go a mile, *go with him a mile; and whosoever shall compel thee to go with him twain, thou shalt* go with him twain.
42 Give to him that asketh thee, and from him that would borrow of thee turn thou not away.	42 Give to him that asketh thee, and from him that would borrow of thee turn not thou away.	44 Give to him that asketh of thee; and from him that would borrow of thee, turn not thou away.
43 **And behold** it **is written also, that** thou shalt love thy neighbor and hate thine enemy;	43 Ye have heard that it hath been said, Thou shalt love thy neigh-bour, and hate thine enemy.	45 Ye have heard that it hath been said, Thou shalt love thy neighbor, and hate thine enemy.
44 But **behold** I say unto you, love your enemies, bless them that curse you, do good to them that hate you, and pray for them **who** despitefully use you and persecute you;	44 But I say unto you, Love your enemies, bless them that curse you, do good to them that hate you, and pray for them which despitefully use you, and persecute you;	46 But I say unto you, love your enemies; bless them that curse you; do good to them that hate you; and pray for them which despitefully use you and persecute you;
45 That ye may be the children of your Father <u>who</u> is in heav-en; for he maketh his sun to rise on the evil and on the good.	45 That ye may be the children of your Father *which* is in heaven: for he maketh his sun to rise on the evil and on the good, and sendeth rain on the just and on the unjust.	47 That ye may be the children of your Father <u>who</u> is in heav-en; for he maketh his sun to rise on the evil and on the good, and sendeth rain on the just and on the unjust.

Book of Mormon 3 Nephi 12–13	King James Version Matthew 5–6	Joseph Smith Translation Matthew 5–6
	46 For if ye love them which love you, what reward have *ye*? do not even the publicans the same?	48 For if ye love *only* them which love you, what reward have *you*? Do not even the publicans the same?
	47 And if ye salute your brethren only, what do ye more than others? do not even the publicans *so*?	49 And if ye salute your brethren only, what do ye more than others? Do not even the publicans *the same*?
46 **Therefore those things which were of old time, which were under the law, in me are all fulfilled.**		
47 **Old things are done away, and all things have become new.**		
48 **Therefore I would that ye should** be perfect even as **I, or** your Father **who** is in heaven is perfect.	48 Be ye therefore perfect, even as your Father which is in heaven is perfect.	50 Ye *are* therefore *commanded to* be perfect, even as your Father which is in heaven is perfect.
		1 *And it came to pass that, as Jesus taught his disciples, he said unto them,*
1 **Verily, verily, I say that I would that ye should do alms unto the poor; but** take heed that ye do not your alms before men to be seen of them; otherwise ye have no reward of your Father <u>who</u> is in heaven.	1 Take heed that ye do not your alms before men, to be seen of them: otherwise ye have no reward of your Father **which** is in heaven .	Take heed that ye do not your alms before men, to be seen of them; otherwise ye have no reward of your Father <u>who</u> is in heaven.
2 Therefore, when **ye shall do your** alms do not sound a trumpet before **you,** as **will** hypocrites do in the synagogues and in the streets, that they may have glory of men. Verily I say unto you, they have their reward.	2 Therefore when thou doest **thine** alms, do not sound a trumpet before thee, as the hypocrites do in the synagogues and in the streets, that they may have glory of men. Verily I say unto you, They have their reward.	2 Therefore, when thou doest alms, do not sound a trumpet before thee, as the hypocrites do, in the synagogues and in the streets, that they may have glory of men. Verily I say unto you, they have their reward.

Book of Mormon 3 Nephi 13	King James Version Matthew 6	Joseph Smith Translation Matthew 6

3 But when thou doest alms let not thy left hand know what thy right hand doeth;
4 That thine alms may be in secret; and thy Father <u>who</u> seeth in secret, himself shall reward thee openly.
5 And when thou prayest thou shalt not **do** as the hypocrites, for they love to pray, standing in the synagogues and in the corners of the streets, that they may be seen of men. Verily I say unto you, they have their reward.

6 But thou, when thou prayest, enter into thy closet, and when thou hast shut thy door, pray to thy Father <u>who</u> is in secret; and thy Father, <u>who</u> seeth in secret, shall reward thee openly.
7 But when ye pray, use not vain repetitions, as the heathen, for they think that they shall be heard for their much speaking.

8 Be not ye therefore like unto them, for your Father knoweth what things ye have need of before ye ask him.
9 After this manner therefore pray ye: Our Father <u>who</u> art in heaven, hallowed be thy name.

3 But when thou doest alms, let not thy left hand know what thy right hand doeth:
4 That thine alms may be in secret: and thy Father **which** seeth in secret himself shall reward thee openly.
5 And when thou prayest, thou shalt not be as the hypocrites **are:** for they love to pray standing in the synagogues and in the corners of the streets, that they may be seen of men. Verily I say unto you, They have their reward.

6 But thou, when thou prayest, enter into thy closet, and when thou hast shut thy door, pray to thy Father **which** is in secret; and thy Father **which** seeth in secret shall reward thee openly.
7 But when ye pray, use not vain repetitions, as the heathen do: for they think that they shall be heard for their much speaking.

8 Be not ye therefore like unto them: for your Father knoweth what things ye have need of, before ye ask him.
9 After this manner therefore pray ye: Our Father **which** art in heaven, Hallowed be thy name.

3 But when thou doest alms, let *it be unto thee as* thy left hand *not knowing* what thy right hand doeth;
4 That thine alms may be in secret; and thy Father <u>who</u> seeth in secret, himself shall reward thee openly.
5 And when thou prayest, thou shalt not be as the hypocrites; for they love to pray standing in the synagogues and in the corners of the streets, that they may be seen of men; *for*, verily, I say unto you, they have their reward.
6 But thou, when thou prayest, enter into thy closet, and when thou hast shut the door, pray to thy Father <u>who</u> is in secret; and thy Father <u>who</u> seeth in secret shall reward thee openly.
7 But when ye pray, use not vain repetitions, as the *hypocrites* do; for they think that they shall be heard for their much speaking.
8 *Therefore* be ye not like unto them; for your Father knoweth what things ye have need of, before ye ask him.
9 *Therefore* after this manner *shall ye pray, saying,*
10 Our Father <u>who</u> art in heaven, Hallowed by thy name.

APPENDIX

Book of Mormon 3 Nephi 13	King James Version Matthew 6	Joseph Smith Translation Matthew 6
10 Thy will be done on earth as it is in heaven.	10 Thy kingdom come. Thy will be done *in* earth, as it is in heaven. 11 Give us this day our daily bread.	11 Thy kingdom come. Thy will be done on earth, as it is *done* in heaven. 12 Give us this day, our daily bread.
11 And forgive us our debts, as we forgive our debtors.	12 And forgive us our debts, as we forgive our debtors.	13 And forgive us our *trespasses*, as we forgive *those who trespass against us.* 14 And *suffer* us not *to be led* into temptation, but deliver us from evil.
12 And lead us not into temptation, but deliver us from evil. 13 For thine is the kingdom, and the power, and the glory, forever. Amen.	13 And lead us not into temptation, but deliver us from evil: For thine is the kingdom, and the power, and the glory, for ever. Amen.	15 For thine is the kingdom, and the power, and the glory, forever *and ever,* Amen.
14 For, if ye forgive men their trespasses your heavenly Father will also forgive you; 15 But if ye forgive not men their trespasses neither will your Father forgive your trespasses.	14 For if ye forgive men their trespasses, your heavenly Father will also forgive you: 15 But if ye forgive not men their trespasses, neither will your Father forgive your trespasses.	16 For if ye forgive men their trespasses, *who trespass against you,* your heavenly Father will also forgive you; but if ye forgive not men their trespasses, neither will your *heavenly* Father forgive *you* your trespasses.
16 Moreover, when ye fast be not as the hypocrites, of a sad countenance, for they disfigure their faces that they may appear unto men to fast. Verily I say unto you, they have their reward. 17 But thou, when thou fastest, anoint <u>thy</u> head, and wash thy face; 18 That thou appear not unto men to fast, but unto thy Father, <u>who</u> is in secret; and thy Father, <u>who</u> seeth in secret, shall reward thee openly.	16 Moreover when ye fast, be not, as the hypocrites, of a sad countenance: for they disfigure their faces, that they may appear unto men to fast. Verily I say unto you, They have their reward. 17 But thou, when thou fastest, anoint thine head, and wash thy face; 18 That thou appear not unto men to fast, but unto thy Father **which** is in secret: and thy Father, **which** seeth in secret, shall reward thee openly.	17 Moreover, when ye fast, be not as the hypocrites, of a sad countenance; for they disfigure their faces, that they may appear unto men to fast. Verily, I say unto you, they have their reward. 18 But thou, when thou fastest, anoint <u>thy</u> head and wash thy face, that thou appear not unto men to fast, but unto thy Father <u>who</u> is in secret; and thy Father <u>who</u> seeth in secret, shall reward thee openly.

Book of Mormon 3 Nephi 13	King James Version Matthew 6	Joseph Smith Translation Matthew 6
19 Lay not up for yourselves treasures upon earth, where moth and rust doth corrupt, and thieves break through and steal;	19 Lay not up for yourselves treasures upon earth, where moth and rust doth corrupt, and where thieves break through and steal:	19 Lay not up for yourselves treasure upon earth, where moth and rust doth corrupt, and where thieves break through and steal.
20 But lay up for yourselves treasures in heaven, where neither moth nor rust doth corrupt, and where thieves do not break through nor steal.	20 But lay up for yourselves treasures in heaven, where neither moth nor rust doth corrupt, and where thieves do not break through nor steal:	20 But lay up for yourselves treasures in heaven, where neither moth nor rust doth corrupt, and where thieves do not break through nor steal.
21 For where your treasure is, there will your heart be also.	21 For where your treasure is, there will your heart be also.	21 For where your treasure is, there will your heart be also.
22 The light of the body is the eye; if, therefore, thine eye be single, thy whole body shall be full of light.	22 The light of the body is the eye: if therefore thine eye be single, thy whole body shall be full of light.	22 The light of the body is the eye; if therefore thine eye be single *to the glory of God*, thy whole body shall be full of light.
23 But if thine eye be evil, thy whole body shall be full of darkness. If, therefore, the light that is in thee be darkness, how great is that darkness!	23 But if thine eye be evil, thy whole body shall be full of darkness. If therefore the light that is in thee be darkness, how great is that darkness!	23 But if thine eye be evil, thy whole body shall be full of darkness. If therefore the light *which* is in thee be darkness, how great *shall* that darkness *be*.
24 No man can serve two masters; for either he will hate the one and love the other, or else he will hold to the one and despise the other. Ye cannot serve God and Mammon.	24 No man can serve two masters: for either he will hate the one, and love the other; or else he will hold to the one, and despise the other. Ye cannot serve God and mammon.	24 No man can serve two masters, for either he will hate the one, and love the other; or else he will hold to the one and despise the other. Ye cannot serve God and Mammon.
		25 *And, again, I say unto you, go ye into the world, and care not for the world; for the world will hate you, and will persecute you, and will turn you out of their synagogues.*

Book of Mormon 3 Nephi 13	King James Version Matthew 6	Joseph Smith Translation Matthew 6
		26 *Nevertheless, ye shall go forth from house to house, teaching the people; and I will go before you.*
		27 *And your heavenly Father will provide for you, whatsoever things ye need for food, what ye shall eat; and for raiment, what ye shall wear or put on.*
25 **And now it came to pass that when Jesus had spoken these words he looked upon the twelve whom he had chosen, and said unto them: Remember the words which I have spoken. For behold, ye are they whom I have chosen to minister unto this people.** Therefore I say unto you, take no thought for your life, what ye shall eat, or what ye shall drink; nor yet for your body, what ye shall put on. Is not the life more than meat, and the body than raiment?	25 Therefore I say unto you, Take no thought for your life, what ye shall eat, or what ye shall drink; nor yet for your body, what ye shall put on. Is not the life more than meat, and the body than raiment?	28 Therefore I say unto you, Take no thought for your life, what ye shall eat, or what ye shall drink; nor yet for your *bodies*, what ye shall put on. Is not the life more than meat, and the body than raiment?
26 Behold the fowls of the air, for they sow not, neither do they reap nor gather into barns; yet your heavenly Father feedeth them. Are ye not much better than they?	26 Behold the fowls of the air: for they sow not, neither do they reap, nor gather into barns; yet your heavenly Father feedeth them. Are ye not much better than they?	29 Behold the fowls of the air, for they sow not, neither do they reap, nor gather into barns; yet your heavenly Father feedeth them. Are ye not much better than they? *How much more will he not feed you?*
		30 *Wherefore take no thought for these things, but keep my commandments wherewith I have commanded you.*
27 Which of you by taking thought can add one cubit unto his stature?	27 Which of you by taking thought can add one cubit unto his stature?	31 *For* which of you by taking thought can add one cubit unto his stature.

Book of Mormon 3 Nephi 13	King James Version Matthew 6	Joseph Smith Translation Matthew 6

28 And why take ye thought for raiment? Consider the lilies of the field how they grow; they toil not, neither do they spin;

29 And yet I say unto you, that even Solomon, in all his glory, was not arrayed like one of these.

30 Wherefore, if God so clothe the grass of the field, which today is, and tomorrow is cast into the oven, **even so will** he clothe you, <u>if</u> ye <u>are not</u> of little faith.

31 Therefore take no thought, saying, What shall we eat? or, What shall we drink? or, Wherewithal shall we be clothed?

32 For your heavenly Father knoweth that ye have need of all these things.

33 But seek ye first the kingdom of God and his righteousness, and all these things shall be added unto you.

---

28 And why take ye thought for raiment? Consider the lilies of the field, how they grow; they toil not, neither do they spin:

29 And yet I say unto you, That even Solomon in all his glory was not arrayed like one of these.

30 Wherefore, if God so clothe the grass of the field, which to day is, and to morrow is cast into the oven, **shall** he **not much more** clothe you, **O** ye of little faith?

31 Therefore take no thought, saying, What shall we eat? or, What shall we drink? or, Wherewithal shall we be clothed?

32 (**For** after all these things do the Gentiles seek:) for your heavenly Father knoweth that ye have need of all these things.

33 But seek ye first the kingdom of God, and his righteousness; and all these things shall be added unto you.

---

32 And why take ye thought for raiment? Consider the lilies of the field, how they grow; they toil not, neither do they spin.

33 And yet I say unto you, that even Solomon, in all his glory, was not arrayed like one of these.

34 *Therefore*, if God so clothe the grass of the field, which today is, and tomorrow is cast into the oven, *how much more will he not provide for* you, <u>if</u> ye <u>are not</u> of little faith.

Therefore take no thought, saying, What shall we eat? or, What shall we drink? or, Wherewithal shall we be clothed?

36 *Why is it that ye murmur among yourselves, saying, We cannot obey thy word because ye have not all these things, and seek to excuse yourselves, saying that,* After all these things do the Gentiles seek.

37 *Behold, I say unto you, that* your heavenly Father knoweth that ye have need of all these things.

38 *Wherefore, seek not the things of this world* but seek ye first *to build up* the kingdom of God, and *to establish* his righteousness, and all these things shall be added unto you.

APPENDIX

Book of Mormon 3 Nephi 13–14	King James Version Matthew 6–7	Joseph Smith Translation Matthew 6–7

34 Take therefore no thought for the morrow, for the morrow shall take thought for the things of itself. Sufficient is the day unto the evil thereof.

1 **And now it came to pass that when Jesus had spoken these words he turned again to the multitude, and did open his mouth unto them again, saying: Verily, verily, I say unto you,** Judge not, that ye be not judged.

2 For with what judgment ye judge, ye shall be judged; and with what measure ye mete, it shall be measured to you again.

3 And why beholdest thou the mote that is in thy brother's eye, but considerest not the beam that is in thine own eye?

4 Or how wilt thou say to thy brother: Let me pull the mote out of thine eye—and behold, a beam is in thine own eye?

---

34 Take therefore no thought for the morrow: for the morrow shall take thought for the things of itself. Sufficient unto the day is the evil thereof.

1 Judge not, that ye be not judged.

2 For with what judgment ye judge, ye shall be judged: and with what measure ye mete, it shall be measured to you again.

3 And why beholdest thou the mote that is in thy brother's eye, but considerest not the beam that is in thine own eye?

4 Or how wilt thou say to thy brother, Let me pull out the mote out of thine eye; and, behold, a beam is in thine own eye?

---

39 Take, therefore, no thought for the morrow; for the morrow shall take thought for the things of itself. Sufficient unto the day *shall be* the evil thereof.

1 Now *these are the words which Jesus taught his disciples that they should say unto the people.*

2 Judge not *unrighteously,* that ye be not judged; *but judge righteous judgment.*

3 For with what judgment ye *shall* judge, ye shall be judged; and with what measure ye mete, it shall be measured to you again.

4 And *again, ye shall say unto them,* Why *is it that* thou beholdest the mote that is in thy brother's eye, but considerest not the beam that is in thine own eye?

5 Or how wilt thou say to thy brother, Let me pull out the mote out of thine eye; and *canst not* behold a beam in thine own eye?

6 *And Jesus said unto his disciples, Beholdest thou the scribes, and the Pharisees, and the priests, and the Levites? They teach in their synagogues, but do not observe the law, nor the commandments; and all have gone out of the way, and are under sin.*

Book of Mormon 3 Nephi 14	King James Version Matthew 7	Joseph Smith Translation Matthew 7
		7 *Go thou and say unto them, Why teach ye men the law and the commandments, when ye yourselves are the children of corruption?*
5 Thou hypocrite, first cast the beam out of thine own eye; and then shalt thou see clearly to cast the mote out of thy brother's eye.	5 Thou hypocrite, first cast out the beam out of thine own eye; and then shalt thou see clearly to cast out the mote out of thy brother's eye.	8 *Say unto them, Ye* hypocrites, first cast out the beam out of thine own eye; and then shalt thou see clearly to cast out the mote out of thy brother's eye. 9 *Go ye into the world, saying unto all, Repent, for the kingdom of heaven has come nigh unto you.* 10 *And the mysteries of the kingdom ye shall keep within yourselves; for it is* not *meet to give that* which is holy unto the dogs; neither cast ye your pearls *unto* swine, lest they trample them under their feet.
6 Give not that which is holy unto the dogs, neither cast ye your pearls before swine, lest they trample them under their feet, and turn again and rend you.	6 Give not that which is holy unto the dogs, neither cast ye your pearls before swine, lest they trample them under their feet, and turn again and rend you.	11 *For the world cannot receive that which ye, yourselves, are not able to bear; wherefore ye shall not give your pearls unto them, lest they* turn again and rend you.
7 Ask, and it shall be given **unto** you; seek, and ye shall find; knock, and it shall be opened unto you.	7 Ask, and it shall be given you; seek, and ye shall find; knock, and it shall be opened unto you:	12 *Say unto them, Ask of God; ask, and it* shall be given you; seek, and ye shall find; knock, and it shall be opened unto you.

Book of Mormon 3 Nephi 14	King James Version Matthew 7	Joseph Smith Translation Matthew 7
8 For every one that asketh, receiveth; and he that seeketh, findeth; and to him that knocketh, it shall be opened.	8 For every one that asketh receiveth; and he that seeketh findeth; and to him that knocketh it shall be opened.	13 For everyone that asketh, receiveth; and he that seeketh, findeth; and *unto* him that knocketh, it shall be opened.
		14 *And then said his disciples unto him, They will say unto us, We ourselves are righteous, and need not that any man should teach us. God, we know, heard Moses and some of the prophets; but us he will not hear.*
		15 *And they will say, We have the law for our salvation, and that is sufficient for us.*
		16 *Then Jesus answered, and said unto his disciples, Thus shall ye say unto them,*
		17 *What man among you, having a son, and he shall be standing out, and shall say, Father, open thy house that I may come in and sup with thee, will not say, Come in my son; for mine is thine, and thine is mine?*
9 Or what man is there of you, <u>who</u>, if his son ask bread, will give him a stone?	9 Or what man is there of you, **whom** if his son ask bread, will **he** give him a stone?	18 Or what man is there *among* you, <u>who</u>, if his son ask bread, will give him a stone?
10 Or if he ask a fish, will he give him a serpent?	10 Or if he ask a fish, will he give him a serpent?	19 Or if he ask a fish, will he give him a serpent?

Book of Mormon 3 Nephi 14	King James Version Matthew 7	Joseph Smith Translation Matthew 7
11 If ye then, being evil, know how to give good gifts unto your children, how much more shall your Father who is in heaven give good things to them that ask him?	11 If ye then, being evil, know how to give good gifts unto your children, how much more shall your Father **which** is in heaven give good things to them that ask him?	20 If ye then, being evil, know how to give good gifts unto your children, how much more shall your Father who is in heaven give good things to them that ask him?
12 Therefore, all things whatsoever ye would that men should do to you, do ye even so to them, for this is the law and the prophets.	12 Therefore all things whatsoever ye would that men should do to you, do ye even so to them: for this is the law and the prophets.	21 Therefore, all things whatsoever ye would that men should do to you, do ye even so to them; for this is the law and the prophets.
		22 *Repent, therefore, and* enter ye in at the strait gate; for wide is the gate, and broad is the way that leadeth to destruction, and many there be who go in thereat.
13 Enter ye in at the strait gate; for wide is the gate, and broad is the way, which leadeth to destruction, and many there be who go in thereat;	13 Enter ye in at the strait gate: for wide is the gate, and broad is the way, that leadeth to destruction, and many there be which go in thereat:	
14 Because strait is the gate, and narrow is the way, which leadeth unto life, and few there be that find it.	14 Because strait is the gate, and narrow is the way, which leadeth unto life, and few there be that find it.	23 Because strait is the gate, and narrow is the way *that* leadeth unto life, and few there be that find it.
		24 *And, again,* beware of false prophets, who come to you in sheep's clothing; but inwardly they are ravening wolves.
15 Beware of false prophets, who come to you in sheep's clothing, but inwardly they are ravening wolves.	15 Beware of false prophets, **which** come to you in sheep's clothing, but inwardly they are ravening wolves.	
16 Ye shall know them by their fruits. Do men gather grapes of thorns, or figs of thistles?	16 Ye shall know them by their fruits. Do men gather grapes of thorns, or figs of thistles?	25 Ye shall know them by their fruits; *for* do men gather grapes of thorns, or figs of thistles?
17 Even so every good tree bringeth forth good fruit; but a corrupt tree bringeth forth evil fruit.	17 Even so every good tree bringeth forth good fruit; but a corrupt tree bringeth forth evil fruit.	26 Even so every good tree bringeth forth good fruit; but a corrupt tree bringeth forth evil fruit.
18 A good tree cannot bring forth evil fruit, neither a corrupt tree bring forth good fruit.	18 A good tree cannot bring forth evil fruit, neither can a corrupt tree bring forth good fruit.	27 A good tree cannot bring forth evil fruit; neither can a corrupt tree bring forth good fruit.

APPENDIX

Book of Mormon 3 Nephi 14	King James Version Matthew 7	Joseph Smith Translation Matthew 7

19 Every tree that bringeth not forth good fruit is hewn down, and cast into the fire.
20 Wherefore, by their fruits ye shall know them.

21 Not every one that saith unto me, Lord, Lord, shall enter into the kingdom of heaven; but he that doeth the will of my Father <u>who</u> is in heaven.

22 Many will say to me in that day: Lord, Lord, have we not prophesied in thy name, and in thy name have cast out devils, and in thy name done many wonderful works?
23 And then will I profess unto them: I never knew you; depart from me, ye that work iniquity.
24 Therefore, **whoso** heareth these sayings of mine and doeth them, I will liken him unto a wise man, <u>who</u> built his house upon a rock—
25 And the rain descended, and the floods came, and the winds blew, and beat upon that house; and it fell not, for it was founded upon a rock.

19 Every tree that bringeth not forth good fruit is hewn down, and cast into the fire.
20 Wherefore by their fruits ye shall know them.

21 Not every one that saith unto me, Lord, Lord, shall enter into the kingdom of heaven; but he that doeth the will of my Father **which** is in heaven.

22 Many will say to me in that day, Lord, Lord, have we not prophesied in thy name? and in thy name have cast out devils? and in thy name done many wonderful works?
23 And then will I profess unto them, I never knew you: depart from me, ye that work iniquity.
24 Therefore whosoever heareth these sayings of mine, and doeth them, I will liken him unto a wise man, **which** built his house upon a rock:
25 And the rain descended, and the floods came, and the winds blew, and beat upon that house; and it fell not: for it was founded upon a rock.

28 Every tree that bringeth not forth good fruit, is hewn down, and cast into the fire.
29 Wherefore by their fruits ye shall know them.
30 *Verily I say unto you, It is* not everyone that saith unto me, Lord, Lord, *that* shall enter into the kingdom of heaven; but he that doeth the will of my Father <u>who</u> is in heaven.
31 *For the day soon cometh, that men shall come before me to judgment, to be judged according to their works.*
32 *And* many will say *unto* me in that day, Lord, Lord, have we not prophesied in thy name; and in thy name cast out devils; and in thy name done many wonderful works?
33 And then will I *say, Ye* never knew *me;* depart from me ye that work iniquity.
34 Therefore, whosoever heareth these sayings of mine and doeth them, I will liken him unto a wise man, <u>who</u> built his house upon a rock, and the rains descended, and the floods came, and the winds blew, and beat upon that house, and it fell not; for it was founded upon a rock.

APPENDIX

Book of Mormon 3 Nephi 14–15	King James Version Matthew 7	Joseph Smith Translation Matthew 7
26 And every one that heareth these sayings of mine and doeth them not shall be likened unto a foolish man, <u>who</u> built his house up on the sand—	26 And every one that heareth these sayings of mine, and doeth them not, shall be likened unto a foolish man, **which** built his house upon the sand:	35 And everyone that heareth these sayings of mine, and doeth them not, shall be likened unto a foolish man, <u>who</u> built his house upon the sand;
27 And the rain descended, and the floods came, and the winds blew, and beat upon that house; and it fell, and great was the fall of it.	27 And the rain descended, and the floods came, and the winds blew, and beat upon that house; and it fell: and great was the fall of it.	and the rains descended, and the floods came, and the winds blew, and beat upon that house, and it fell; and great was the fall of it.
	28 And it came to pass, when Jesus had ended these sayings, the people were astonished at his doctrine:	36 And it came to pass when Jesus had ended these sayings *with his disciples*, the people were astonished at his doctrine;
	29 For he taught them as one having authority, and not as the scribes.	37 For he taught them as one having authority *from God*, and not as *having authority from* the scribes.
1 And **now** it came to pass **that** when Jesus had ended these sayings **he cast his eyes round about on the multitude, and said unto them: Behold, ye have heard the things which I taught before I ascended to my Father; therefore, whoso remembereth these sayings of mine and doeth them, him will I raise up at the last day.**		

202

SELECTED BIBLIOGRAPHY

BOOKS

Albright, W. F. and C. S. Mann. *Matthew*. Garden City, New York: Doubleday, 1971.

Barth, Gerhard. *Tradition and Interpretation in Matthew*. Philadelphia: Westminster, 1963.

Betz, Hans Dieter. *Essays on the Sermon on the Mount*. Philadelphia: Fortress, 1985.

Black, Matthew. *An Aramaic Approach to the Gospels and Acts*. 3rd ed. Oxford: Clarendon, 1967.

Bornkamm, Günther. *Tradition and Interpretation in Matthew*. Philadelphia: Westminster, 1963.

Davies, W. D. *The Sermon on the Mount*. Cambridge: Cambridge University Press, 1966.

Dupont, J. *Les Béatitudes: Le problème littéraire — Les deux versions du Sermon sur la montagne et des Béatitudes*. 2nd ed. Paris: Gabalda, 1969.

Fitzmyer, Joseph A. *Essays on the Semitic Background of the New Testament*. London: Geoffrey Chapman, 1971.

Jeremias, Joachim. *The Prayers of Jesus*. London: SCM, 1967.

————. *The Sermon on the Mount*. Philadelphia: Fortress, 1963.

Kissinger, Warren S. *The Sermon on the Mount: A History of Interpretation and Bibliography*. American Theological Library Association Bibliography Series, No. 3. Metuchen, New Jersey: Scarecrow Press, 1975.

McArthur, Harvey K. *Understanding the Sermon on the Mount*. Westport, Connecticut: Greenwood, 1978.

203

Montefiore, C. G. *The Synoptic Gospels*. New York: KTAV, 1968.

Moule, C. F. D. *Essays in New Testament Interpretation*. Cambridge: Cambridge University Press, 1982.

Nibley, Hugh W. *Mormonism and Early Christianity*. Salt Lake City: Deseret Book and F.A.R.M.S., 1987.

————. *The Message of the Joseph Smith Papyri*. Salt Lake City: Deseret Book, 1975.

Smith, Morton. *Clement of Alexandria and a Secret Gospel of Mark*. Cambridge: Harvard University Press, 1973.

Sperry, Sidney B. *Problems of the Book of Mormon*. Salt Lake City: Bookcraft, 1964.

Stendahl, Krister. *The School of St. Matthew*. Philadelphia: Fortress, 1968.

Strack, Hermann, and Paul Billerbeck. *Kommentar zum Neuen Testament aus Talmud und Midrasch*. Munich: Beck, 1922.

Strecker, Georg. *The Sermon on the Mount: An Exegetical Commentary*. Tr. O. C. Dean, Jr. Nashville: Abingdon, 1988.

Talmage, James E. *Jesus the Christ*. Salt Lake City: Deseret Book, 1976.

Vermes, G. *Jesus the Jew*. London: Collins, 1973.

Werner, Eric. *The Sacred Bridge*. New York: Schocken, 1970.

Windisch, Hans. *Der Sinn der Bergpredigt*. Leipzig: Hinrich, 1929. English translation, *The Meaning of the Sermon on the Mount*. Philadelphia: Westminster, 1951.

Zimmermann, Frank. *The Aramaic Origin of the Four Gospels*. New York: KTAV, 1979.

ARTICLES

Allison, Dale C., Jr. "The Eye is the Lamp of the Body." *New Testament Studies* 33 (1987): 61–83.

————. "The Structure of the Sermon on the Mount." *Journal of Biblical Literature* 106 (1987): 423–45.

Anderson, Richard L. "Religious Validity: The Sacramental Covenant in 3 Nephi." In *By Study and Also By Faith: Essays in Honor of Hugh Nibley*. 2 vols. Ed. J. Lundquist and S. Ricks. Salt Lake City: Deseret Book and F.A.R.M.S., 1990, 2:1–51; first annual F.A.R.M.S. Book of Mormon Lecture, 1988.

Bandstra, Andrew J. "The Lord's Prayer and Textual Criticism: A Response." *Calvin Theological Journal* 17 (1982): 88–97.

————. "The Original Form of the Lord's Prayer." *Calvin Theological Journal* 16 (1981): 15–37.

Banks, Robert. "Matthew's Understanding of the Law: Authenticity and

Interpretation in Matthew 5:17–20." *Journal of Biblical Literature* 93 (1974): 226–42.

Beyschlag, Karlmann. "Zur Geschichte der Bergpredigt in der Alten Kirche." *Zeitschrift für Theologie und Kirche* 74 (1977).

Black, David Alan. "Jesus on Anger: The Text of Matthew 5:22a Revisited." *Novum Testamentum* 30 (1988): 1–8.

Branscomb, Harvie. "Jesus' Attitude to the Law of Moses." *Journal of Biblical Literature* 47 (1928): 32–40.

Brown, Raymond E. "The Pater Noster as an Eschatalogical Prayer." In *New Testament Essays.* London: Chapman, 1965, 217–53.

————. "The Pre-Christian Semitic Concept of 'Mystery.' " *Catholic Biblical Quarterly* 20 (1958): 417–23.

Brown, S. Kent, John A. Tvedtnes, and John W. Welch. "When Did Jesus Appear to the Nephites in Bountiful?" F.A.R.M.S. Paper, 1989.

Burkhardt, H. "Die Bergpredigt—Eine allgemeine Handlungsanweisung?" *Theologische Beiträge* 15 (1984): 137–40.

Burtness, John E. "Life Style and Law: Some Reflections on Matthew 5: 17." *Dialog* 14 (1975): 13–20.

Cadbury, Henry J. "The Single Eye." *Harvard Theological Review* 47 (1954): 59–74.

Cahill, Lisa Sowle. "The Ethical Implications of the Sermon on the Mount." *Interpretation* 41 (1987): 144–56.

Cloward, Robert A. "The Sermon on the Mount in the Joseph Smith Translation and the Book of Mormon." In *The Joseph Smith Translation.* Ed. M. Nyman and R. Millet. Provo: Religious Studies Center, 1985, 163–200.

Davison, James E. "*Anomia* and the Question of an Antinomian Polemic in Matthew." *Journal of Biblical Literature* 104 (1985): 617–35.

Dumbrell, W. J. "The Logic of the Role of the Law in Matthew V 1–20." *Novum Testamentum* 23 (1981): 1–21.

Durham, John I. "Shalom and the Presence of God." In *Proclamation and Presence.* Ed. John I. Durham and J. R. Porter. Richmond, Virginia: John Knox, 1970, 272–93.

Ellingworth, Paul. "Translating Parallel Passages in the Gospels." *Bible Translator* 34 (1983): 401–7.

Elliott, J. K. "Can We Recover the Original New Testament?" *Theology* 77 (1974): 338–53.

Filson, Floyd V. "Broken Patterns in the Gospel of Matthew." *Journal of Biblical Literature* 75 (1956): 227–31.

Flusser, David. "Blessed Are the Poor in Spirit." *Israel Exploration Journal* 10 (1960): 1–13.

————. "Some Notes to the Beatitudes (Matthew 5:3-12, Luke 6:20-26)." *Immanuel* 8 (1978): 37-47.

Frankmolle, H. "Die Makarismen (Matt 5:1-12; Luke 6:20-23) — Motive und Umfang der redaktionellen Komposition." *Biblische Zeitschrift* 15 (1971): 52-75.

Friesen, B. "Approaches to the Interpretation and Application of the Sermon on the Mount." *Direction* 10 (1981): 19-25.

Gee, John. "Use of the Sermon on the Mount in the Earliest Christian Church." Unpublished paper, F.A.R.M.S. Archive, 1989, 88 pp.

Goulder, M. D. "The Composition of the Lord's Prayer." *Journal of Theological Studies* 14 (1963): 32-45.

Grant, Robert M. "The Sermon on the Mount in Early Christianity." *Semeia* 12 (1978): 215-31.

Greenwood, David. "Moral Obligation in the Sermon on the Mount." *Theological Studies* 31 (1970): 301-9.

Guelich, Robert A. "The Antitheses of Matthew V. 21-48: Traditional and/or Redactional?" *New Testament Studies* 22 (1976): 444-57.

————. "Interpretation of the Sermon on the Mount." *Interpretation* 41 (1987): 117-30.

————. "The Matthean Beatitudes: 'Entrance Requirements' or Eschatological Blessings?" *Journal of Biblical Literature* 95 (1976): 415-34.

Hamblin, William J. "Aspects of an Early Christian Initiation Ritual." In *By Study and Also by Faith: Essays in Honor of Hugh Nibley*, 2 vols. Ed. J. Lundquist and S. Ricks. Salt Lake City: Deseret Book and F.A.R.M.S., 1990, 1:202-21.

Hamerton-Kelly, R. G. "Attitudes to the Law in Matthew's Gospel: A Discussion of Matthew 5:18." *Biblical Research* 17 (1972): 19-32.

Harner, Philip B. "Matthew 6:5-15." *Interpretation* 41 (1987): 173-78.

Hasler, V. E. "Das Herzstück der Bergpredigt: Zum Verständnis der Antithesen in Matt V:21-48." *Theologische Zeitschrift* 15 (1959): 90-106.

Hill, David. "False Prophets and Charismatics: Structure and Interpretation in Matthew 7, 15-23." *Biblica* 57 (1976): 327-48.

Hoerber, Robert G. "Implications of the Imperative in the Sermon on the Mount." *Concordia Journal* 7 (1981): 100-103.

Kennard, J. Spencer, Jr. " 'Hosanna' and the Purpose of Jesus." *Journal of Biblical Literature* 67 (1948): 171-76.

Kilgallen, John J. "To What Are the Matthean Exception-Texts an Exception?" *Biblica* 61 (1980): 102-5.

Kingsbury, Jack Dean. "The Place, Structure, and Meaning of the Sermon on the Mount within Matthew." *Interpretation* 41 (1987): 131-43.

Lachs, Samuel Tobias. "Some Textual Observations on the Sermon on the Mount." *Jewish Quarterly Review* 69 (1978): 98–111.

Larson, Stanley R. "The Sermon on the Mount: What Its Textual Transformation Discloses Concerning the Historicity of the Book of Mormon." *Trinity Journal* 7 (1986): 23–45.

Lundquist, John M. "The Common Temple Ideology of the Ancient Near East." In *The Temple in Antiquity: Ancient Records and Modern Perspectives*. Ed. T. Madsen. Provo: Religious Studies Center, 1984, 53–76.

————. "Temple, Covenant, and Law in the Ancient Near East and in the Old Testament." In *Israel's Apostasy and Restoration*. Ed. A. Gileadi. Grand Rapids, Michigan: Baker, 1988, 293–305.

Malina, Bruce. "Does *Porneia* Mean Fornication?" *Novum Testamentum* 14 (1972): 10–17.

McEleney, Neil J. "The Beatitudes of the Sermon on the Mount/Plain." *Catholic Biblical Quarterly* 43 (1981): 1–13.

————. "The Principles of the Sermon on the Mount." *Catholic Biblical Quarterly* 41 (1979): 552–70.

Minear, P. S. "Yes or No: The Demand for Honesty in the Early Church." *Novum Testamentum* 13 (1971): 1–13.

Montefiore, H. W. "God as Father in the Synoptic Gospels." *New Testament Studies* 3 (1956): 31–46.

Moo, Douglas J. "Jesus and the Authority of the Mosaic Law." *Journal for the Study of the New Testament* (1984): 3–49.

Nibley, Hugh W. "Literary Style Used in the Book of Mormon Insured Accurate Translation." In *The Prophetic Book of Mormon*. Salt Lake City: Deseret Book and F.A.R.M.S., 1989, in *CWHN* 8:212–16.

————. "The Early Christian Prayer Circle." *BYU Studies* 19 (1978): 41–78. Reprinted in *Mormonism and Early Christianity*. Salt Lake City: Deseret Book and F.A.R.M.S., 1987, in *CWHN* 4:45–99.

Perry, Alfred M. "The Framework of the Sermon on the Mount." *Journal of Biblical Literature* 54 (1935): 103–15.

Plooij, D. "The Attitude of the Outspread Hands ('Orante') in Early Christian Literature and Art." *Expository Times* 23 (1912): 199–203, 265–69.

Powell, J. Enoch. "Those 'Lilies of the Field' Again." *Journal of Theological Studies* 33 (1982): 490–92.

Ricks, Stephen D. "Liturgy and Cosmogony: The Ritual Use of Creation Accounts in the Ancient Near East." F.A.R.M.S. Preliminary Report, 1981.

Roberts, B. H. "Bible Quotations in the Book of Mormon, and Reasonableness of Nephi's Prophecies." *Improvement Era* 7 (1904): 179–96.

SELECTED BIBLIOGRAPHY

————. "Translation of the Book of Mormon." *Improvement Era* 9 (1906): 425–36.

Schattenmann, J. "Jesus und Pythagoras." *Kairos* 21 (1979): 118–28.

Schubert, Kurt. "The Sermon on the Mount and the Qumran Texts." In *The Scrolls and the New Testament.* Ed. Krister Stendahl. New York: Harper, 1957, 118–28.

Schweizer, Eduard. "Observance of the Law and Charismatic Activity in Matthew." *New Testament Studies* 16 (1970): 213–30.

Seitz, O. J. F. "Love Your Enemies." *New Testament Studies* 16 (1969): 39–54.

Sjöberg, Erik. "Das Licht in dir. Zur Deutung von Matth. 6,22f Par." In *Studia Theologica.* Lund: Gleerup, 1952, 5:89–105.

Stapley, Delbert L. "Salt of the Earth." *Improvement Era* 67 (December 1964): 1069–71.

Stendahl, Krister. "The Sermon on the Mount and Third Nephi." In *Reflections on Mormonism.* Ed. T. Madsen. Provo: Religious Studies Center, 1978, 139–54.

Stuhlmacher, Peter. "Jesu vollkommenes Gesetz der Freiheit: Zum Verständnis der Bergpredigt." *Zeitschrift für Theologie und Kirche* 79 (1982): 283–332.

Thurston, Bennie Bowman. "Matthew 5:43–48." *Interpretation* 41 (1987): 170–73.

Tuckett, C. M. "The Beatitudes: A Source-Critical Study, with a Reply by M. D. Goulder." *Novum Testamentum* 25 (1983): 193–216.

Tuttle, Gary A. "The Sermon on the Mount: Its Wisdom Affinities and Their Relation to Its Structure." *Journal of the Evangelical Theological Society* 20 (1977): 213–30.

van Bruggen, Jacob. "The Lord's Prayer and Textual Criticism." *Calvin Theological Journal* 17 (1982): 78–87.

van Tilberg, S. "A Form-Criticism of the Lord's Prayer." *Novum Testamentum* 14 (1972): 94–105.

van Zyl, H. C. " 'n Moontlike verklaring vir Matteus 7:6 [A Possible Explanation of Matthew 7:6]." *Theologia Evangelica* 15 (1982): 67–82.

Walker, William O., Jr. "The Lord's Prayer in Matthew and John." *New Testament Studies* 28 (1982): 237–56.

Weinfeld, Moshe. "The Decalogue: Its Significance, Uniqueness, and Place in Israel's Tradition." In *Religion and Law: Biblical-Judaic and Islamic Perspectives.* Ed. E. Firmage, B. Weiss, and J. Welch. Winona Lake, Indiana: Eisenbrauns, 1990, 3–48.

Weise, Manfred. "Mt 5:21 – ein Zeugnis sakraler Rechtsprechung in der

Urgemeinde." *Zeitschrift der neutestamentliche Wissenschaft* 49 (1958).

Welch, John W. "How Long Did It Take Joseph Smith to Translate the Book of Mormon?" *Ensign* 18 (January 1988): 46–47.

————, comp. "King Benjamin's Speech in the Context of Ancient Israelite Festivals." F.A.R.M.S. Preliminary Report 1985, and "Abinadi and Pentecost." F.A.R.M.S. Update, September 1985.

————. "The Melchizedek Materials in Alma 13." In *By Study and Also By Faith: Essays in Honor of Hugh Nibley.* 2 vols. Ed. J. Lundquist and S. Ricks. Salt Lake City: Deseret Book and F.A.R.M.S., 1990, 2:238–72.

Wenham, David. "Guelich on the Sermon on the Mount: Critical Review of R. A. Guelich's 'The Sermon on the Mount: Foundation for Understanding.' " *Trinity Journal* 4 (1983): 92–108.

Wernberg-Moeller, P. "A Semitic Idiom in Matthew V.22." *New Testament Studies* 3 (1956): 71–73.

Yarnold, E. "Teleios in St. Matthew's Gospel." *Studia Evangelica* 4. In *Texte und Untersuchungen* 102 (1968): 269–73.

NAME INDEX

Note: In the index, the words *Sermon on the Mount* have been abbreviated SM.

Albright, William F., 103
Allison, Dale C., 5, 35 n. 1
Anthon, Charles, 133

Bahr, Gordon J., 63–64
Barth, G., 60–61
Batdorf, Irvin W., 9
Benson, Ezra Taft, 86
Betz, Hans Dieter: on state of interpretation of SM, 4; on SM as early Christian *didache*, 6; on instruction of baptismal candidates, 7; on use of beatitudes in initiation rituals, 44; on total commitment to Lord, 67–68; on possible uses of SM, 87; on prominent place of SM, 104; on anti-Pharisaical influence on SM, 106; on anti-Gentile bias in SM, 107; on anti-Pauline elements in SM, 108; on pre-Matthean sources, 168; on the composition of SM, 176
Beyschlag, Karlmann, 7

Billerbeck, Paul, 45, 65, 159
Black, Matthew, 125, 149, 154
Bloch, Abraham, 29
Bonhoeffer, Dietrich, 5
Bornkamm, G., 60–61
Brown, Kent, 27, 30, 31
Brown, Raymond E., 128 n. 3
Bultmann, 5
Burkhardt, H., 87
Burtness, John E., 4

Cadbury, Henry J., 67
Cazelles, Henri, 152
Charlesworth, James H., 43–44, 76–77 n. 1
Clark, John A., 133
Clement of Alexandria, 59
Clifford, Richard J., 18
Conrad, Sarah Heller, 131
Cowdery, Oliver, 131–34

Davies, W. D., 7, 18–19, 87
Dodd, 5
Duling, Dennis C., 97–98 n. 2
Durham, John I., 60–61, 101

Ebeling, Gerhard, 7
Eisenman, Robert, 150
Ellingworth, Paul, 152–53

211

INDEX OF PASSAGES

216

SUBJECT INDEX

223